Although the concept of precedent is basic to the operation of the legal system, there has not yet been a full-length empirical study of why U.S. Supreme Court justices have chosen to alter precedent. This book attempts to fill this gap by analyzing those decisions of the Vinson, Warren, and Burger Courts, as well as the first six terms of the Rehnquist Court – a span of 47 years (1946–1992) – that formally altered precedent. The authors summarize previous studies of precedent and the Court, assess the conference voting of justices, and compile a list of overruling and overruled cases. Additionally, the authors draw a distinction between personal and institutional stare decisis. By using the attitudinal model of Supreme Court decision making, which is normally seen as antithetical to the legal model of voting, the authors find that it is the individual justices' ideologies which explain their voting behavior.

STARE INDECISIS

STARE INDECISIS

THE ALTERATION OF PRECEDENT ON THE SUPREME COURT, 1946–1992

SAUL BRENNER
University of North Carolina, Charlotte

HAROLD J. SPAETH
Michigan State University

CAMBRIDGE
UNIVERSITY PRESS

Published by the Press Syndicate of the University of Cambridge
The Pitt Building, Trumpington Street, Cambridge CB2 1RP
40 West 20th Street, New York, NY 10011-4211, USA
10 Stamford Road, Oakleigh, Melbourne 3166, Australia

First published 1995

Printed in the United States of America

Library of Congress Cataloging-in-Publication Data
Brenner, Saul, 1932–

Stare indecisis : the alteration of precedent on the Supreme
Court, 1946–1992 / Saul Brenner, Harold J. Spaeth.

p. cm.

Includes index.

ISBN 0-521-45188-4

1. Stare decisis – United States. 2. Judicial review – United
States. 3. Judges – United States – Attitudes. I. Spaeth, Harold J.
KF429.S68 1994
347.73′12 – dc20
[347.30712] 94–33753
CIP

A catalog record for this book is available from the British Library.

ISBN 0-521-45188-4 Hardback

For Martha – for sharing my joys and pains
For David, Daniel, and my sister Deena – for the great pleasure
you gave me seeing you grow from birth to adulthood
Saul Brenner

For Mary Kay – who is truly Number 1, except in Latin
Harold J. Spaeth

Contents

Tables and figure

TABLES

FIGURE

Preface

The scientific study of the United States Supreme Court had its genesis in the legal realism of the 1920s and 1930s. It flowered with the onset of the behavioral revolution in political science during the 1950s. Both the legal realists and the behavioralists championed the empirical, scientific study of decision making. But most legal realists were also legal reformers, who criticized the conservative appellate court bench of their day by arguing that these judges were not deciding cases on the basis of law, but rather used legal arguments only to support their conservative values. The legal realists favored liberal values.

Since the 1950s almost all behavioral scholars who have attempted to explain decision making on the United States Supreme Court have investigated extra-legal variables: the attitudes and ideologies of the justices, the fact patterns of the cases in various issues areas, the justices' social background characteristics, their role perceptions, small group variables, game theoretic strategies, and the influence of interest groups, public opinion, Congress, and the solicitor general. But despite the skepticism of the legal realists and that of the modern critical legal studies movement, it is possible that legal variables also influence the justices' votes.

In this book we will partly test whether legal variables are influential. More specifically, we will test whether stare decisis, one of the elements of the legal model of decision making, influences the justices' votes in cases that alter precedent. We will also test whether the attitudinal model, a model antithetical to the legal model, explains the votes. The analyses regarding the testing of these two models are located in Chapters 6, 7, and 8. The data we rely on are the decisions of the Vinson, Warren, and Burger Courts and the first six terms of the Rehnquist Court, a span of 47 years: 1946–1992.

In addition, we will investigate some of the characteristics of the overruling and overruled cases. This material is presented in Chapters 4 and 5 and, to a lesser extent, in Chapter 3.

We could not have written the book without using the data contained in the United States Supreme Court Judicial Database, which Harold Spaeth has compiled for use by the scholarly community, and which is available to students and scholars at member institutions of the Interuniversity Consortium for Political and Social Research in Ann Arbor, Michigan. The National Science Foundation has financially assisted in the formation and maturation of the database since its inception in the mid-1980s (grants SES-8313773, 71-1675, 8503060, 8842925, and 9211452). Without its support, the data on which this book is based would not exist. Saul Brenner acknowledges the assistance of 1993 and 1994 summer research grants from the Foundation of the University of North Carolina – Charlotte.

We thank Lawrence Baum of the Ohio State University for his scholarly critique of the first draft of our manuscript. We also appreciate greatly the support and encouragement provided to us by the past and present political science editors at Cambridge University Press: Emily Loose and Alex Holzman.

1

Introduction

In *Gulliver's Travels,* Jonathan Swift satirized stare decisis in the following language:

It is a maxim among . . . lawyers, that whatever has been done before may legally be done again: and therefore they take special care to record all the decisions formerly made against common justice and the general reason of mankind. These, under the name of *precedents,* they produce as authorities, to justify the most inquitious opinions; and the judges never fail of directing accordingly.[1]

Swift was deriding the strict version of stare decisis; a version which binds judges to follow precedent. The United States Supreme Court has always used a more liberal version.[2] According to this version, the justices have a prima facie duty to conform to the precedents of the Court, but that obligation can be overridden if they offer a cogent reason for so doing. What constitutes a "cogent" reason in this context is uncertain; one certainly would exist if it could be shown that the law in the prior case is no longer workable or never was.

Before we explore stare decisis, it is necessary to define it. "Stare decisis" is a shortened form of the Latin phrase "stare decisis et non quieta movere," which *Black's Law Dictionary* defines as "To adhere to precedents, and not to unsettle things which are established."[3] It takes two forms: vertical stare decisis and horizontal stare decisis. The former refers to the obligation of lower court judges to adhere to the precedents of higher courts within the same jurisdiction. Horizontal stare decisis concerns the duty of a court to conform to its own precedents or that of a sister court, if any. Because this study pertains only to the United States Supreme Court, we are solely interested in horizontal stare decisis: the duty of the justices of the Court to abide by their own precedents.

In examining horizontal stare decisis, the ambiguities involved in deciding what constitutes a precedent must be explicated. It is unclear, for example, whether the justices ought to respect: 1) the result or outcome of a prior case, 2) the rule of law in that case, or 3) the reasons for the result or for the rule of law. Most scholars, we suspect, would contend that the justices ought to respect the

---

[1] (New York: Dodd Mead & Co., 1950), p. 256.
[2] See the concurring opinion of Justice Scalia in *Harper v. Virginia Dept. of Taxation,* 125 L Ed 2d 74 (1993), at 90.
[3] 6th ed. (St. Paul: West Publishing Co., 1990), p. 1406.

rule of law in the prior case. But if the justices adopt this standard, should they opt for the broad view of the rule of law; i.e., the rule of law as set forth in the controlling opinion in the prior case, or the narrow view; i.e., the rule of law necessary for the decision in that case? A rule of law is almost always stated in terms of some given facts. The question arises: Should the justices examine the relevant and material facts as presented by the author of the controlling opinion in the prior case or are they free to decide which facts in the former case are relevant and material? Finally, whether the justices respect the result, the rule of law, or the reasons, they must decide whether they ought to look at the relevant prior decision exclusively or whether they also should examine all the other decisions that may shed light on that decision.

The discussion in the former paragraph is heavily influenced by our reading of Bodenheimer.[4] Bodenheimer treated this topic under the rubric of the "ratio decidendi" of the case; i.e., the principle of the case.

Wise[5] points out that how one treats precedent is more art than science or, to use his language, is "a matter of drawing on a complex of habits, experiences, and skills which are more or less the common property of people trained in a particular legal tradition." We concur, for we have not seen any operational definitions which a justice or a scholar could follow which tell him or her whether a given prior decision is a precedent for a subsequent case.

We believe, however, that while it is easy to point out the ambiguities involved in deciding what constitutes a precedent, it is also possible to overemphasize them. In this regard it is striking to note that in most of the decisions we list as overturning decisions of the Supreme Court, the justices in their opinions do not disagree that the Court has overturned a precedent. Disagreement, if any, only concerns the propriety of overturning the prior decision.

Whether the Supreme Court ought to follow or overturn precedent in any given case ought to depend on the reasons for following or abandoning the precedent in question. Some of these reasons may be grouped together. We will do so by focusing on the justification for stare decisis.

JUSTIFICATION FOR STARE DECISIS

The justification for stare decisis usually rests on the values it fosters. Among such values are efficiency, continuity of the law, justice or fairness, legitimacy, and the enhancement of the Court's decision. Although we make no attempt to determine the relative worth of each, others have. Justice Scalia, for example, has written: "[T]he principal purposes of stare decisis . . . are to protect reliance interests and to foster stability in the law."[6] For him, justice or fairness and legitimacy are apparently of secondary importance, at most.

---

4   Edgar Bodenheimer, *Jurisprudence: The Philosophy and Method of the Law,* rev. ed. (Cambridge: Harvard University Press, 1974), pp. 432–439.
5   E. M. Wise, "The Doctrine of Stare Decisis," 21 *Wayne Law Review* 1043 (1975), at 1052.
6   *Itel Containers International Corp. v. Huddleston,* 122 L Ed 2d 421 (1993), at 439.

First, regarding efficiency, one may argue that a de novo solution to all problems requires too much time and effort. It is much easier to simply conform to the past. As Cardozo stated, "[T]he labor of judges would be increased almost to the breaking point if every past decision could be reopened in every case, and one could not lay one's own course of bricks on the secure foundation of the courses laid by others who have gone before him."[7] Similarly, Walter F. Murphy, a student of judicial politics, noted that stare decisis provides the "harried judges who face difficult choices with a welcome decision-making crutch."[8]

At times, of course, the justices must attempt to find a better solution to the dispute before them. For the past solution may no longer be workable, if indeed it ever was.

Economists, who claim expertise in efficiency, have considered it with regard to stare decisis. Landes and Posner, for example, view precedents "as a capital stock that yields a flow of information services which depreciates over time as new conditions arise that were not foreseen by the framers of the existing precedents."[9] Stare decisis, in other words, is a public good. And Jonathan F. Macey claims that stare decisis, or at least the lax form of stare decisis used by the Supreme Court, is efficient because: 1) it enables judges "to *avoid* having to rethink the merits of particular legal doctrine" in many cases; 2) it "enables higher courts to select cases for review more efficiently. Those cases that depart dramatically from established precedent can be easily identified and singled out for special attention"; and 3) "It increases the effects of the opinions reached by the intellectually active judges, while simultaneously easing the burden of deciding cases that falls on the shoulders of lazy judges."[10]

The views of these economists are backward looking, while stare decisis is more Janus-like – looking both ways simultaneously. One might argue that stare decisis facilitates better decisions because it forces the decision maker to think more deeply about the future uses of his decision. But the argument also has another side. At times, the decision maker will be handing down a suboptimal decision because he considers the precedential aspects of the decision.[11]

Second, adherence to precedent also assures continuity in the law. Such continuity is often desirable because many people rely on the law in conducting their affairs. In this connection, former Justice Lewis Powell contended that "This is especially important in cases involving property rights and commercial transac-

---

7 Benjamin N. Cardozo, *The Nature of the Judicial Process* (New Haven: Yale University Press, 1921), p. 149.
8 *Elements of Judicial Strategy* (Chicago: University of Chicago Press, 1964), p. 23.
9 William M. Landes and Richard A. Posner, "Legal Precedent: A Theoretical and Empirical Analysis," 19 *Journal of Law and Economics* 249 (1976), at 250–251. Posner was appointed by Reagan to the Seventh Circuit Court of Appeals and is an advocate of an economic approach to the law.
10 "The Internal and External Costs and Benefits of Stare Decisis," 65 *Chicago-Kent Law Review* 93 (1989), at 102, 108, 112.
11 See Frederick Schauer, "Precedent," 39 *Stanford Law Review* 571 (1987), at 572–574.

tions. Even in the area of personal rights, stare decisis is necessary to have a predictable set of rules on which citizens may rely in shaping their behavior."[12]

Continuity, of course, entails costs. For when the Court chooses continuity, it disregards changes in American society that might warrant legal alteration.

Certain decisions, however, are so basic to our understanding of the Constitution or have so changed American society that the probability of their being overruled approximates zero. Law Professor Henry Paul Monaghan,[13] for example, argues that it is inconceivable that the Court will overrule *Brown v. Board of Education,* 347 U.S. 483 (1954); *the Second Legal Tender Case,* 12 Wallace 457 (1871), which upheld Congress's power to make paper money legal tender for the payment of debts; or Congress's power to enact the New Deal legislation or to create the administrative state. One might easily add to the list such nineteenth century decisions as *Marbury v. Madison,* 1 Cranch 137 (1803); *Martin v. Hunter's Lessee,* 1 Wheaton 304 (1816); the interpretation of the necessary and proper clause in *M'Culloch v. Maryland,* 4 Wheaton 316 (1819); the definition of interstate commerce in *Gibbons v. Ogden,* 9 Wheaton 1 (1824); *Barron v. Baltimore,* 7 Peters 243 (1833); *Cooley v. Board of Wardens,* 12 Howard 299 (1852); the scope of the privileges and immunities clause of the Fourteenth Amendment in *The Slaughterhouse Cases,* 16 Wallace 36 (1873); or such twentieth century decisions as the series that incorporated most of the provisions of the Bill of Rights into the due process clause of the Fourteenth Amendment; *Bolling v. Sharpe,* 347 U.S. 497 (1954); *Baker v. Carr,* 369 U.S. 186 (1962); *Gideon v. Wainwright,* 372 U.S. 335 (1963) *Reynolds v. Sims,* 377 U.S. 533 (1964); or *Wesberry v. Sanders,* 376 U.S. 1 (1964). Justice William O. Douglas's discussion of *Santa Clara County v. Southern Pacific R. Co.,* 118 U.S. 394 (1886),[14] suggests that this case could appear among the foregoing as well, for it held that the Fourteenth Amendment's due process clause protects corporations, clearly a decision which cannot be overturned without basically changing the economic system. Finally, Michael J. Gerhardt argues that three precedents from the Great Society – *Katzenbach v. Morgan,* 384 U.S. 681 (1966); *Heart of Atlanta Motel v. United States,* 379 U.S. 241 (1964); and *Katzenbach v. McClung,* 379 U.S. 294 (1964) – are also immune from overruling.[15] The foregoing do not comprise a complete or a definitive list. What cases ought to appear is obviously a matter of opinion. But it is clear that even justices whose attachment to stare decisis is weak are unwilling to reexamine a host of decisions, even if they believe that these decisions were wrongly decided.

Third, one may argue that stare decisis is fairer or more just because it treats like cases alike. Justice Douglas contends that "there will be no equal justice

---

[12] "Stare Decisis and Judicial Restraint," 47 *Washington and Lee Law Review* 281 (1990), at 286.

[13] "Stare Decisis and Constitutional Adjudication," 88 *Columbia Law Review* 723 (1988), at 723, 744, 745.

[14] "Stare Decisis," 49 *Columbia Law Review* 735 (1949), at 737.

[15] "The Role of Precedent in Constitutional Decisionmaking and Theory," 60 *George Washington Law Review* 68 (1991), at 89.

under law if a negligence rule is applied in the morning but not in the afternoon."[16]

But if the early decision did not treat like cases alike (e.g., because it discriminated against women or blacks), it would not further the value of fairness or justice to follow it. In addition, Richard A. Wasserstrom points out that, at times, one might be able to argue persuasively that the rule of law announced in the early case should not be applied to other members of the class in the later case.[17] To fail to make such an argument and to follow stare decisis instead would not be the fair or the just way of deciding cases. Thus, adherence to stare decisis does not always foster fairness or justice.

Fourth, some scholars maintain that stare decisis fosters legitimacy. Walter Murphy, for example, asserts that "When the Court reverses itself or makes new law out of whole cloth – reveals its policy-making role for all to see – the holy rite of judges consulting a higher law loses some of its mysterious power."[18] Similarly, Justice Douglas contends that "*Stare decisis* serves to take the capricious element out of law."[19] And Justice Powell argues that "the elimination of constitutional stare decisis would represent an explicit endorsement of the idea that the Constitution is nothing more than what five Justices say it is. This would undermine the rule of law."[20]

We are uncertain whether these three people are concerned with the Supreme Court's legitimacy in the eyes of Court commentators or in the eyes of the general public. The general public, of course, knows and cares about few Supreme Court decisions, and we suspect that its reaction to these decisions rarely depends on whether the Court followed precedent, overturned precedent, or ignored precedent. Rather, the public's reaction is heavily influenced by whether it likes the outcome or not.

Court commentators, or at least some of them, pay attention to whether the Court followed precedent or not. But they also realize that, at times, it is legitimate for the Court to overturn precedent as long as the Court supplies a persuasive reason for so doing. In addition, we would find it quaint – given our knowledge of Supreme Court decision making – to suggest that commentators would be shocked to learn that the justices' attitudes influence their votes. Indeed, we believe that the arguments of Justices Douglas and Powell and of Murphy regarding legitimacy confuses two different questions. The first is: Why do justices decide cases the way they do? A partial but important answer to this question is that they are voting in accord with their attitudes. The second question is: Have they justified their decision by presenting a good argument? Whether a decision is legitimate, we believe, concerns only the second question. Thus, it is hardly illegitimate for a justice to vote in conformity with his attitudes, while

---

[16] Op. cit. fn. 14 *supra*, p. 736.

[17] *The Judicial Decision: Toward a Theory of Legal Justification* (Stanford: Stanford University Press, 1961), p. 71. Alternatively, one might argue that the two cases are dissimilar.

[18] Op. cit. fn. 8 *supra*, p. 204.   [19] Op. cit. fn. 14 *supra*, p. 736.

[20] Op. cit. fn. 12 *supra*, p. 288.

voting to overturn a precedent, when he advances cogent reasons why the precedent should be overturned. Does this suggest that we reject the legitimacy argument altogether? Not at all. Particularly in constitutional cases, when the justices are almost always dealing with an ambiguous text, it might be easier for a justice to justify his position when he follows precedent than when he votes to overturn it. But not always, of course.

Finally, some scholars contend that the justices ought to adhere to stare decisis because to do otherwise would undermine the precedential weight of their own decisions. In some cases, of course, a justice believes that it is more important to change direction and, thereby, create a new precedent than to support stare decisis. A given justice might attempt to free ride on the system by refusing to conform to precedent, while expecting his present and future colleagues to respect his decisions. But as in other situations, if there are too many free riders, no one will play the game and the precedential system will break down.

Analysis of the values associated with stare decisis suggests both advantages and disadvantages. Perhaps the best advice comes from Benjamin Cardozo, who stated that "Somewhere between worship of the past and exaltation of the present, the path of safety will be found."[21]

To this point we have discussed stare decisis in the abstract. It is also useful to attempt to understand it within the context of a particular case. A focus on the recent decision, *Payne v. Tennessee,* 115 L Ed 2d 720 (1991), may prove helpful.

STARE DECISIS APPLIED: *PAYNE V. TENNESSEE*

On Saturday morning, June 17, 1987, Pervis Tyrone Payne, a man with a low I.Q. and no previous criminal record, entered the apartment of Charisee Christopher, a 28-year-old mother. He sexually attacked her notwithstanding her resistance. Using a butcher knife he killed her and her 2-year-old daughter, Lacie Jo. Payne also attempted to kill her 3-year-old son Nicholas, but, with substantial help from modern medicine, Nicholas survived. Payne was convicted of two counts of first-degree murder and one count of assault with intent to commit first-degree murder. During the sentencing phase of the trial the state of Tennessee presented testimony by Nicholas's grandmother that Nicholas cried for his mother and sister. And in his closing argument the prosecutor also claimed that the murder affected Nicholas. He stated:

(Petitioner's attorney) . . . doesn't want you to think about . . . The brother who mourns for [little Lacie Jo] . . . every single day and wants to know where his best little playmate is. He doesn't have anybody to watch cartoons with him, a little one. These are the things that go into why it is especially cruel, heinous, and atrocious, the burden that that child will carry forever.[22]

In *Booth v. Maryland,* 482 US 496 (1987), the Supreme Court had held that the introduction into the trial of victim impact testimony violates the Eighth

---

[21]   Op. cit. fn. 7 *supra,* p. 160.   [22]   115 L ed 2d 720 (1991), at 729.

Amendment to the United States Constitution. And in *South Carolina v. Gathers,* 490 US 805 (1989), the Court had held that the prosecutor's presentation of a victim impact statement also violates the Eighth Amendment.

The jury sentenced Payne to death on each of the two murder counts and to a 30-year term on the assault count. The Tennessee Supreme Court affirmed the conviction and the sentence. On certiorari, the United States Supreme Court affirmed. In an opinion written by Chief Justice Rehnquist and joined by five of his colleagues, *Booth* and *Gathers* were overruled. Justices Marshall, Blackmun, and Stevens dissented. The decision and opinions were handed down on June 27, 1991, Justice Marshall's last day on the Court and the last day of the Court's October 1990 term.

In five of the six opinions in this case the author not only offered arguments regarding whether victim impact testimony and statements by the prosecutor violated the Constitution, but also presented his or her views regarding stare decisis. We examine these views.

In the opinion of the Court, Chief Justice Rehnquist argued that

Booth and Gathers were decided by the narrowest of margins, over spirited dissents challenging the basic underpinnings of those decisions. They have been questioned by members of the Court in later decisions, and have defied consistent application by the lower courts. . . . Reconsidering these decisions now, we conclude for the reasons heretofore stated, that they were wrongly decided and should be, and now are, over-ruled. [23]

One wonders why Rehnquist is telling us that *Booth* and *Gathers* were decided "by the narrowest of margins." Is he advancing the untenable and dangerous argument that we ought to judge the legitimacy of a position based on the number of people who support it, or is he merely bragging that he now has the votes to overturn these two decisions? And why should we care whether the dissent in these two cases was "spirited" or whether the decisions of the Court in these two cases were "questioned" in later decisions? The relevant consideration is not whether the dissents were "spirited" or whether the decisions were "questioned" but, rather, whether the justices writing these spirited dissents or questioning the decisions were advancing persuasive arguments.

Rehnquist is not the only justice who can be criticized in this case. In his concurring opinion, Scalia states that "The response to Justice Marshall's strenuous defense of the virtues of stare decisis can be found in the writings of Justice Marshall himself."[24] Marshall previously held, according to Scalia, that the Court should not follow stare decisis if the earlier decision was contrary to reason. Scalia argues that *Booth* defies reason. We find it somewhat ironic that Marshall ended his career on the Court as a strong defender of stare decisis. He did so fearing that the conservative Rehnquist Court was attempting to over-turn many of the civil liberties decisions of the Warren and Burger Courts: "The majority today sends a clear signal that scores of established constitutional

---

[23] Id. at 737–739.   [24] Id. at 741.

liberties are now ripe for reconsideration."[25] Marshall, of course, had not championed stare decisis when many of these cases were decided. This suggests the question: Is stare decisis a rule of convenience advanced by justices when it helps them to justify their decisions, or does it influence their decision making?

A third theme running through these opinions is the standards used to overturn precedent. Justice Souter, in his concurring opinion, held that a departure from precedent must be supported by "special justification" and he found special justification in this case. Marshall also favored the special justification standard but found none in this case. More specifically, he stated that precedent ought to be followed unless there were "subsequent changes or development in the law" that undermined the rationale of the earlier decision; there is a need "to bring [a decision] into agreement with experience and with facts newly ascertained"; or it can be shown that the precedent has become "a detriment to coherence and consistency in the law."[26]

Contrastingly, Scalia argues that no special justification is needed to overrule precedent. A mistake suffices to warrant overturning. Rehnquist also shows little respect for stare decisis in two different ways. First, he argues that the Court is not "constrained to follow precedent" if the governing decision is unworkable or "badly reasoned."[27] A case, of course, is presumably badly reasoned because a justice who disagrees with the outcome says so. Second, Rehnquist asserts that stare decisis is not particularly important in cases involving "procedural and evidentiary rules":

> Considerations in favor of stare decisis are at their acme in cases involving property and contract rights, where reliance interests are involved . . . the opposite is true in cases such as the present one involving procedural and evidentiary rules.[28]

And O'Connor merely holds that *Booth* and *Gathers* were "wrongly decided," implying that is all that is necessary.[29]

We believe that the positions taken by Scalia, Rehnquist, and O'Connor represent an abandonment of stare decisis. For if the doctrine of precedent means anything, it clearly does not allow a justice to overrule a former decision simply because he or she believes that it was wrongly decided, as these three justices intimate. In this connection, Justice Stevens stated:

> [T]he question whether a case should be overruled is not simply answered by demonstrating that the case was erroneously decided and that the Court has the power to correct its mistakes. The doctrine of *stare decisis* requires a separate examination. Among the questions to be considered are the possible significance of intervening events, the possible impact of settled expectations, and risk of undermining public confidence in the stability of our basic rules of law.[30]

---

[25] Id. at 748.   [26] Id. at 751.   [27] Id. at 737.   [28] Id. at 737.   [29] Id. at 740.
[30] John Paul Stevens, "The Life Span of a Judge-Made Rule," 58 *New York University Law Review* 1 (1983), at 9.

CONCLUSION

The material we have covered in this introduction has been explored time and again by law professors and by other judicial scholars. But the main purpose of this study is not to deal with the legalistic, doctrinal, and philosophical positions espoused by commentators, practitioners, and judges regarding stare decisis. Our main purpose, rather, is to present an empirical study of the alteration of precedent by the Vinson, Warren, Burger, and Rehnquist Courts through the 1991 term. The first step in such a study is to inspect the existing body of empirical research concerning stare decisis. To this material we now turn.

2

A survey of the empirical literature

In this chapter we will survey the empirical literature concerning the alteration of precedent on the United States Supreme Court. Because it is exceedingly difficult, if not impossible, to evaluate claims of knowledge when precise measures are not used, we will examine only the quantitative literature.

ULMER'S STUDY

Four people have conducted empirical studies of precedent: S. Sidney Ulmer,[1] John R. Schmidhauser,[2] David J. Danelski,[3] and Christopher P. Banks.[4] Ulmer, Schmidhauser, and Danelski are prominent political scientists, while Banks was a Ph.D. candidate in political science at the time he published his analysis. Ulmer, one of the three most important pioneers in the scientific study of judicial behavior,[5] investigated the overruling decisions from the beginning of the Court through the 1957 term. He defined a decision as "overruled": 1) "if the majority opinion expressly so states"; 2) if a justice so states in another opinion or in his outside writings; 3) if the Court reporter cites the case as overruled in the case summary; or 4) if *Shepard's Citations* lists the case as overruled.[6] Ulmer's list contains 81 overruling cases. These 81 cases overturned 103 decisions.

The following are the major findings of Ulmer's study:

The infrequency of overruling decisions. Ulmer concluded that precedents are rarely overruled. He pointed out that since 1880 the Supreme Court had decided more than 55,000 appellate decisions. The 65 decisions that he identified as

[1] "An Empirical Analysis of Selected Aspects of Lawmaking of the United States Supreme Court," 8 *Journal of Public Law* 414 (1959).

[2] "*Stare Decisis*, Dissent, and the Background of the Justices of the Supreme Court of the United States," 14 *University of Toronto Law Review* 194 (1962).

[3] "Causes and Consequences of Conflict and Its Resolution in the Supreme Court," in Sheldon Goldman and Charles M. Lamb, eds., *Judicial Conflict and Consensus* (Lexington: University of Kentucky Press, 1986).

[4] "The Supreme Court and Precedent: An Analysis of Natural Courts and Reversal Trends," 75 *Judicature* 262 (1992).

[5] The other two are Glendon Schubert and Harold J. Spaeth.

[6] Op. cit. fn. 1 *supra*, p. 416.

overturned since 1880 comprise only one-tenth of 1 percent of the total. This result does not surprise us. Small groups that meet regularly usually solve similar problems in similar ways. To do otherwise would greatly increase decision-making costs.

A minimum of five votes to overrule. Ulmer found that in only one of the 81 overruling decisions did the Court overturn a former decision by less than a majority of the entire Court. The vote in that case was 4 to 3. This finding is trivial because justices rarely vote 4 to 3 when the Court consists of nine justices.

The age of the overruled cases. Ulmer's chart of overruling and overruled decisions shows that 29 percent (or 30) of the overturned cases were 10 years old or less; 35 percent (or 35) were 11 to 20 years old; 14 percent (or 14) were 21 to 30 years old; 12 percent (or 12) were 31 to 40 years old; and the remaining 12 percent exceeded 41 years, or to be more precise, were between 43 and 98 years old. These findings are somewhat surprising in two respects. First, it is interesting that cases 11 to 20 years old were overturned at a somewhat greater rate than cases of briefer age (35 percent versus 29 percent). Second, only three of the overturned cases were older than 75 years – 95, 96, and 98.

Concerning the latter finding, one may argue that many decisions that have existed for more than 75 years are either so fundamental to the Court's view of the Constitution (if they are constitutional decisions) or so influenced practices in American society that they cannot be undone. Alternatively, older precedents may no longer be relevant to the resolution of modern controversies. And like antiquated statutes, they merely harmlessly clutter the Court's Reports.

On the other hand, it might appear somewhat illegitimate for the Court to overturn more recent precedents. To do so might give the impression that the justices merely vote on the basis of their attitudes and have no respect for precedent. It is also possible that the resolution decreed by the new precedent may still be workable. Finally, newer precedents might be favored by a majority of the justices on the Court, most of whom can be expected to follow "personal stare decisis"; i.e., vote for the same outcome in a subsequent case as they did in the original one.

The subject matter of the overruling decisions. Ulmer ascertained that most of the altering decisions concerned commerce or taxation. This finding also does not surprise us. In the era Ulmer examined, a large number of cases concerned these two areas of the law.

The size of decision coalitions in the overruling and overruled cases. In 32 of the 81 cases (40 percent) the majority bloc in the overruling case was either 8 or 9 votes larger than the minority bloc; in 14 cases (17 percent) the majority bloc was only 1 or 2 votes larger; and in 35 cases (43 percent) it was 3 to 7 votes larger. That the differences listed by Ulmer in 60 percent of the cases were less than 8 or

9 is expected. Despite suggestions to the contrary by Howard[7] and Rohde,[8] no evidence supports a judgment that the justices vote as a unit when acting boldly; e.g., when overruling their own precedents. Massing of votes occasionally occurs, of course, as *Brown v. Board of Education,* 347 US 483 (1954), and *United States v. Nixon,* 418 US 683 (1974), indicate, but these two cases are unusual.

From Ulmer's data on the size of the coalitions in the overruling cases[9] one can compile parallel statistics for the overruled cases. We discovered that in 35 of the 103 overruled decisions (34 percent) the majority bloc was either 8 or 9 votes larger than the minority bloc, and in 24 decisions (23 percent) the majority bloc was only 1 or 2 votes larger. Thus, the coalitions were slightly smaller in the overruled cases.

The occurrence of overrulings. Ulmer discovered that 53 percent of the overruling decisions (43 cases) occurred after 1925, a period of 32 terms, while only 47 percent (38 cases) took place in the earlier 135 terms. The modern Supreme Court's break with the past is not peculiar to itself, however. Similar departures have also characterized the legislative and executive branches of government. The New Deal serves as an apt example.

Related change activities of the Court. Ulmer found that between 1940 and 1954 not only did the number of overrulings increase but so did the number of cases modified, reversed, and questioned. He obtained these data by Shepardizing the cases, using *United States Citations.* Although Ulmer discovered a relationship between these four change-oriented activities, he found none between overruling and distinguishing cases. Apparently distinguishing cases is not a change-oriented activity.

The prior history of overruled cases. Ulmer discovered that 64 of the 103 overruled cases (62 percent) were not distinguished by the Court prior to overruling, 32 cases (31 percent) were distinguished once or twice, with only 7 cases (7 percent) distinguished three or more times. One case was distinguished eight times. This finding dramatically undermines the traditional image of the alteration process. According to that view, cases are distinguished time and again and when the exceptions have swallowed the rule, abandonment occurs. Overrulings on the Supreme Court apparently happen much more suddenly.

Ulmer also discovered that 76 (74 percent) of the 103 overruled cases were never cited by the Court as authority for a subsequent decision prior to their being overruled and an additional 18 cases (17 percent) were cited only once. Ulmer

---

7   J. Woodford Howard, Jr., "On the Fluidity of Judicial Choice," 62 *American Political Science Review* 43 (1968).

8   David W. Rohde, "Policy Goals, Strategic Choice, and Majority Opinion Assignments in the U.S. Supreme Court," 16 *American Journal of Political Science* 652 (1972).

9   Op. cit. fn. 1 *supra,* pp. 418–423.

concludes that cases that are used as authority for a subsequent decision two or more times are unlikely to be overruled.

Case load size and the number of overrulings. Ulmer found no close relationship between the size of the case load and the number of overruling decisions. He discovered, however, that of the 64 cases overruled since 1880, in 57 cases (89 percent), the case load was greater in the term in which the case was overruled than in the term which originally decided it. This finding comports with the increase in case load over time.

New justices and overruling decisions. Sixty-four of the 81 overrulings (79 percent) took place within five years of the seating of a new justice. This period covers only 41.6 percent of Ulmer's study. Twenty-three of these overrulings occurred during or five years after 1939–1941, a period in which Franklin Roosevelt made six appointments to the Court. An additional 10 overrulings happened during or five years after 1880–1882, a time in which three Republican presidents appointed five new justices. These findings, of course, are not surprising. They comport with the dominant view of judicial behavioralists that the attitudes of the justices strongly influence the Court's decision making, and that new justices can be expected to have attitudes different from their predecessors.

Justices who opposed overruling six or more times. Ulmer discovered that five of the six justices (all except Jackson) who voted against overruling a precedent six or more times did so more often in the second half of the cases in which they participated than in the first half. All six – McReynolds, Butler, Roberts, Reed, Frankfurter, and Jackson – are perceived as generally conservative justices who faced an increasingly liberal court during their later years.

Political party affiliation. Ulmer failed to find any relationship between the justices' political party affiliation and the frequency with which they overruled precedent. This finding also comes as no surprise, for no theoretical reason suggests the contrary.

Although Ulmer's pioneering study lacks a theoretical basis, his findings show that an imaginative social scientist, committed to quantification, can tell us much about the alteration of precedent.

SCHMIDHAUSER'S STUDY

The author of the second study we examine, John Schmidhauser,[10] used Ulmer's list of overruling decisions to test the relationship between stare decisis and certain background characteristics of the justices who participated in these decisions. He classified all 71 justices who voted in at least one overruling decision

---

[10] Op. cit. fn. 2 *supra.*

in terms of either a strong propensity to abandon stare decisis (defined as supporting the overruling decision in at least 80 percent of the cases) or a weak propensity (supporting the overruling decision in 79 percent of the cases or less). He compared this dependent variable with six background characteristics: 1) at least five years of prior judicial experience; 2) a family tradition of judicial service; 3) socio-economic status; 4) political party affiliation; 5) type of legal career; and 6) geographical origin.

We will not summarize Schmidhauser's findings because we are not persuaded that they are meaningful. We arrived at this conclusion for the following reasons: First, no theoretical reason supports a relation between any of the six background characteristics and the propensity to abandon stare decisis or the converse. One might argue, for example, that justices who come from poor origins are less likely to be self-confident, and that it takes a certain amount of self-confidence to abandon stare decisis. But we question both assumptions. No empirical evidence of which we are aware supports the conclusion that justices from poor homes are less likely to be self-confident than justices who come from rich homes. Nor does anyone know whether it takes more self-confidence to conform to the majority (and, therefore, to vote to abandon stare decisis) or to dissent (and, therefore, to vote to adhere to precedent). Note further that psychological concepts such as "self-confidence" are exceedingly difficult to measure and, therefore, one ought to be suspicious of any findings that relate this variable to specific behavior. Although disciplines often borrow concepts from one another, danger lurks when the borrower does so blindly.

Second, as mentioned above, Schmidhauser includes all 71 justices who voted in any of Ulmer's overruling decisions. But five justices (7 percent) voted in only one decision, and 27 others (38 percent) voted in no more than four. Only 24 of the 71 justices (34 percent) participated in at least 10 decisions. In short, many, if not most, of the justices did not vote a sufficient number of times to enable one to state with any confidence that they possessed a strong or a weak propensity to abandon stare decisis.

Third, when a justice votes to uphold stare decisis when his colleagues are abandoning it, he dissents from the majority's position and usually dissents in the case as well. Yet, at different stages of the Court's history different traditions governed the legitimacy of dissent.[11] As a consequence, the score a justice receives using Schmidhauser's measure not only reflects the propensity to abandon stare decisis but also is influenced by the Court's dissent norms. In short, Schmidhauser allows an external matter to contaminate the measurement of his dependent variable.

Fourth, Schmidhauser's category of support for stare decisis includes justices who voted to abandon stare decisis 79 percent of the time. We understand why he used such a high cut-off point: he needed a sufficient number of justices in this category. But this is not a good theoretical reason for such an arbitrary classification.

---

[11]   Thomas G. Walker, Lee Epstein, and William J. Dixon, "On the Mysterious Demise of Consensual Norms in the United States Supreme Court," 50 *Journal of Politics* 361 (1988).

Fifth, it is uncertain whether the propensity to abandon stare decisis ought to be investigated independently of the ideological outcome of the particular decisions involved. And because justices confront different ideological situations, it is not obvious that a high score by one justice means the same thing as the same score by another justice, especially when the justices in question did not participate in the same cases.

Sixth, Schmidhauser dichotomizes all variables, notwithstanding the fact that the propensity to abandon stare decisis and many of his background variables are continuous.

Finally, we suspect that some of his background characteristics have different meaning in the life experiences of the justices at different stages of the Court's history. The most obvious examples are political party affiliation and place of origin, but it may even be true of socio-economic status.

Some of these criticisms not only pertain to Schmidhauser's work but also are germane to other background studies that attempt to relate the backgrounds of the justices to their behavior. Simply put, background analysis has not proven fruitful as an explanation of judicial behavior.[12]

It may be somewhat unfair to criticize Schmidhauser. He wrote early in the study of judicial behavior, at a time when only a few scholars had sufficient theoretical understanding and adequate methodological skills to conduct good scientific research. We have benefitted from thirty years of judicial behavior research and the attendant sophistication that it generated. Schmidhauser's work simply fails to meet these modern standards.

DANELSKI'S STUDY

The third study we examine is that of David Danelski.[13] Danelski claimed to inspect *all* overrulings between the 1958 and 1980 terms of the Court. He identified 50 such decisions. For the same period we found 74 decisions.[14] Missing from Danelski's list are such salient cases as *Malloy v. Hogan,* 378 U.S. 1 (1964), and *Escobedo v. Illinois,* 378 US 478 (1964).[15] We do not know why Danelski listed so few cases. Perhaps he depended on unreliable research assistants to locate the cases. Danelski's truncated list, of course, makes one wary about the validity of his work. With this caveat, we present his findings.

---

[12] See, generally, S. Sidney Ulmer, "Are Social Background Models Time-Bound?" 80 *American Political Science Review* 957 (1986); and Jeffrey A. Segal and Harold J. Spaeth, *The Supreme Court and the Attitudinal Model* (Cambridge: Cambridge University Press, 1993), pp. 231–234.

[13] Op. cit. fn. 3 *supra.*   [14] See Appendix I.

[15] *Malloy* appears not only on our list, but also on the ones compiled by the Congressional Research Service, *The Constitution of the United States of America: Analysis and Interpretation* (Washington, DC: Government Printing Office, 1987); Jon D. Noland, "Stare Decisis and the Overruling of Constitutional Decisions in the Warren Years," 4 *Valparaiso University Law Review* 101 (1969); and Michael J. Gerhardt, "The Role of Precedent in Constitutional Decisionmaking and Theory," 60 *George Washington Law Review* 68 (1991). *Escobedo* is on our list, the Congressional Research Service's, and Gerhardt's, but not on Noland's.

Danelski reported that of the 41 overruled cases in which a dissenting opinion appeared, the Court specifically cited a prior dissenting opinion in 16 cases (39 percent), and in an additional 15 cases (37 percent) the ideas expressed in the dissenting opinions were used as the basis for the overruling decisions.[16] Thus, Danelski's finding supports the view that dissenting opinions sometimes serve as forerunners of future developments in the law.

Danelski also found that in 8 of the 41 voided cases (20 percent) the overruling opinion stated that the precedent was being overturned either because one or more of the subsequent cases on related issues had eroded the precedent or because time or changed circumstances suggested a different outcome. Finally, Danelski discovered that the dissenting opinions of Justices Frankfurter, Douglas, Warren, Black, and Murphy appeared to be the basis for three-fourths of the 31 overruled cases (16 and 15) mentioned above.

BANKS'S STUDY

Christopher Banks conducted the remaining empirical study.[17] Banks mainly used the Congressional Research Service list and supplement to compile a list of overturned and overturning cases from the Court's inception through the 1991 term. His most important findings are:

1) Three Courts rendered 59 percent of the overruling cases (118 of 201): Hughes (21), Warren (45), and Burger (52). Yet even in these three Courts the number of overrulings constituted only a small percentage of the total number of decisions: Hughes (1.25 percent), Warren (2.54 percent), and Burger (2 percent).
2) Constitutionally based decisions were formally altered more than twice as often as those based on statutory construction (121 versus 54).
3) Four of the Courts that disproportionately altered precedent were characterized by multiple membership changes. The Hughes Court, for example, was entirely transformed between June 2, 1937 and July 8, 1941. Simultaneously, 15 decisions voided precedents between the seventh and the sixteenth (or last) natural courts of the Hughes Court. The successor to the Hughes Court, presided over by Harlan Fiske Stone, continued to overturn a substantial number of decisions. Most of the altering decisions of the Warren Court were handed down after Frankfurter's retirement in 1962, while in the Burger Court most occurred after Douglas's retirement in November 1975.

THE EPSTEIN ET AL. STUDY

In addition to these four quantitative studies, Lee Epstein, Tracey George, Micheal W. Giles, and Thomas G. Walker[18] (hereafter Epstein et al.) used the

---

[16]   Op. cit. fn. 3 *supra*, p. 43.   [17]   Op. cit. fn. 4 *supra*.

[18]   "Rating the Justices: Lessons from Another Court," paper presented at the annual meeting of the Midwest Political Science Association, Chicago, April 1992.

Congressional Research list to ascertain which justices, from 1810 through the end of the 1988 term, voted most often with the majority in overruling decisions. Although their purpose was not a scholarly one, they discovered that Douglas and Brennan were tied for first, each casting 67 votes to overrule. Following them were Byron White (66), Black (56), Stewart (53), Blackmun (39), Thurgood Marshall (39), Warren (36), Powell (34), and Burger (33). They noted that all of the top ten justices served in the post-New Deal era, a period in which overruling decisions predominated, and that the list includes liberal, conservative, and moderate justices.

Even more interesting is their "prophetic vision" list, the top 10 justices who dissented in cases later overturned. Black ranked first (30 cases), followed by Douglas (27), Brandeis (16), Holmes (13), Warren (11), Stone (10), Harlan I (10), and Brennan, Murphy, Rutledge, and Stewart (8 each). The first four names also appear among those justices prominently featured as subjects of judicial biography.[19] Holmes ranked second in this regard (after John Marshall), Brandeis third, Black fourth, and Douglas seventh (after Taft and Frankfurter).

In summary, then, the prior research provides us with some understanding of the characteristics of the overruling and overruled cases. But we still need a more comprehensive view. The first step in pursuit of this goal is to identify the cases appropriate to our study.

---

[19] Henry J. Abraham, *Justices and Presidents,* 3d ed. (New York: Oxford University Press, 1992); Fenton S. Martin and Robert U. Goehlert, *The U.S. Supreme Court: A Bibliography* (Washington, DC: Congressional Quarterly, 1990).

3

A list of cases

As the previous chapters indicate, our study concerns the cases that altered precedent and the precedents that were altered. Researchers studying stare decisis would not necessarily examine these cases. They might, for example, investigate the cases that followed precedent, or those in which one of the parties asked the Court to overturn precedent. The first enterprise would be exceedingly difficult to undertake because it is not easy to distinguish between the citation of a precedent and adherence to it. Even *Shepard's Citations,* the most authoritative source of this information, does not set forth the guidelines it uses to assemble its list. The second venture would entail an examination of written briefs over a period of time. This would depend on access to the briefs themselves and is also difficult and time consuming. How, for example, should the consequences of a litigant's request to overturn precedent be determined? What about cases overturned even when no litigant so requests?

Both kinds of research might be worth doing. We, however, chose a different path: cases that formally alter precedent. In choosing this course, our initial problem is to select a list of overruling and overruled cases.

As indicated in Chapter 2, Banks and Epstein turned to the Congressional Research Service (CRS) to obtain a list of overturned and overturning cases. This list is unreliable, however, for one fundamental and four ad hoc reasons. Fundamentally, those who compiled it failed to indicate the guidelines which they used and which others could follow to determine the accuracy of the list. Also militating against reliability are the following considerations:

1) Although most of the overruling cases from 1810 to 1957 were compiled by Justice Brandeis, Emmet Wilson, Justice Douglas, or Albert P. Blaustein and Andrew H. Field, CRS also includes 40 cases which it claims were expressly overruled, but do not appear in any of these four lists. If these sources omitted so many cases, why does CRS use them in the first place?

2) Starting with 1957, CRS is on its own. From 1957 to 1979 CRS indicates that 73 of 82 cases (89 percent) were overruled in "express terms by the Supreme Court," while no case decided between 1980 and 1990 is so characterized. Because most of these alterations contain indisputably overruling language,

we suspect that CRS simply neglected to indicate whether the cases identified from 1980 to 1990 were expressly overruled.

3) CRS tells us that "in a great many instances the overruling must be deduced from the principles of related cases" and admits that "there is a chance here for a difference of opinion and this will be reflected in any listing."[1] This statement does not surprise us because we do not know of any two judges or scholars who deduce principles from related cases in the same way. Nevertheless, we believe that if CRS had specified the criteria it used and others could follow, the "difference of opinion" regarding these cases would have been minimized.

4) We have found wrong dates and wrong citations in the Congressional list, although their number is not great. In the post-1953 period, for example, *Cohen v. Hurley* is wrongly cited, while *Hoyt v. Florida* and *Jones v. United States* show the wrong date.[2]

Because of these problems with the CRS list we chose to compile our own. For the period covered by both (1946–1990) and excluding reargued and reheard cases, which we omit, a comparison between the CRS and our list shows that 94 of the overruling cases appear on both lists; 15 overruling cases appear on our list but not on theirs; and 25 of the overruling cases appear on theirs but not on ours. In short, 70 percent of all cases alleged to overrule a precedent are found on both lists and 30 percent in one or the other.[3] These differences are not trivial and indicate that we need to specify and justify the criteria we use to identify our list of overruling and overruled cases.

CRITERIA FOR DETERMINING
THE ALTERATION OF PRECEDENT

Our basic rule for determining whether a precedent was formally altered is a statement in the Court's majority or plurality opinion that the decision overrules one or more of the Supreme Court's precedents. All formal alterations are included: decisions that are constitutionally grounded, that rest on statutory construction, or that are based on the common law. We embrace both complete and partial overrulings, for both kinds of cases formally alter precedent. We omit, however, cases in which the Court overrules decisions of lower courts. To include overruled lower court decisions would extend the meaning of stare decisis far beyond its established limits. Higher courts are expected to overturn or modify the decisions of lower courts. Their so doing should not be viewed as an alteration of precedent. If it were, every time the Supreme Court resolved a

---

[1] Congressional Research Service, *The Constitution of the United States of America: Analysis and Interpretation* (Washington, DC: Government Printing Office, 1987), p. 2117.

[2] Id. at 2124, 2125, and 2127.

[3] We focus here on the overruling cases, rather than the overruled ones, because they are more important. When lists of overruling cases differ, the overruled cases will differ as well.

conflict between two or more circuit courts of appeals the alteration of precedent would necessarily be involved.

The requirement that the majority or plurality opinion state that a precedent was altered enables us to avoid pitting our judgment against that of the Court's majority opinion writer. Not uncommonly, a dissenter will assert that the majority has done violence to various precedents, or Supreme Court scholars will so allege. Rather than debate the truth of such statements, we believe it preferable to rely on the majority opinion's own language, or, in a case decided by a judgment of the Court, the plurality opinion. We depart from this rule in a couple of cases where the language of a dissenting opinion empirically establishes that an alteration took place that the majority has seen fit to obfuscate. Thus, in *Schneider v. Rusk,* 377 U.S. 163 (1964), the majority opinion fails to note that a provision of the Immigration and Nationality Act of 1952 revoking the citizenship of naturalized citizens who resided in their country of origin for three continuous years was at variance with a 1915 decision, *Mackenzie v. Hare,* 239 U.S. 299, which upheld the power of Congress to enact statutes similar to the one voided here.[4] In his dissent, Justice Clark systematically documents the incompatibility of the majority's ruling with the indisputable holding of *Mackenzie.*[5]

Note also that the votes to overrule a precedent are not necessarily the same as those that resolve the merits of the controversy. For example, the vote in *Thomas v. Washington Gas Light Co.,* 448 U.S. 261 (1980), was 7 to 2, while the vote on the overruled precedent was 6 to 3. The two dissenters voted to overrule. Similarly, the vote to overrule the affected precedents in *Planned Parenthood v. Casey,* 120 L Ed 2d 674 (1992), was 7 to 2, while the decision vote was 5 to 4. The two justices who opposed overruling – Blackmun and Stevens – were simultaneously members of the decision's majority opinion coalition, while the four dissenters were not!

Usually the Court speaks plainly when it overrules a precedent. There are some exceptions, however, as we shall see. A previous decision is "overruled," "disapproved," "no longer good law," "can no longer be considered controlling," "modified and narrowed," or the controlling opinion employs other analogous language such as "we decline to follow . . ."[6] or "can no longer be regarded as the law."[7] Occasionally, the Court will state that an earlier decision overruled a precedent even though the overruling opinion contains no language to this effect. Thus, for example, the majority in *International Paper Co. v. Ouellette,* 479 U.S. 481 (1987), at 488, stated that *Illinois v. Milwaukee,* 406 U.S. 91 (1972), overruled *Ohio v. Wyandotte Chemicals Corp.,* 401 U.S. 493 (1973). We accept such statements at face value. In these situations, we will assume that the deci-

---

4   *Mackenzie* sustained a statute that suspended the citizenship of a native-born American woman during coverture to a foreigner. See 377 U.S. at 174.
5   Id. at 170, 174–178. Significantly, nowhere in its opinion does the majority dispute Clark's assertions that *Mackenzie* held the contrary.
6   *Construction & General Laborers' Union v. Curry,* 371 U.S. 542 (1962), at 552.
7   *Pointer v. Texas,* 380 U.S. 400 (1965), at 406.

sion referred to by the later Court overruled the case(s) in question. Accordingly, we list *Illinois v. Milwaukee,* rather than *International Paper,* as overruling *Ohio v. Wyandotte Chemical.* Consider the following language from an early Vinson Court decision, *Angel v. Bullington,* 330 U.S. 183 (1947):

Cases like *David Lupton's Sons Co. v. Automobile Club,* 225 U.S. 489 . . . are obsolete insofar as they are based on a view of diversity jurisdiction which came to an end with *Erie R. Co. v. Tompkins* . . . (330 U.S. at 192)

According to our criteria, *Erie Railroad* rather than *Angel v. Bullington* overruled *Lupton's Sons.* To give a third example, 28 years after the decision in question a unanimous Court in *Kirkpatrick & Co., Inc. v. Environmental Tectonics,* 493 U.S. 400 (1990), at 407, stated that "American Banana was squarely decided on the ground (later substantially overruled, see *Continental Ore Co. v. Union Carbide & Carbon Corp.,* 370 U.S. 690 . . . (1962)) that the antitrust laws had no extraterritorial application . . ." Accordingly, we list *Continental Ore* as overruling *American Banana.*

We do, however, pay a price for this decision rule: our list of overrulings for the Vinson, Warren, Burger, and Rehnquist Courts is not necessarily permanent. Language in the majority opinion of some decision of a future Court may indicate that cases other than those we have identified have been overruled, even though the opinion in question in no way so states.[8]

Note that the language of alteration excludes "distinguished" precedent. Distinguished precedents retain their vitality; the majority merely considers them inapposite to the decision it has reached. The material facts on which the distinguished precedent rests are viewed as sufficiently different from those in the case at hand so as not to control the Court's decision. If, however, the opinion states that a precedent is limited "to its facts" (e.g., *Rutkin v. United States,* 343 U.S. 130 (1952), at 138), we will treat this situation as a formal alteration. Words such as "limit" and "confine" are not legal synonyms for "distinguished."[9] Indeed, *Shepard's Citations* uses two separate categories, "distinguished" and "limited."

Note further that we exclude the expansion of precedent from our definition of alteration. The Court rarely states that it is expanding a precedent beyond its original scope, even though that may be the effect of its subsequent decision. Thus, for example, we do not read *Brown v. Board of Education,* 347 U.S. 483 (1954), to have been formally altered by way of expansion because the Court

---

[8] A recent example, one that postdates the period that our analysis covers, occurred in *Bray v. Alexandria Women's Health Clinic,* 122 L Ed 2d 34 (1993), wherein the majority stated that the Burger Court decision, *Griffin v. Breckinridge,* 403 U.S. 88 (1971), overruled the Vinson Court case, *Collins v. Handyman,* 341 U.S. 651 (1951) (122 L Ed 2d at 45).

[9] Note, however, that we do not include *Rutkin* among our overruling decisions. We would have included it but for the fact that a Warren Court decision, *James v. United States,* 366 U.S. 213 (1961), uses the unequivocal word "overruled" with reference to the altered precedent, *Commissioner v. Wilcox,* 327 U.S. 404 (1946). We do not count as two overrulings separate cases that overturn a single antecedent decision, unless the overrulings void separate portions of the earlier decision.

cited it as authority for courtroom desegregation in *Johnson v. Virginia,* 373 U.S. 61 (1963).

Finally, unlike CRS, we do not consider the rehearing of a case originally decided by a tied vote to alter whatever precedent the summary affirmation established; e.g., *Halliburton Oil Well Cementing Co. v. Walker,* 329 U.S. 1 (1946); *MacGregor v. Westinghouse Co.,* 329 U.S. 402 (1947); and *Ladner v. United States,* 358 U.S. 169 (1958). Neither do we include memorandum or other non-orally argued cases among our set of altered precedents; e.g., *Zap v. United States,* 330 U.S. 800 (1947); *Dove v. United States,* 423 U.S. 325 (1976); and *Standard Oil of California v. United States,* 429 U.S. 17 (1976). We exclude such summarily decided cases, whether they appear among the formally decided cases in the front portion of the Reports or in the back of the Reports among the so-called "Orders" (most of which are denials of petitions for writs of certiorari), because they do not contain the full complement of conference votes – jurisdictional or certiorari, original vote on the merits, and final vote on the merits – as orally argued cases do. Conversely, we do not include formally decided cases which purportedly overrule summary per curiams; e.g., *Wesberry v. Sanders,* 376 U.S. 1 (1964), overruling *Colegrove v. Barrett,* 330 U.S. 804 (1947). We exclude such decisions because, in analyzing the justices' behavior, we want to pay attention to their votes in conference as well as those published in the Reports.

The unit of analysis throughout this book is the case citation rather than the docket number. The overruling of precedent is a function of a single opinion or judgment of the Court. A precedent is not altered differently because several docketed cases are combined under a single citation. Thus, *Brown v. Board of Education,* 347 U.S. 483 (1954), counts as a single overruling rather than four, as would be true if we had used the docket number as our unit of analysis.

On the other hand, while a given citation constitutes only a single overruling, the number of cases overruled is a separate and independent question. Although most alterations pertain to a single precedent, exceptions abound. The most numerically extreme exception is *Michigan v. Long,* 463 U.S. 1032 (1983), which overruled an unspecified – and probably unspecifiable – number of precedents. This, however, is the only case in which we are unable to identify the overruled decision(s).

On the basis of these decision rules, we identified 115 overruling decisions. These decisions formally altered 154 precedents. (See Table 3.1.) During its first six terms, the Rehnquist Court handed down more altering decisions (3.3 per term) than its predecessors; the Vinson Court the least (.9 per term). The Warren and Burger Courts were equally active, generating 2.7 overturning decisions per term. The Warren Court, however, formally altered more precedents per term than did the Burger Court, 3.7 versus 3.3. Again, the Rehnquist and Vinson Courts ranked first (4.7) and last (1.4). Not surprisingly, a large proportion of the altered precedents (41 percent) antedate the Vinson Court.

Table 3.1. *Overruling and overruled decisions by Court*

	Pre-Vinson	Vinson	Warren	Burger	Rehnquist	Total
N of terms		7	16	17	6	46
Overruling decisions		6	43	46	20	115
Overrulings per term		.9	2.7	2.7	3.3	2.5
Overruled per term		1.4	3.7	3.3	4.7	3.3
Overruled Court						
Vinson	8	2				10
Warren	29	14	17			60
Burger	18	10	19	9		56*
Rehnquist	8	2	8	8	2	28
Totals	63	28	44	17	2	154

*Excludes the decisions overruled by <u>Michigan v. Long</u>.

CRITERIA FOR ASCERTAINING THE SALIENCE OF THE OVERRULED AND OVERRULING DECISIONS

Not only are we interested in determining the identity of the overruled and overruling decisions, but we also want to ascertain which of these decisions are salient or important. Determining the importance of Supreme Court decisions has long bedeviled commentators. We will use the Congressional Quarterly's *Guide to the United States Supreme Court,* supplemented by the *Congressional Quarterly Weekly Report* (CQWR) for the 1989, 1990, and 1991 terms of the Court, to measure this variable.[10] Not all scholars agree that the *Guide* is the best possible source for this purpose, but we will employ it because we believe it is better than the four measures proposed by others, and also because it possesses additional characteristics that are attractive for our purposes.

The most widely used measure of salience is usually attributed to Elliot Slotnick,[11] although David Danelski,[12] and David W. Rohde[13] employed similar measures. If two of five constitutional law casebooks reprinted a case, Slotnick considered it "salient." Slotnick's measure can be criticized on at least three grounds: 1) The list of salient cases obtained by examining constitutional law casebooks obviously includes only constitutional law cases, while some important Supreme Court cases involve the construction of either statutes or of administrative regulations.[14] The underinclusiveness of Slotnick's sources is a more

[10] Elder Witt, ed. (Washington, DC: Congressional Quarterly, 1990), pp. 885–929; 48 *CQWR* 2131 (1990); 49 *CQWR* 1830 (1991); and 50 *CQWR* 1960 (1992).

[11] "Judicial Career Patterns and Majority Opinion Assignment on the Supreme Court," 41 *Journal of Politics* 640 (1979), at 642.

[12] "The Influence of the Chief Justice in the Decisional Process of the Supreme Court," paper delivered at the 1960 annual meeting of the American Political Science Association, New York.

[13] "Policy Goals, Strategic Choice and Majority Opinion Assignment in the U.S. Supreme Court," 16 *American Journal of Political Science* 652 (1972), at 680.

[14] Saul Brenner, "Fluidity on the United States Supreme Court: A Reexamination," 24 *American Journal of Political Science* 526 (1980), at 528.

serious problem in the earlier periods of the Supreme Court's history when a much larger percentage of the Court's decisions were nonconstitutional. 2) The authors of constitutional law casebooks do not claim that they are compiling a list of salient constitutional cases. Instead, they include a case because they believe that students in constitutional law courses ought to read and analyze it. Cases that serve educational purposes would undoubtedly be selected even if not salient, while some salient cases are likely to be omitted if too difficult, if another case in the casebook made the same or a similar point, if a later case overturned it, or even if the case could not easily be combined with other cases to form a chapter. In the third edition of Rossum and Tarr,[15] for example, the editors failed to include *Scott v. Sandford* (1857), the case that declared the Missouri Compromise unconstitutional, although they included it in their second edition.[16] Clearly *Scott* was one of the most important decisions in the Court's history. But it is apparently beyond the comprehension of many college students. 3) Finally, as Slotnick[17] himself recognizes, constitutional law texts contain few early cases and many recent ones. In Goldman's casebook,[18] for example, 39 cases date from 1793 to 1908 (a period of 115 years) and 116 were decided by the Burger and Rehnquist Courts (a period of 21 years, through the 1989 term.) Thus, a period less than one-fifth as long contains almost three times as many cases.

Sidney Ulmer[19] classified cases as "significant" by determining the number of times the Supreme Court cited a case within five years after the date of decision. He treated those cases that ranked in the top 10 percent as significant. There are a number of serious problems with this measure: 1) Some cases are cited less often in future decisions of the Court, not because they are less important, but because the Supreme Court infrequently deals with this area of the law (e.g., church-state relations), while other cases are cited more often because the Court regularly revisits the area (e.g., search and seizure).[20] 2) Cases that resolve an issue (e.g., *Marbury v. Madison*) are less likely to be cited in future decisions than cases that introduce a question. Yet, no intuitive reason posits the first kind of case as less important than the second. 3) Some cases might be "sleepers"; i.e., they might lie dormant during a period of time and then come to life. Ulmer's approach misses these cases. 4) Finally, the number of salient cases within a given five-

---

[15] Ralph A. Rossum and G. Allan Tarr, *American Constitutional Law: Cases and Interpretation,* 3d ed. (New York: St. Martin's Press, 1991).

[16] Ralph A. Rossum and G. Allan Tarr, *American Constitutional Law: Cases and Interpretation,* 2d ed. (New York: St. Martin's Press, 1987).

[17] Elliot Slotnick, "The Chief Justices and Self-Assignment of Majority Opinions" 31 *Western Political Quarterly* 219 (1978), at 220.

[18] Sheldon Goldman, *Constitutional Law: Cases and Essays,* 2d ed. (New York: HarperCollins, 1991.)

[19] "The Use of Power in the Supreme Court: The Opinion Assignments of Earl Warren, 1953–1960," 19 *Journal of Public Law* 49 (1970), at 51–52.

[20] Harold J. Spaeth, "Distributive Justice: Majority Opinion Assignments in the Burger Court, 67 *Judicature* 299 (1984).

year period based on Ulmer's measure depends entirely on the total number of cases in that period, an arbitrary result.

Dennis Haines[21] treated cases as "noteworthy" if they were discussed in at least 8 law review notes contained in the *Index to Legal Periodicals*[22] within two years of the decision. This is a curious measure, for the law students writing these notes are not like news reporters covering the Supreme Court, who presumably want to make sure that they report all the major decisions of the Court. Rather, they are more like local columnists who wish to comment on a legal problem of specialized interest. For example, in the two years after *Brown v. Board of Education* (1954), only 11 law review notes featured it, while *Fuentes v. Shevin,* 407 US 67 (1972), was the subject of 63 notes in its first two years. *Fuentes* held that replevin statutes, which authorized state officials to seize property on the application of any person who claimed ownership, violated the Fourteenth Amendment's due process clause. Apparently, *Fuentes* addressed more interesting legal questions than *Brown*. Note also that *Brown* was unanimous, a condition associated with fewer law review notes, while *Fuentes,* in contrast, was decided by a 4 to 3 vote. Haines, of course, would have classified both of these cases as "noteworthy," but we are not particularly interested in this result. For if law review notes are a valid measure of salience, cases with 63 review notes ought to be appreciably more salient than those with only 11 review notes.

There are additional problems with this measure. First, the *Index to Legal Periodicals* was initially published in 1887. Therefore, it cannot be used to measure the salience of pre-1885 cases. Second, the *Index's* first volume is much thinner than the latest one, reflecting the fewer law reviews in the early period. Thus, if we employ the *Index* for the entire period of its publication, we would have to vary the number of notes necessary to classify a case as "salient."

Harold Spaeth[23] measured salience by treating as "important" cases headlined on the cover of the advance sheets of the *Lawyer's Edition of the United States Supreme Court Reports*. The major difficulty with Spaeth's measure is that it generates too many salient cases. In the 1988 term, for example, 106 cases were so headlined, while in the 1989 term the number reached 109. Salience lacks utility if it includes so many cases. In addition, some of these cases were apparently selected because they might interest the attorneys who subscribe to this publication. In the 1988 term, for example, headlined cases included attorneys' fees, bar admission, mandatory representation of indigents in civil cases, and the activities of the American Bar Association's Committee on the Federal Judiciary. Note further that this measure cannot be employed to measure salience on the early Supreme Court because there were no advance sheets at that time.

---

[21] "Rolling Back the Top on Chief Justice Burger's Opinion Assignment Desk," 38 *University of Pittsburg Law Review* 631 (1977).
[22] New York: H. Wilson Company.   [23] Op. cit. fn. 20 *supra*.

Finally, Epstein et al.[24] classified a case as salient if the Congressional Quarterly's *Guide to the United States Supreme Court*[25] lists it as a "major decision." This is the measure we use. It, however, is also subject to criticism. First, its compilers failed to indicate the guidelines they used. Indeed, we do not even know what they mean by the term "major decision." But we should not cavil because we know of no better criteria. Lists of this kind, like lists of the greatest films of all time, inevitably mirror the subjective judgment of the compiler or the people who were surveyed.

We have selected the Congressional Quarterly measure because it possesses a number of virtues not shared by the other four.

1) Its compilers attempted to list the major decisions of the Supreme Court. The other four lists reflect other purposes.
2) The list is probably an informed one. The compilers inspected two multi-volume studies of constitutional history, one of which is the nine-volume *History of the Supreme Court of the United States*[26] written by some of America's most distinguished legal scholars.
3) It includes both constitutional and nonconstitutional cases and is therefore more inclusive than Slotnick's list.
4) It contains more early Court decisions. It lists 113 cases for the 1793–1908 period, while Goldman,[27] as previously mentioned, includes only 39. By contrast, Goldman provides 116 cases for the Burger and Rehnquist Courts through the 1989 term, while the Congressional Quarterly contains 187 cases through the 1991 term. The Congressional Quarterly ratio of new to old cases is 1.65, while the Goldman ratio is almost three to one.

As already indicated, neither the *Index to Legal Periodicals* nor the advance sheets of the *Lawyer's Edition of the U.S. Supreme Court Reports* can be employed to measure the salience of the Court's early decisions, while Ulmer's measure makes no sense for any period. Using Congressional Quarterly we discovered that 38 of 115 overruling decisions are salient (33 percent), as were 25 of 154 overruled cases (18 percent).[28] The results are presented in Table 3.2.

PRECEDENTS ALTERED BY THE COURT

On the basis of the decision rules presented above, in Appendix I we list the overruling and overruled cases in chronological order. In Appendix II we briefly describe each of the cases in which the Vinson, Warren, Burger, and Rehnquist

---

[24]   Lee Epstein, Tracey George, Micheal W. Giles, and Thomas G. Walker, "Rating the Justices: Lessons from Another Court," paper presented at the annual meeting of the Midwest Political Science Association, Chicago, 1992.

[25]   Op. cit. fn. 10 *supra.*

[26]   Edited by Paul Freund and Stanley N. Katz (New York: Macmillan, 1971–1984).

[27]   Op. cit. fn. 18 *supra.*

[28]   Because the CQ *Guide* was published prior to the 1989, 1990, and 1991 terms, we inspected the *Congressional Quarterly Weekly Report* to obtain a list of salient cases for these three terms. These are indicated by a double asterisk in Appendix I.

Table 3.2. *Salient overruling and overruled decisions by Court*

Court	Vinson	Warren	Burger	Rehnquist	total
No. of terms	7	16	17	6	46
Salient overruling	1	20	11	6	38
Salient overruled	0	13	5	7	25

Sources: Elder Witt, ed., Guide to the United States Supreme Court (Washington, DC: Congressional Quarterly, 1990), pp. 885-929; 48 CQWR 2131 (1990); 49 CQWR 1830 (1991); and 50 CQWR 1960 (1992).

Courts overruled the Court's previous decisions. Table 3.1 complements the Appendices by presenting a numerical summary of the overruling and overruled decisions for each term of each Court. Appendix I also provides the name and citation of each of the overruling and overruled cases, as well as the legal provision(s) at issue and the policy question(s) that the case contains. The decision rules governing the legal provisions at issue in a given case and the policy issue to which it pertains are those specified in the documentation to the *United States Supreme Court Judicial Database, 1953–1992 Terms.*[29] The basic criterion for determining the relevant legal provisions is a reference to it in the summary of one of the numbered headings in the "syllabus" compiled by the Reporter of the Court's decisions. A case's issue, by contrast, depends on the justices' own statements as to what a case concerns. The objective is to categorize cases from a public policy standpoint, a perspective that the legal basis for decision often disregards. But not always. A number of overrulings have the same legal provision and policy issue: e.g., double jeopardy, habeas corpus. Prior analysis indicates that the coding of cases decided by the Warren and Burger Courts was reliable. The cases decided by the Vinson and Rehnquist Courts have not yet been subject to a similar analysis. But because the same codes were used and the same person, Harold Spaeth, coded all the cases in all four Courts, it is reasonable to assume that the coding in these two Courts is also reliable.

Appendix I asterisks the cases that are listed in the Congressional Quarterly. In our description of the cases in Appendix II, we indicate whether a case is salient by referring to it as "salient," "important," "major," "landmark," or "listed in Congressional Quarterly." We use these terms for variety only. We do not suggest, for example, that "landmark" decisions are more important than "salient" ones.

Some readers may consider Appendix II, our chronological term-by-term description, analytically superfluous. We, however, believe that a historical overview sets the analytical stage, identifies pertinent judicial actors, and summarizes the cases that constitute our units of analysis. Readers interested in referencing specific overrulings should find Appendix II especially useful.

[29] Compiled by Harold J. Spaeth, Ann Arbor: Interuniversity Consortium for Political and Social Research, 1993, pp. 41–44, 56–58.

The statutory and constitutional provisions at issue in the overruling cases are among those that were most litigated during the Warren, Burger, and early Rehnquist Courts.[30] The statutory provisions are habeas corpus, internal revenue, labor relations, civil rights, antitrust, and immigration. The constitutional provisions supporting overrulings also reflect the overall pattern, although with marked differences in rank order: Fourth Amendment (12), equal protection clause (10), interstate commerce clause (9), Fourteenth Amendment due process and First Amendment (7 each), and self-incrimination, double jeopardy, and the case or controversy requirement of Article III (4 each).

Table 4.7 in Chapter 4 shows that almost two-thirds of the overrulings rest on constitutional grounds, as compared with a fifth on statutory bases. This difference conforms to the Court's policy – dating at least to the time of Chief Justice Taney – that the justices are less concerned about conforming to stare decisis in constitutional cases than in statutory cases.[31] Congress can correct statutory errors, but only the Court can change its constitutional decisions.

The policy aspects of the overruling decisions also reflect the frequency with which the Court addressed the various issue areas overall. Over one-third of the overruling decisions pertain to criminal procedure, followed by economic regulation at slightly less than 20 percent. Tied for third in the overrulings are the civil rights and judicial power issue areas at 13.3 percent. The next largest areas are federalism (7.4 percent) and First Amendment (5.2 percent). The totality of the Warren, Burger, and early Rehnquist Court decisions produce virtually the same rankings for the first four issue areas: criminal procedure (21.2 percent), economic regulation (20.3 percent), civil rights (16.7 percent), and judicial process (12 percent). First Amendment is fifth (8.6 percent), while federalism is seventh (4.3 percent).

CONCLUSION

In this chapter we presented the decision rules we used to determine which decisions of the Vinson, Warren, Burger, and Rehnquist Courts – the last though the end of the 1991 term – formally altered the Court's precedents. We also identified the overruling and overruled decisions that the Congressional Quarterly classifies as salient. Applying these decision rules, we identified and described the overruling and the overruled decisions of these four Courts. (See Appendices I and II.) Although our list differs somewhat from the list compiled by the Congressional Research Service, we specified the criteria for overruling and thereby provided a measure for determining the reliability of our list. Not surprisingly, we find that a substantial majority of the overruling decisions rest on constitutional bases and primarily pertain to the legal and policy issue areas that the Court most frequently considers.

[30] Lee Epstein, Jeffrey A. Segal, Harold J. Spaeth, Thomas G. Walker, *The Supreme Court Compendium: Data, Decisions & Developments* (Washington, DC: CQ Press, 1994), pp. 553–556.

[31] *Passenger Cases,* 7 Howard 283 (1849), at 470.

4

Some characteristics of the overruling and overruled cases

In this chapter we will attempt to ascertain some of the characteristics of the overruling and overruled cases. Although we will mainly examine the overruling and overruled cases themselves, at times we will also compare these cases with the non-overruling and the non-overruled cases. We will both present descriptive data and test hypotheses.

THE AGES OF THE OVERRULED PRECEDENTS

As we indicated in Chapter 2, Ulmer[1] discovered that the Supreme Court's 11- to 20-year-old decisions were more likely to be overruled than those of any other age. He also found that only 3 percent of the overturned precedents exceeded 95 years of age.[2] Blaustein and Field,[3] whose study covered the Court through the 1956 term, found that the mean life-span of overruled cases was 24 years and the median life-span was 17 years.

We inspected the ages of the 154 overruled precedents of our study and discovered that the most frequently overruled decisions were 0 to 10 years old (26.6 percent), followed by those decided 11 to 20 years previously (23.4 percent). (See Table 4.1.) In other words, half the overruled decisions survived less than 21 years. (Ulmer's comparable proportion is 64 percent.) We also found that 6.4 percent of the overturned cases (10 cases) were over 90 years old. (Ulmer's comparable figure is 3 percent, or 3 cases.)

The conventional wisdom does not specify an age at which precedents become sacrosanct. Nonetheless, we certainly feel safe in assuming that cases decided in the nineteenth century and earlier qualify in this regard. Inspection of the list of overruled decisions in Appendix I shows that slightly more than 10 percent of them predate 1900 (16 of 154). This low proportion seems to support the conventional wisdom, even though we recognize that far more decisions of the Court were handed down in the twentieth century than in the nineteenth century. (See Table 4.2.)

---

[1] S. Sidney Ulmer, "An Empirical Analysis of Selected Aspects of Lawmaking of the United States Supreme Court, "8 *Journal of Public Law* 414 (1959) at 420–423.

[2] Id. at 424.

[3] Albert P. Blaustein and Andrew H. Field, "Overruling Opinions in the Supreme Court," 57 *Michigan Law Review* 151 (1958), at 161.

Table 4.1. *Ages of overruled decisions*

Years	N	%	Years	N	%
0-10	41	26.6%	61-70	4	2.6%
11-20	36	23.4%	71-80	1	.6%
21-30	21	13.6%	81-90	2	1.3%
31-40	21	13.6%	91-100	5	3.2%
41-50	10	6.5%	Over 100	5	.2%
51-60	8	5.2%			
			Total	154	99.8%

Table 4.2. *Overruled nineteenth century precedents by Court*

Court	Vinson	Warren	Burger	Rehnquist	Total
N	0	4	7	5	16
%	0.0	6.7	12.5	17.9	10.4

Which of the four Courts in our study was likely to have overturned the most recent precedents? Although a number of variables relate to this question, at least two are particularly pertinent: first, the period during the Court's tenure in which most of its overturnings took place and, second, the time between that period and the probable targeted period of the overturned cases. In focusing on the probable targeted period, we do not assume that most of the overruled decisions of any Court are likely to have been decided in that period. The Court's alterations range much more widely than that. We are simply attempting to identify a likely major target with the hope that it reflects the overall picture.

Banks[4] tells us that most of the altering decisions of the Warren Court were handed down after Frankfurter's retirement in 1962. Our list of overruling decisions, which differs somewhat from the list used by Banks, indicates that the Warren Court overruled 43 decisions and all except 9 (21 percent) were decided during or after the 1962 term. We also know that the transformation of the Court from moderate to strong support of civil liberties began with the 1961 term. Segal and Spaeth[5] report that in the early Warren Court (1953–1960) term-by-term support for civil liberties mostly ranged between 50 and 59 percent, while in its later terms (1961–1968) support mainly varied from the low 70s to the low 80s. It is likely, therefore, that a major targeted period for the overturning decisions of the Warren Court was the 1953–1960 era of that Court.

In contrast, it is likely that the gap between the overrulings and the overruled decisions of the Burger Court spanned a longer time. Banks[6] indicates that most

---

4   Christopher P. Banks, "The Supreme Court and Precedent: An Analysis of Natural Courts and
     Reversal Trends," 75 *Judicature* 262 (1992), at 266.
5   Jeffrey A. Segal and Harold J. Spaeth, "Decisional Trends on the Warren and Burger Courts:
     Results from the Supreme Court Data Base Project," 73 *Judicature* 103 (1989), at 104.
6   Op. cit. fn. 4 *supra*.

of the altering decisions of the Burger Court were handed down after Douglas's retirement in November 1975. We list 46 overruling decisions during the Burger Court and all but 13 (28 percent) date from or after the 1975 term. Yet, it is likely that a major target of the conservative Burger Court was the liberal Warren Court decisions from 1961 to 1968. Thus, when we compare the Burger Court with the Warren Court we are dealing with an additional six-year gap. The Rehnquist Court probably overturned even older precedents than the Burger Court. For a major targeted era of this conservative Court was likely to be this same liberal 1961–1968 period. The conservative Vinson Court overturned only 10 precedents and, therefore, it makes little sense to talk about a likely major targeted area.

In short, we expected the Warren Court to alter the most recent precedents, and also expected the Burger Court to overturn somewhat more recent precedents than those overruled by the Rehnquist Court. To determine whether our hypothesis was supported, we examined the average and median age scores of the four Courts. Table 4.3 contains the results.

We discovered that the *median* score results support the Warren Court portion of the hypothesis. The median age of the Warren Court overrulings was 18, exactly 6 points below the Burger Court (24.0) and below the Vinson Court (24.5) and Rehnquist Court (23.0) as well. The Warren Court also had the second lowest *average* score (26.2), which was 5.8 points lower than the Burger Court's (32.0) and 12.6 points lower than the Rehnquist's Court (38.8). The Vinson Court's score of 20.5 should be substantially ignored because of its paucity of overrulings (10).

We also found, as indicated above, that the Burger Court's *average* score was 6.3 points lower than the average score for the Rehnquist Court (32.0 versus 38.3), but its *median* score was virtually the same (24.0 versus 23.0). In short, we received mixed results for this part of the hypothesis.

The Warren Court was the only Court of the four which underwent a major ideological shift, at least in the important civil liberties area. As already indicated, in the early period the term-by-term support for civil liberties mostly ranged between 50 and 59 percent, while in its later terms the range was mostly between the low 70s and the low 80s. Goldman[7] reports a 35 percent support for civil liberties in the first Vinson Court (1946 through 1948 terms) and a 29 percent score in the second Vinson Court (1949 through 1952). His list includes only nonunanimous cases and was derived from Schubert's dataset.[8] Segal and Spaeth[9] report that the Burger Court gradually became more conservative as it aged. Its term-by-term support for civil liberties ranged from 54.5 percent (1969 term) to 33.7 percent (1983 and 1985 terms). The gap between its highest and

---

[7] Sheldon Goldman, *Constitutional Law, Cases and Essays,* 2nd ed. (New York: Harper Collins, 1991), p. 131.

[8] Glendon Schubert, *The Judicial Mind* (Evanston, IL: Northwestern University Press, 1965).

[9] Op. cit. fn. 5 *supra.*

Table 4.3. *The average and median age of overruled precedents by Court*

Court	Vinson	Warren	Burger	Rehnquist
Average	20.5	26.2	32.0	38.8
Median	24.5	18.0	24.0	23.0

lowest term score was 20.8, while the gap between the highest and lowest term score on the Warren Court was 36.1. And the Rehnquist Court remained conservative throughout the period of our study. Thus, it might be expected that the Warren Court would be more likely to overrule its own precedents than the other three Courts. The results, set out in Table 4.4, conform to our expectations. We discovered that 28.3 percent of the Warren Court's overrulings involved precedents of its own making. The comparable statistics were 20 percent for the Vinson Court (but based on a small number of cases), 16.1 percent for the Burger Court, and 7.1 percent for the Rehnquist Court.

Another aspect of the age of altered precedents warranted testing. We expected that the older precedents would tend to be overruled by a unanimous or nearly unanimous vote (9 to 0, 8 to 0, 8 to 1), while newer precedents would tend to be overruled by a minimum winning or a close vote (5 to 4, 5 to 3). We based this hypothesis on our belief that not all justices would be willing to overturn the more recent precedents. Indeed, justices on the overruling Court who voted in favor of the precedent being overruled might wish to adhere to their previous position. In contrast, there was no reason to believe that the older precedents would generate any such loyalty.

We tested this hypothesis for all the overturning cases in our dataset. If a given overturning decision altered more than one precedent we, first, tested it by using the older or the oldest overruled precedent. Then we tested it employing the more recent or the most recent precedent. We doubted, however, that the results would substantially differ when we used the first procedure rather than the second.

We grouped the altering cases by vote into three categories: 1) 9-to-0, 8-to-0, 8-to-1; 2) 5-to-4, 5-to-3; and 3) an intermediate category of 7-to-1, 7-to-2, 6-to-2, 6-to-3, and 5-to-2.[10] We also divided the precedents into three age groups: 1) 0 to 10 years, 2) 11 to 39 years, and 3) 40 years or more.

---

[10]   We adopted this division in part because the size of the difference between the majority and the minority (if any) may range from 9 to 1. We chose to group the cases into three groups of three (9-0, 8-0, 8-1), (7-1, 7-2, 6-2), and (6-3, 5-3, 5-4). We added the 6-3 division to the intermediate group, however, because of the distinctive behavior that tends to characterize the minimum winning coalition. See, for example, Saul Brenner and Harold J. Spaeth, "Majority Opinion Assignment and the Maintenance of the Original Coalition on the Warren Court," 32 *American Journal of Political Science* 72 (1988); Saul Brenner, Timothy Hagle, and Harold J. Spaeth, "Increasing the Size of Minimum Winning Original Coalitions on the Warren Court," 23 *Polity* 309 (1990). The 5-3 vote falls into this category when the Court reverses or otherwise fails to affirm the decision of the court that it is reviewing.

Table 4.4. *The frequency with which the Courts overruled one another*

Court	Vinson	Warren	Burger	Rehnquist	Total
Pre-Vinson	8 (80%)	29 (48.3%)	18 (32.1%)	8 (28.6%)	63
Vinson	2 (20%)	14 (23.3%)	10 (17.9%)	2 (7.1%)	28
Warren		17 (28.3%)	19 (33.9%)	8 (28.6%)	44
Burger			9 (16.1%)	8 (28.6%)	17
Rehnquist				2 (7.1%)	2
Totals	10	60	56	28	154

When we examined the older or the oldest precedent (when there was more than one), we obtained results that conformed to our hypothesis. More specifically, precedents 40 years or older were more likely to be overruled by a 9-to-0, 8-to-0, or 8-to-1 vote (58 percent) than by a 5-to-4 or 5-to-3 vote (13 percent), while precedents that were 0 to 10 years old were more likely to be overturned by a 5-to-4 or 5-to-3 vote (48 percent) than by a 9-to-0, 8-to-0, or 8-to-1 vote (21 percent). The full results appear in Table 4.5. The resulting association between the age of the precedent and the size of the vote is a robust GAMMA of .477.

Comparable results occurred when we inspected the more recent or the most recent precedent (when there was more than one). We discovered that precedents that were 40 or more years old were more likely to be altered by a 9-to-0, 8-to-0, or 8-to-1 vote (64 percent) than by a 5-to-4 or 5-to-3 vote (4 percent), while precedents of a vintage of 10 years or less were more likely to be altered by a 5-to-4 or 5-to-3 vote (47 percent) than by a 9-to-0, 8-to-0, or 8-to-1 vote (21 percent). The resulting GAMMA is a still more substantial .531.

THE IMPORTANCE OF THE OVERRULING AND OVERRULED CASES

As reported in Chapter 3, 38 of the overruling decisions in our dataset (33 percent) are salient cases, as are 25 of the 154 overruled cases (16.2 percent). (See Table 4.6.) Not surprisingly, the Warren Court produced an appreciably higher proportion of important overrulings than the other three Courts. The Warren Court's percentage is 46.5. The Rehnquist Court occupies second place (30.0 percent), ahead of the Burger Court (23.9).

Should we be impressed with these percentages? One way of judging them is to compare them with the percentage of salient cases among the non-overruling cases. We will do so for the Warren and Burger Courts. The Warren Court decided 2095 orally argued, non-overruling cases.[11] The Congressional Quar-

---

[11] Excluding cases decided by a tied vote and those arising under the Court's original jurisdiction. In these kinds of cases the precedent is unlikely to be overruled. Indeed, it is doubtful whether a tied vote constitutes a precedent.

Table 4.5. *Relationship between the age of the overruled precedent and the size of the vote to overrule*

Age of oldest overruled precedent	Size of overruling vote			Total
	9-0, 8-0, 8-1	7-1, 7-2, 6-2, 6-3, 5-2	5-4, 5-3	
40 years or more	18	9	4	31
11 to 39 years	13	31	10	54
0 to 10 years	6	9	14	29
Total	37	49	28	114

Age of most recently overruled precedent	Size of overruling vote			Total
	9-0, 8-0, 8-1	7-1, 7-2, 6-2, 6-3, 5-2	5-4, 5-3	
40 years or more	16	8	1	25
11 to 39 years	14	30	11	55
0 to 10 years	7	11	16	34
Total	37	49	28	114

Table 4.6. *Number of important overruling and overruled cases*

Court	Overruling	%	Overruled	%
Vinson	1/6	16.7	0/10	0.0
Warren	20/43	46.5	13/60	21.7
Burger	11/46	23.9	5/56	8.9
Rehnquist	6/20	30.0	7/28	25.0
Totals	38/115	33.0%	25/154	16.2%

terly lists 53 of them as salient (2.5 percent). This is obviously a dramatically different statistic than the 46.5 percent we obtained for the overruling cases of this Court. Comparable figures for the Burger Court are 138 salient, non-altering decisions out of a total of 2552 (5.4 percent), as compared with 23.9 percent salient among the overruling cases. Clearly, decisions altering precedent are much more likely to be salient.

Regarding overruled cases, the Rehnquist Court ranks first, producing a slightly higher proportion of important cases than did the Warren Court (25.0 versus 21.7 percent). The other two Courts trail distantly. All four Courts generated a higher percentage of important overruling cases than overruled cases.

There were a number of cases in our dataset in which the overruled case was listed as salient, but the case that overruled it was not so listed. We consider it incongruous that a voided case is treated as more important than the one that overruled it. One would certainly expect that if someone classifies a given case as important, he would *a fortiori* judge the case that overrules it important as well.

THE BASES ON WHICH THE COURT ALTERS PRECEDENT

The Court may alter precedents on the basis of constitutional interpretation, statutory construction, common law, or its supervisory authority over the lower federal courts. Justices have frequently stated that decisions based on the Constitution are always open to reconsideration. In the words of Chief Justice Taney, the Court's "opinion upon the construction of the Constitution is always open to discussion when it is supposed to have been founded in error, and that its judicial authority should hereafter depend altogether on the force of the reasoning by which it is supported."[12] Justice Powell elaborates:

To be sure, *stare decisis* promotes the important considerations of consistency and predictability in judicial decisions and represents a wise and appropriate policy in most instances. But that doctrine has never been thought to stand as an absolute bar to reconsideration of a prior decision, especially with respect to matters of constitutional interpretation. Where the Court errs in its construction of a statute, correction may always be accomplished by legislative action. Revision of a constitutional interpretation, on the other hand, is often impossible as a practical matter, for it requires the cumbersome route of constitutional amendment. It is thus not only our prerogative but also our duty to re-examine a precedent where its reasoning or understanding of the Constitution is fairly called into question. And if the precedent or its rationale is of doubtful validity, then it should not stand.[13]

Some justices take a more radical view toward stare decisis in constitutional cases. Justice Scalia, for example, recently adopted Justice Douglas's perspective:

With some reservation concerning decisions that have become so embedded in our system of government that return is no longer possible . . . I agree with Justice Douglas: "A judge looking at a constitutional decision may have compulsions to revere past history and accept what was once written. But he remembers above all else that it is the Constitution which he swore to support and defend, not the gloss which his predecessors have put on it."[14]

The foregoing statements suggest that the Court is more likely to overturn a constitutional precedent. Whether the Court is likely to overrule a common law precedent depends on whether the issue involved concerns the judiciary. Examples of such issues are those concerning comity and its abstention doctrine, and the doctrine of primary jurisdiction as it applied to administrative agency activity. Similarly, the Court is likely to overrule cases involving its supervisory authority over the lower federal courts, for this is an area that tends to be exclusively under the Court's power.

[12] *Passenger Cases,* 7 Howard 283 (1849), at 470.
[13] *Mitchell v. W. T. Grant Co.,* 416 U.S. 600 (1974), at 627–628 (footnote omitted).
[14] *South Carolina v. Gathers,* 490 U.S. 805 (1989), at 825.

Table 4.7. *The bases for overruling precedent*

Court	Constitution	Statute	Common law	Supervisory authority over federal courts	Total
Vinson	2(33.3%)	2(33.3%)	2 (33.3%)		6
Warren	29(67.4%)	10(23.3%)	2 (4.7%)	2(4.7%)	43
Burger	29.5(64.1%)	7(15.2%)	9.5 (20.7%)		46
Rehnquist	13(65.0%)	4(20.0%)	2 (10.0%)	1(5.0%)	20
Total	73.5(63.9%)	23(20.0%)	15.5(13.5%)	3(2.6%)	115

Table 4.7 displays by Court the bases on which alteration of precedent has occurred. Overall, almost 64 percent of the overruling decisions were based on constitutional grounds, while only 20 percent rested on statutory grounds. In addition, 13.5 percent of the overruling cases were based on the common law and 2.6 percent were based on the Court's supervisory authority over the lower federal courts. A Court-by-Court breakdown, presented in Table 4.7, indicates that there were no substantial differences among the Courts. Ignoring the Vinson Court, in which there were only six overruling cases, we see that the Warren, Burger, and Rehnquist Court had virtually the same percentage of constitutional overrulings, i.e., 67.4 percent (Warren Court),[15] 64.1 percent (Burger Court),[16] and 65 percent (Rehnquist Court).[17] Regarding statutory overrulings, however,

[15] The Warren Court's 29 constitutional overrulings occurred in *Brown v. Board of Education, Reid v. Covert, Vanderbilt v. Vanderbilt, Mapp v. Ohio, Gideon v. Wainwright, Gray v. Sanders, Ferguson v. Skrupa, Schneider v. Rusk, Malloy v. Hogan, Murphy v. Waterfront Commission, Jackson v. Denno, Escobedo v. Illinois, Pointer v. Texas, Harper v. Virginia Board of Elections, Miranda v. Arizona, Spevack v. Klein, Keyishian v. Board of Regents, Afroyim v. Rusk, Warden v. Hayden, Camara v. Municipal Court, Katz v United States, Marchetti v. United States, Bruton v. United States, Duncan v. Louisiana, Jones v. Alfred H. Mayer Co., Moore v. Ogilvie, Brandenburg v. Ohio, Chimel v. California,* and *Benton v. Maryland.*

[16] The Burger Court's 29½ constitutional overrulings occurred in *Perez v. Campbell, Lehnhausen v. Lake Shore Auto Parts, Miller v. California, North Dakota State Board of Pharmacy v. Snyder's Drug Stores, Edelman v. Jordan, Taylor v. Louisiana, Michelin Tire Corp. v. Wages, Hudgens v. National Labor Relations Board, Virginia State Board of Pharmacy v. Virginia Citizens Consumer Council, National League of Cities v. Usery, New Orleans v. Dukes, Gregg v. Georgia, Craig v. Boren, Complete Auto Transit v. Brady, Shaffer v. Heitner, Washington Revenue Dept. v. Stevedoring Assn., Burks v. United States, United States v. Scott, Hughes v. Oklahoma, Thomas v. Washington Gas Light Co., Commonwealth Edison Co. v. Montana, United States v. Ross, Illinois v. Gates, United States v. One Assortment of 89 Firearms* (½ constitutionally based, ½ common law based), *Limbach v. Hooven & Allison Co., Garcia v. San Antonio Metropolitan Transit Authority, United States v. Miller, Daniels v. Williams, Batson v. Kentucky,* and *Brown-Forman Distillers Corp. v. New York State Liquor Authority.*

[17] The Rehnquist Court altered precedents on the basis of the Constitution in *Puerto Rico v. Bransted,* 483 U.S. 219 (1987); *Tyler Pipe Industries, Inc. v. Dept. of Revenue,* 483 U.S. 232 (1987); *American Trucking Assns. v. Scheiner,* 483 U.S. 266 (1987); *Solorio v. United States,*

the results differed; i.e., Warren Court (23.3 percent), Burger Court (15.2 percent), and Rehnquist Court (20).

We could also obtain statistics concerning the bases of the overruled decisions, but we have no reason to believe that they would be substantially different from the results we secured for the overruling decisions. Here, however, it makes less sense to present a Court-by-Court summary, for only two of the Rehnquist Court's decisions, and only 17 of those of the Burger Court, were formally altered. Only the Warren Court had a large number of its decisions overruled: 44. (See Table 4.4.)

We can ask, concerning the Warren Court, whether the bases of the overruled decisions differ from the bases of the non-overruled. We discovered that the overruled decisions of the Warren Court were dramatically more likely to be constitutionally based than statutorily based. Twenty-six of 44 overruled decisions of the Warren Court (59 percent) were constitutional, 10 (23 percent) were statutory, while four each rested on the Court's supervisory authority over the lower federal courts and on common law. Focusing only on the first two categories, 72.2 percent were constitutionally based and 27.8 percent were statutorily based. In contrast, only 37.1 percent of the non-overruled decisions of the Warren Court (462 out of 1245) were constitutionally based, while 62.9 percent (783 out of 1245) were statutorily based.

Note also that the overruled decisions of the Warren Court were more likely to pertain to civil liberties than the non-overruled decisions. The relevant statistics are 75 percent for the overruled decisions (33 out of 44) and 42.1 percent for the non-overruled decisions (737 out of 1749).

These results are hardly surprising. Clearly when they decide constitutional issues, and particularly when they decide civil liberties issues, the justices believe they are free to void precedents.

OPINION ASSIGNMENT IN THE OVERRULING CASES

Who is assigned to write the majority or the plurality opinions in the overruling cases? We know that each justice tends to write approximately the same number of opinions per term,[18] and that the chief justices tend to self-assign in salient cases.[19] We indicated that 33 percent of the overruling cases in our dataset can be classified as salient. Thus, we expect that the chief justices will tend to self-

483 U.S. 435 (1987); *Welch v. Texas Dept. of Highways and Public Transportation,* 483 U.S. 468 (1987); *South Carolina v. Baker,* 485 U.S. 505 (1988); *Thornburgh v. Abbott,* 490 U.S. 401 (1989); *Alabama v. Smith,* 490 U.S. 794 (1989); *Webster v. Reproductive Health Services,* 492 U.S. 490 (1989); *Collins v. Youngblood,* 497 U.S. 37 (1990); *California v. Acevedo,* 114 L Ed 2d 619 (1991); *Payne v. Tennessee,* 115 L Ed 2d 720 (1991); and *Planned Parenthood v. Casey,* 120 L Ed 2d 674 (1992).

[18] See Harold J. Spaeth, "Distributive Justice: Majority Opinion Assignments in the Burger Court," 67 *Judicature* 299 (1984), and the work therein cited.

[19] Saul Brenner, "The Chief Justices' Self Assignment of Majority Opinions in Salient Cases," 30 *Social Science Quarterly* 143 (1993).

assign in the cases altering precedent. We also know that the other opinion assigners tend to self-assign even more often than the chief justices.[20] This is true regarding cases in general. These justices will have an even greater incentive to self-assign in overturning cases, many of which are salient. Thus, we expect that the other opinion assigners will also self-assign.

To test whether the opinion assigners tended to self-assign we ascertained whether they wrote more majority or plurality opinions than can be expected based on random assignment. If, for example, Warren was a member of a five-person opinion coalition in a given case, we assume that he had a one-fifth probability of writing the majority opinion in that case.[21] We compared the number of expected opinion assignments of the opinion assigners with the actual number of such assignments.

Our results are set forth in Table 4.8. In none of the four Courts did we find statistically significant support at the .05 level for our hypothesis. We used Z values and a one tail test to test for statistical significance. Overall, the opinion assigners were expected to write 19.74 opinions. They authored 20 opinions, the closest whole number to 19.74. In short, opinion assigners do not favor themselves in the overruling cases.

An alternative approach might prove more helpful: Law Professor Maurice Kelman has gratuitously advised the Court which justice should be selected to author the majority or the plurality opinion when precedent is altered. We quote the entire text of his advice:

In the category of outright overruling, I advise against handing the opinion assignment to an original dissenter. As Jerold Israel has shown, a vindicated dissenter is given to gloating and less inclined to make use of the traditional arts of overruling, which is to say, the diplomatic techniques available for correcting the Court's mistakes with a minimum of reproach. According to my public relations precepts, the best qualified justice for an overruling assignment would seem to be a converted member of the original majority, or best still, the author of the discredited opinion. ('Joy shall be in heaven over one sinner that repenteth, more than ninety and nine just persons, which need no repentance'.) The occasional act of contrition cleans the judicial soul and is, as well, a powerful demonstration of intellectual openness. But there is a complication in using the recanter as the

---

[20]   Jeffrey A. Segal and Harold J. Spaeth, *The Supreme Court and the Attitudinal Model* (Cambridge: Cambridge University Press, 1993), p. 264.

[21]   In conducting this research we inspected the *final* vote on the merits, instead of the *original* vote cast in conference. It is better to use original vote data because the majority opinion is assigned to a justice who is a member of the majority decision coalition at the original vote. Indeed, we do not even know who is the opinion assigner in any given case unless we examine original vote data. But original vote data for the entire period of our study is presently unavailable to scholars. We, therefore, assumed that the justices voted the same way at both votes. It should be noted that no one has conducted an opinion assignment study using final vote data, instead of original vote data, that obtained substantially different findings.

   Instead of focusing on *decision* coalitions at the final vote, we inspected *opinion* coalitions at that vote. We proceeded this way because it is reasonable to assume that a justice who is a member of the decision majority, but is not a member of the opinion coalition, would be an inappropriate opinion writer. If such a justice was originally assigned to author the majority opinion, he or she would lose the assignment.

Table 4.8. *Self-assignment of majority and plurality opinions in the overruling cases*

Court	# of cases*	Expected**	Actual
Vinson	6	1.09	0
Warren	42	7.48	6
Burger	45	7.32	8
Rehnquist	20	3.85	6
Overall	113	19.74	20

*We excluded cases in which there was no opinion writer.
**Based on random assignment.

Court's voice, which is that the justice will have an autobiographical urge to explain his flip flop, and that is something that is done more comfortably through the first-person medium of a separate concurring opinion. Consequently, though the choice is close, I give the edge to a newcomer as the spokesman for overruling.[22]

To what extent did the Court follow Kelman's advice? If adhered to, new justices (or, more precisely, justices who did not participate in the overruled case) are likely to write more majority opinions than can be expected by chance, while justices who dissented in the overruled case (whom we call "dissenting justices") are likely to be disadvantaged. The justices who were in the majority in the overruled case (whom we call "majority justices") could be expected to occupy an intermediate position.

We only inspected those overruling cases in which justices from at least two of the preceding categories joined the opinion coalition. Almost all of the excluded cases consisted of opinion coalitions containing only new justices. There are 59 cases in this dataset, 51 percent of the altering decisions. If more than one precedent was overruled, we used the most recent precedent.

There were an insufficient number of opinions assigned in any of the four Courts for us to expect statistically significant results in that Court. In the Vinson Court there were only 3 opinions assigned, in the Warren Court 25, in the Burger Court 21, and in the Rehnquist Court 10. Perhaps statistically significant results can be expected if we use the overall statistics. Overall, the new justices were expected – based on random assignment – to write 30.42 opinions and wrote 34, the dissenting justices were expected to write 18.25 and wrote 17, while the majority justices were expected to write 9.97 and wrote 8. These data

[22] Maurice Kelman, "The Forked Path of Dissent," 1985 *Supreme Court Review* 227 (1986), at 293–294. Note that Kelman's advice is contrary to an investment rationale. According to that rationale, the best candidate to write the majority opinion in the overruling case would be one of the authors of the dissenting opinions in the overruled case. Such an author would have already invested his time and energy in defending the position that was victorious in the overruling case. It would, therefore, take little effort for him to write the majority opinion in that case.

Table 4.9. *Assignment of majority or plurality opinion to the new justice,
the dissenting justice from the overruled case, or the majority justice
from that case – overruling cases*

Vinson Court - 3 (# of cases)*

Warren Court - 25 (# of cases)*								
New Justices			Dissenting			Majority		
N	Expected	Actual	N	Expected	Actual	N	Expected	Actual
76	12.72	16	53	9.85	8	12	2.06	1

Burger Court - 19 (# of cases)*								
New Justices			Dissenting			Majority		
N	Expected	Actual	N	Expected	Actual	N	Expected	Actual
68	10.74	13	17	3.3	3	38	6.52	3

Rehnquist Court - 10 (# of cases)**								
New Justices			Dissenting			Majority		
N	Expected	Actual	N	Expected	Actual	N	Expected	Actual
31	5.76	4	14	3.30	4	8	1.39	2

*We excluded cases in which there was no opinion writer.
**We excluded Planned Parenthood v. Casey (1992) in which 3 justices
wrote the plurality opinion.

are presented in Table 4.9. These results, however, are not statistically significant at the .05 level.

Thus, we have not found any evidence which supports the hypothesis that the
status of the justice (i.e., newcomer, dissenting justice, or majority justice)
influences assignment to write the majority or plurality opinion in the overruling
cases.

Aside from a focus on opinion assignment, we also wanted to know which
justices wrote the most majority or plurality opinions in the overruling cases. The
number of overruling opinions written by a given justice probably reflects: 1) the
number of overturning decisions handed down by the Court during his tenure; 2)
how often the justice was in the winning decision coalition in the overturning
case at the original vote on the merits and, therefore, available for opinion
assignment;[23] and 3) whether the justice was a particularly able majority or
plurality opinion writer. Justice Brennan, who scored well on the first two
variables but might not have on the third,[24] authored 15 overruling opinions.
(See Table 4.10.) Rehnquist ranked second with 13. The long-tenured White
ranked third with 12 opinions, while Douglas, who was equally long-serving in
the post-1946 era, was next with 9.

[23] The size of these coalitions is also relevant because the probability of being assigned to write the
      majority opinion is, of course, greater when that coalition is minimum winning than when it is
      unanimous.
[24] Op. cit. fn. 20 *supra*, pp. 296–297.

Table 4.10. *Frequency of authorship of the overruling decisions*

Author of overruling decision*		Dates of service**
1) Brennan	15	10/16/56 to 7/20/90
2) Rehnquist	13	1/7/72 to present
3) White	12	4/16/62 to present
4) Douglas	9	'46 term to 11/12/75
5) Blackmun	8	6/9/60 to present
5) Marshall	8	10/2/67 to 6/27/91
5) Stewart	8	10/14/58 to 7/3/81
8) Black	7	'46 term to 9/17/71
9) Burger	5	6/23/69 to 9/26/86
10) Harlan	4	3/28/55 to 9/23/71
10) Powell	4	1/7/72 to 6/26/87
10) Stevens	4	12/19/75 to present
10) Warren	4	10/5/53 to 6/23/69
14) O'Connor	3	9/25/81 to present
15) Clark	2	8/24/49 to 6/12/67
15) Goldberg	2	10/1/62 to 7/25/65
15) Kennedy	2	2/18/88 to present
15) Reed	2	'46 term to 2/25/57
19) Fortas	1	10/4/65 to 5/14/69
19) Minton	1	10/12/49 to 10/15/56
19) Rutledge	1	'46 term to 9/10/49
19) Souter	1	10/9/90 to present

*The following justices did not author any overruling opinions:
  Burton, Frankfurter, Jackson, Murphy, Scalia, Thomas, Vinson,
  and Whittaker.
**Beginning '46 term through the '91 term.

We also wanted to ascertain who wrote the most majority or plurality opinions in the overruled cases. We included here only those writers who served on at least one of the four Courts of our study (see Table 4.11). The ranking of the justices on this list probably reflects the same three variables specified for the overruling cases and may also reflect 4) the elapsed time between a justice's departure from the Court and the end of the 1991 term, and 5) whether subsequent Courts differed ideologically from the justice in question.

The most overturned authors were Frankfurter and Harlan, with a striking 9 opinions each, Minton with 7, and Reed and Stewart with 6 each. The Warren Court voided five of Frankfurter's nine opinions, including his opinions in the salient cases of *Wolf v. Colorado*, 338 U.S. 25 (1949), and *Colegrove v. Green*, 328 U.S. 549 (1946). It is curious that all five of these justices were conservatives or moderates. This is a surprising result. We would have expected the liberal Warren Court justices to have been most overturned.

Note that it makes little sense to compare Table 4.10 with Table 4.11 to obtain overall success rates (i.e., successes over the total number of successes and defeats) for the individual justices. As suggested above, somewhat different variables determine both lists, and justices who write the majority or plurality opinions in a large number of overruled cases are not necessarily losers. Indeed, they might be perceived as Court leaders, at least when they are writing a large number of majority opinions. The losers are those justices who wrote few major-

Table 4.11. *Frequency of authorship of the overruled decisions*

Author of overruled decision*		Dates of service**
1) Frankfurter	10	'46 term to 8/28/62
2) Harlan	9	3/28/55 to 9/23/71
3) Minton	7	10/12/49 to 10/15/56
4) Clark	6	8/24/49 to 6/12/67
4) Reed	6	'46 term to 2/25/57
4) Stewart	6	10/14/58 to 7/3/81
7) Powell	5	1/7/72 to 6/16/87
7) Murphy	5	'46 term to 7/19/49
9) Black	4	'46 term to 9/17/71
9) Brennan	4	10/16/56 to 7/20/90
11) Blackmun	3	6/9/70 to present
11) Burton	3	'46 term to 10/13/58
11) Douglas	3	'46 term to 11/22/75
11) Rehnquist	3	1/7/72 to present
15) Jackson	2	'46 term to 10/9/54
15) Marshall	2	10/2/67 to 6/27/91
15) Rutledge	2	'46 term to 9/10/49
15) White	2	4/16/62 to present
19) Burger	1	6/23/69 to 9/26/86
19) Fortas	1	10/4/65 to 5/14/69
19) Goldberg	1	10/1/62 to 7/25/65
19) Vinson	1	'46 term to 9/8/53
19) Warren	1	10/5/53 to 6/23/69

*The following justices did not write any overruled opinions:
  Kennedy, O'Connor, Scalia, Stevens, Souter, Thomas, and
  Whittaker.
**Beginning '46 term through '91 term.

ity or plurality opinions in both overruling and overruled cases. Justice Whittaker, for example, who wrote neither an overruled nor an overturning majority or plurality opinion during his six terms on the Warren Court, might be viewed as such.

Finally, we wanted to determine the percentage of majority or plurality opinions overturned for each of the justices. In examining this topic we excluded the Vinson Court because no one has calculated the total number of majority opinions those justices authored. We discovered (see Table 4.12) that a higher proportion of Justice Frankfurter's opinions were overturned than those of any other justice: 7 of 84 (8.3 percent); next came Burton at 5.6 percent, followed by Harlan at 5.3 percent, and Minton and Reed at 4.5 percent and 3.7 percent. All five justices tended to oppose civil liberties. At the other extreme, we found that of the eight justices who were never overruled seven were conservatives (all except Stevens). The other justices are O'Connor, Scalia, Kennedy, Whittaker, Souter, Thomas, and Jackson. Not surprisingly, the rank of the justices on Table 4.12 correlates with the Court's current membership. Six of these eight justices who have never been overruled were members of the Court at the end of the 1991 term, while none of the 12 most overruled justices were on the Court at that time. The highest-ranking active justice is Blackmun, with 3 of his 297 opinions overruled (1 percent).

We also ascertained which justices wrote dissenting opinions that were vindi-

Table 4.12. *Frequency of authorship of overruled opinions*
(excluding those of the Vinson Court)

Author and number of overruled opinions		Total number of authored majority and plurality opinions	% overruled
1) Frankfurter	7	84	8.3
2) Burton	2	36	5.6
3) Harlan	9	171	5.3
4) Minton	1	22	4.5
5) Reed	1	27	3.7
6) Clark	5	172	2.9
7) Goldberg	1	36	2.8
8) Fortas	1	40	2.5
9) Powell	5	254	2.0
10) Stewart	6	314	1.9
11) Black	3	200	1.5
12) Brennan	5	452	1.1
13) Blackmun	3	297	1.0
14) Rehnquist	3	328	.9
15) Douglas	2	260	.8
16) Marshall	2	322	.6
16) Warren	1	170	.6
18) White	2	463	.4
18) Burger	1	258	.4
20) Jackson	0	7	0
20) Thomas	0	8	0
20) Souter	0	22	0
20) Whittaker	0	42	0
20) Kennedy	0	59	0
20) Scalia	0	77	0
20) O'Connor	0	174	0
20) Stevens	0	245	0

cated in a subsequent overruling. Table 4.13 contains these data. We discovered that Chief Justice Warren garnered the highest score, 17.9 percent, more than twice as high as that of the second-ranked Goldberg (7.4 percent). Ten of Warren's 56 dissenting opinions were subsequently vindicated. Note also that Warren infrequently wrote dissenting opinions. Only Souter, during his first two terms, wrote fewer dissenting opinions than Warren's 16-year average of 3.5 per term. Fortas and Frankfurter occupy third and fourth place with percentages of 6.1 and 5.8. Black and Douglas rank fifth and sixth. Five of these six justices (all except Frankfurter) can be classified as liberals. In contrast, all eight of the justices who were never vindicated were conservatives: Powell, Burton, Kennedy, Reed, Minton, Jackson, Thomas, and Souter.

THE NUMBER AND KINDS OF OPINIONS IN THE OVERRULING AND OVERRULED CASES

In this section we determine how many and what kinds of opinions the justices wrote in the altering and altered cases. Because of the unsettling effect that overrulings have on the legal model of decision making we expect overruling

Table 4.13. *Authorship of dissenting opinion in decisions that were subsequently overruled*

Author and number of dissenting opinions		Total number of dissenting opinions authored	% vindicated
1)	Warren 10	56	17.9
2)	Goldberg 2	27	7.4
3)	Fortas 2	33	6.1
4)	Frankfurter 6	104	5.8
5)	Black 11	238	4.6
6)	Douglas 17	481	3.5
7)	O'Connor 3	98	3.1
8)	Scalia 2	67	3.0
9)	Clark 3	103	2.9
9)	Harlan 9	311	2.9
11)	White 7	298	2.3
12)	Whittaker 1	52	1.9
13)	Stewart 4	225	1.8
14)	Brennan 6	456	1.3
15)	Blackmun 2	231	.9
16)	Burger 1	118	.8
16)	Stevens 3	372	.8
16)	Rehnquist 2	259	.8
19)	Marshall 2	328	.6
20)	Souter 0	5	0
20)	Thomas 0	6	0
20)	Jackson 0	7	0
20)	Minton 0	17	0
20)	Reed 0	23	0
20)	Kennedy 0	29	0
20)	Burton 0	35	0
20)	Powell 0	152	0

cases to produce appreciably more opinions than cases that do not overrule precedent. On the other hand, we know of no a priori reason why overruled cases should deviate in opinion frequency from the mass of orally argued cases. We also want to know if the four Courts differ in the frequency with which their members write opinions in overruling decisions. If they do not, it will increase our confidence that overruling decisions are fungible across the four Courts.

In ascertaining the number of opinions a justice wrote, we count each author of a joint opinion as an individual writer. This rule proportionately increases the number of Vinson Court opinions as compared with those of the successor Courts. Each member of the Vinson Court wrote at least one such opinion, with Black appearing as a joint author of 24 opinions, Douglas 22, and Frankfurter 19. By contrast, we count a per curiam opinion as authorless. As for the number of cases, we count only those citations that were orally argued.

Compatibly with our expectation, Table 4.14 shows that the average number of opinions written in overruling cases exceeds the average number written in non-overruling decisions. The Warren and Rehnquist Courts produce the most marked discrepancy, i.e., a difference 1.09 and 1.04 opinions. By contrast, the Burger Court justices authored only .37 more opinions in altering than in non-altering decisions, while those on the Vinson Court did so at a lesser frequency of only .26. Of course, the Vinson Court's proportion may be skewed because its voiding decisions numbered only six.

Among the Courts themselves, dissents slightly exceed the majority or plurality opinion in all except the Vinson Court, where six prevailing opinions

Table 4.14. *The number of opinions authored per case*

Court	Precedent	
	Overruling	Non-overruling
Vinson	2.33	2.07
Warren	3.12	2.03
Burger	2.78	2.41
Rehnquist	3.35	2.31

matched six dissents. The justices wrote slightly fewer concurrences than they did dissents, again except for the Vinson justices, who wrote only two concurrences, both of which were special.[25] Interestingly, the number of regular concurrences (those which support the result as well as the majority's reasoning) exceeds special concurrences in the Warren and Burger Courts, 23 to 20 in the former, 22 to 17 in the latter. The opposite pattern prevails in the Rehnquist Court: 9 regular and 12 special.

These findings suggest that the opinion-writing proclivities of our Courts do not vary much from one another either in the decisions altering precedent or those that do not. Only .38 of an opinion separates the most from the least prolific of the Courts in the number of opinions per unaltered decision: Burger at 2.41, Warren at 2.03. More likely than not this discrepancy results from an increase in the number of clerks available to the Burger Court justices. The number of law clerks, however, does not explain why the Warren Court justices on average wrote substantially more opinions in cases altering precedent than did the members of the Burger Court (3.12 versus 2.78).

COALITION SIZE IN THE OVERRULING AND OVERRULED CASES

We suspect that both the decision coalitions and the opinion coalitions will tend toward a minimum winning size rather than a unanimous size. We expect this result in both the overruling and the overruled cases for the following reasons:

1) Ulmer's finding[26] that in 60 percent of the decision coalitions in the overruling cases during the earlier period the majority bloc exceeded the size of the minority bloc by less than eight or nine votes.

---

[25] A special concurrence supports the result the majority has reached, but disagrees with the reasoning it gives for its decision.

The opinion breakdown is as follows: Vinson Court, 6 opinions of the Court, 6 dissents, and 2 special concurrences; Warren Court, 40 opinions of the Court, 3 judgments of the Court, 48 dissents, 23 regular concurrences; and 20 special concurrences. Burger Court, 43 opinions of the Court, 2 judgments of the Court, 44 dissents, 22 regular concurrences, and 17 special concurrences; Rehnquist Court, 21 opinions of the Court, 1 judgment of the Court, 24 dissents, 9 regular concurrences, and 12 special concurrences.

[26] Op. cit. fn. 1 *supra*, p. 426.

2) Our analysis based on Ulmer's table[27] which shows that in 66 percent of the overruled decision coalitions the majority bloc also exceeded the size of the minority bloc by less than eight or nine votes.
3) The likeliness of overturned decisions to be weak in some respect. One measure of weakness is the small size of the decision or opinion coalition. This is particularly true in the absence of norms against dissent.
4) Our finding that justices wrote a disproportionate number of opinions in overruling cases.

We test this hypothesis by examining each Court separately. In breaking down coalition data by Court, we count a decision that overrules precedents from two or more Courts as voiding the more recent one only. That is, if a Burger Court decision alters decisions from both the Vinson and Warren Court the overruling decision would be counted only against the Warren Court. This decision rule precludes double counting the number of overruling decisions, while simultaneously locating the voided precedents with those of the overruling Court.

Table 4.15 presents the results of our analysis. Coalition sizes in all four Courts for overruling as well as overruled decisions and opinions (in other words, in 16 situations: $4 \times 2 \times 2$) ranged from 5.0 to 6.7. Thus, our hypothesis is supported. Coalition sizes tend to be closer to the minimum for winning than to unanimous.

We are interested in not only coalition sizes in general, but whether the size will be greater in the altering or the altered cases. Only two Courts contain a sufficient number of overruled and overruling cases to conduct a statistical comparison. We discovered that the size of decision coalitions in the overruled cases of the Warren Court was smaller (overruling 6.7; overruled 5.9), while the size of these coalitions in the Burger Court was virtually the same (overruling 6.5; overruled 6.6). With regard to opinion coalitions, we discovered that overruled Warren Court opinions were smaller (overruling 6.1; overruled 5.4), a matter also true of the Burger Court (overruling 6.5; overruled 6.2.). In short, coalition sizes tend to be somewhat smaller in the overruled case than in the overruling case.

We also found that 33 of the 115 overruling decisions produced a unanimous decision coalition (28.7 percent), 21 of which also formed a unanimous opinion coalition (18.3 percent). But when we omit the 23 decision coalitions and the 15 opinion coalitions that voided pre-Vinson Court precedents, the proportion of unanimous decision coalitions falls to a low 8.7 percent (10 of 115), with the proportion of unanimous opinion coalitions at a still lower 5.2 percent (6 of 115). By contrast, the unanimous fraction of the orally argued decisions in the non-overruling cases in each of our Courts is appreciably higher: Vinson Court 31.1 percent, Warren Court 36.6 percent, Burger Court 41.4 percent, and Rehnquist Court 38.5 percent.

---

[27]   Id. at 418–423.

Table 4.15. *The size of the decision and opinion coalition
in the overruling and overruled cases*

Court	Overruling decisions		Overruled decisions	
Vinson	6.6	(N = 6)	6.3	(N = 30)
Warren	6.7	(N = 43)	5.9	(N = 43)
Burger	6.5	(N = 46)	6.6	(N = 16)
Rehnquist	6.35	(N = 20)	5.0	(N = 2)
	Overruling opinions		Overruled opinions	
Vinson	5.7	(N = 6)	6.0	(N = 30)
Warren	6.1	(N = 43)	5.4	(N = 43)
Burger	6.5	(N = 46)	6.2	(N = 16)
Rehnquist	5.7	(N = 20)	5.0	(N = 2)

CONCLUSION

The major findings of this chapter are the following:

1) Half the overruled decisions survived less than 21 years.
2) Slightly more than 10 percent of the overruled decisions predate 1900.
3) Of the four Courts, the Warren Court overturned the most recent precedents.
4) The Warren Court as well was more likely to have overruled its own precedents.
5) Older precedents tended to be overturned by a unanimous or a nearly unanimous vote, while new precedents tended to be altered by a minimum winning or close vote.
6) The Warren Court generated a higher proportion of salient overrulings (46.5 percent) than the other three Courts. The percentage for the Burger Court was 30 percent.
7) In contrast, only 2.5 percent of the Warren Court's decisions and 5.4 percent of Burger Court's non-overruling decisions were salient.
8) Almost 64 percent of the overrulings were based on constitutional grounds, while only 20 percent rested on statutory grounds.
9) While 72.2 percent of the overruled decisions of the Warren Court were constitutionally based (as compared to statutorily based), only 37.1 percent of the non-overruled decisions were constitutionally based.
10) Seventy-five percent of the overruled decisions of the Warren Court pertained to civil liberties, while only 42.1 percent of the non-overruled decisions of that Court concerned civil liberties.
11) There were wide differences in the number of overruling opinions written by the justices. Justices Brennan, Rehnquist, and White wrote the most.

12) There were also wide differences in the number of overruled opinions authored by them. Justices Frankfurter, Burton, Harlan, and Reed had their opinions voided more often than the other justices.

13) On the Warren Court Chief Justice Warren wrote a higher proportion of dissenting opinions in cases that were subsequently overturned than any other justice. We found that 16.1 percent of his dissenting opinions were subsequently vindicated. Others vindicated more than 6 percent of the time were Fortas and Goldberg. Conversely, 8 of the 27 justices were never vindicated.

14) The average number of opinions written in overruling cases exceeds the average number written in non-overruling cases.

15) Decision and opinion coalitions in overruling cases tend to be closer to a minimum winning size than to a unanimous size.

We turn next to the overturning decisions in conference.

5

The conference votes

In most fully argued and fully decided cases the justices vote at least three times. The first vote, cast in secret conference, determines whether the Court will hear the case. During the period of our study, about 75 percent of the cases heard by the Supreme Court came to the Court via a petition for a writ of certiorari (hereinafter cert), while the remaining cases, with few exceptions, arrived via a petition for a writ of appeal.[1]

If the Court votes to grant cert, the case is scheduled for oral argument. After oral argument the justices again meet in conference to decide whether to reverse or to affirm the decision of the lower court. This vote is called the original vote on the merits. It is not a permanent vote, for any of the justices may change their vote at any time prior to the announcement of the Court's decision.

The final vote on the merits determines whether the decision below is, in fact, affirmed or reversed. This vote is cast by the justices during the course of their writing or joining the various opinions and can be ascertained by reading the published reports of these opinions.

In this chapter we examine the overturning cases to determine: 1) the cert grant rate (i.e, the vote to grant cert over the total number of votes) in these cases; 2) whether the justices, in their cert voting, vote in accord with the error-correcting and prediction strategies; 3) the extent to which the justices and the Court shift between the original vote on the merits and the final vote; and 4) the extent to which the shifts by the individual justices consist of minority-majority voting (i.e., voting with the minority at the original vote and with the majority at the final vote) or majority-minority voting.

Note that we will not be examining the justices' votes regarding petitions for a writ of appeal. Behavioral scholars rarely study the appeal votes.[2] These votes are less numerous and are more difficult to investigate than the votes for the cert

---

[1] Segal and Spaeth tell us that from the beginning of the Warren Court in 1953 through the end of the fourth term of the Rehnquist Court in 1990, excluding cases on the original docket and using the docket number as the unit of analysis, 25.2 percent of the Warren Court cases did not come to the Court via the cert route. The comparable statistics for the Burger and Rehnquist Courts are 26.5 percent and 18.1 percent. See Jeffrey A. Segal and Harold J. Spaeth, *The Supreme Court and the Attitudinal Model* (Cambridge: Cambridge University Press, 1993), p. 191.

[2] Id., at 187, 191.

petition. When the justices face a cert petition they either vote to grant or deny. But when they confront an appeal petition they have four options: note probable jurisdiction, postpone further consideration of jurisdiction until the decision on the merits, summarily affirm the decision of the lower court, or dismiss the writ for lack of a substantial federal question or for want of jurisdiction.

We obtained the conference vote data for the overruling decisions of the Vinson and Warren Courts from Jan Palmer of Ohio University and for the overruling decisions of the Burger and Rehnquist Courts from Saul Brenner. We also used Brenner's previously collected conference vote data for the Warren and Burger Courts.[3]

THE VOTE TO GRANT OR DENY CERT

As we saw in Chapter 3, overruling cases are substantially more salient or important than non-overruling cases. Because salience is one of the variables that determines whether the Supreme Court will grant cert,[4] we can expect high salience to increase the number of justices voting to grant cert.[5] As a consequence, the cert grant rate in the overruling cases can be expected to be higher than the cert grant rate of cases in general.

We computed cert grant rates for the four Courts of our study. The results, presented in Table 5.1, show the following cert grant rates: Vinson Court .82; Warren Court .75; Burger Court .65; and Rehnquist Court .69. The overall rate is .71.

How does the overall grant rate of .71 compare with the cert grant rate for cases in general? On the basis of Brenner's conference vote data we computed cert grant rates for all the cases in the 1958 and 1963 terms of the Warren Court and for the 1974 term of the Burger Court, the last term collected by Brenner. The cert grant rates are .70 (1958 term), .73 (1963 term), and .66 (1974 term). These results parallel the .71 we obtained for the altering cases. Thus, there is no evidence of a higher grant rate in the overruling cases than for cases in general.[6]

---

[3] Jan Palmer's Vinson Court data was published in *The Vinson Court Era* (New York: AMS Press, 1990), pp. 159–392. He is currently gathering Warren Court data and has supplied us with data sheets for the cases on that Court which altered precedent. Saul Brenner inspected the docket books of Justice Brennan from the 1969 term through the 1985 term and the docket books of Justice Marshall from the 1969 term through the 1990 term to obtain data for the overturning decisions of the Burger and Rehnquist Courts. No data are available for the two 1991 term cases that altered precedent. Brenner previously collected data for the Warren Court from the docket books of Justices Burton, Clark, and Brennan and for the Burger Court from the docket books of Justice Brennan.

[4] Lawrence Baum, *The Supreme Court*, 4th ed. (Washington, DC: Congressional Quarterly, 1992), pp. 104–105.

[5] See Doris Marie Provine, *Case Selection in the United States Supreme Court* (Chicago: University of Chicago Press, 1980), pp. 110–111.

[6] We do not run a statistical test of significance on these differences for two obvious reasons. First, the numbers are virtually identical. Second, the data are not comparable because the overruling cases come from the 1946–1992 era, while the general grant rate is based on cases from three discrete terms.

Table 5.1. *Certiorari grant rates*

Court	Total votes to grant	Total votes to deny	Grant rate
Vinson	36	8	.82
Warren	222	73	.75
Burger	157	84	.65
Rehnquist	73	33	.69
Overall	488	198	.71

Possibly the justices do not react to the salience of the overturning cases by voting to grant cert. They may react, instead, to the salience of these cases by voting more strategically than they do in other cases. Various scholars[7] discovered a relationship, on the one hand, between a justice's vote to grant cert and a vote to reverse on the merits and, on the other, between a vote to deny cert and a vote to affirm on the merits. This relationship suggests an error-correcting strategy; i.e., justices vote to grant cert to correct the lower court's "errors" and vote to deny cert because they approve of these decisions.

Some scholars[8] contend that the justices pursue a second strategy in their cert voting – a prediction strategy. These scholars discovered a strong relationship between the vote to grant cert and winning at the final vote on the merits and the vote to deny cert and losing at the final vote. This relationship suggests that a justice votes to grant cert because of a likely victory at the final vote and votes to deny cert because of the likelihood of losing. Two recent studies, however, found only weak support for this strategy.[9]

In an attempt to evaluate why the recent studies regarding the prediction strategy differ from the earlier studies, Brenner[10] discovered that 1) support for the prediction strategy is strongly related to the extent to which the Court reverses; 2) support for the error-correcting strategy is weakly related to the extent

[7] S. Sidney Ulmer, "The Decision to Grant Certiorari as an Indicator to Decision 'On the Merits,'" 4 *Polity* 429 (1972); Provine, op. cit. fn. 5 *supra;* Jan Palmer, "An Econometric Analysis of the U.S. Supreme Court's Certiorari Decisions," 39 *Public Choice* 387 (1982); Saul Brenner and John F. Krol, "Strategies in Certiorari Voting on the United States Supreme Court," 51 *Journal of Politics* 828 (1989); Palmer, op. cit. fn. 3 *supra;* John F. Krol and Saul Brenner, "Strategies in Certiorari Voting on the United States Supreme Court: A Reevaluation," 43 *Western Political Quarterly* 335 (1990).

[8] Saul Brenner, "The New Certiorari Game," 41 *Journal of Politics* 649 (1979); Palmer, "An Econometric Analysis,: id.; Brenner and Krol, id.

[9] Palmer , op. cit. fn. 3 *supra* , p. 62; Krol and Brenner, op. cit., fn. 7 *supra,* p. 340. In "The Prediction Strategy in Certiorari Voting on the Supreme Court Revisited," a paper presented at the 1994 Interim Meeting of the International Political Science Association Research Committee on Comparative Judicial Studies, Florence, Italy, 1994, Brenner argued that the prediction strategy does not usually motivate the justices' cert decisions. We nevertheless explore the prediction strategy here for two reasons: Brenner could be mistaken, and other judicial scholars accept this strategy as operative.

[10] Saul Brenner, "Strategies in Certiorari Voting on the U.S. Supreme Court: Examining Reverse and Affirm Cases Separately," unpublished paper, 1994.

to which the Court reverses; 3) when the Court reverses, a justice can either vote in accord with both cert strategies (i.e., vote to grant cert and reverse or vote to deny cert and affirm), or vote in conflict with both strategies; and 4) when the Court affirms, a justice can either vote in conformity with the error-correcting strategy (i.e., vote to grant and reverse or deny-affirm) or vote in conformity with the prediction strategy (i.e., grant-affirm or deny-reverse), but cannot vote non-strategically.

In the light of these findings, Brenner[11] urged researchers to examine reverse and affirm cases separately. We follow his advice in our examination of the overturning cases.

When the Court reverses and overturns a precedent, we expect the justices to vote strategically, i.e., in accord with both cert strategies, a large percentage of the time, for we expect the justices to be sensitive to consequences of their cert vote. But when the Court affirms and overturns a precedent, we expect the justices to vote more often for the prediction strategy than for the error-correcting strategy mainly because the latter is counter-productive. Why, for example, should a justice vote to grant cert in order to reverse, when, as a result of the cert vote, the lower court's decision will be affirmed at a more authoritative level? In advancing this argument, however, we are assuming that at the cert vote the justices know or are able to guess accurately what outcome they favor, what outcome the Court is likely to support, and what the Court is likely to overturn. In some cases, it is unreasonable to make these three assumptions.

In testing the two hypotheses presented above, we used only the votes of those justices who voted for the same outcome (i.e., reverse or affirm) at both the original and final vote on the merits, in cases in which the Court voted for the same outcome at both votes. In short, we inspected stable voting in a stable environment.

We discovered that in the reverse cases the justices were likely to vote strategically; i.e., in accord with both cert strategies, in 82.1 percent of the votes in the Vinson Court, in 78.7 percent in the Warren Court, in 70.1 percent in the Burger Court, and in 89.1 percent in the Rehnquist Court. Our findings for the four Courts are presented in Table 5.2.

But contrary to our expectation we obtained mixed results in the affirm cases (see Table 5.3). In two courts (Vinson and Warren) the justices voted more often in accord with the prediction strategy, in one court (Rehnquist) they voted more often in conformity with the error-correcting strategy, and in the final court (Burger) the voting was tied for the two cert strategies. Note, however, that there were few affirm votes in any of the four Courts and, therefore, our findings ought to be considered tentative.

One might wonder how our findings compare with cert voting in other cases. Brenner[12] addressed this question for the Warren Court. He inspected 18 data-sets: 1) the nonsalient cases for the 16 terms of this Court, 2) the salient cases

[11] Id.   [12] Id.

Table 5.2. *Certiorari strategies: reverse cases*

Court	Votes	% in accord with both strategies
Vinson	28	82.1
Warren	169	78.7
Burger	144	70.1
Rehnquist	46	89.1

Table 5.3. *Certiorari strategies: affirm cases*

Court	Votes	% in accord with prediction strategy	% in accord with error-corrrecting strategy
Vinson	4	75.0	25.0
Warren	29	79.3	20.7
Burger	20	50.0	50.0
Rehnquist	39	46.1	53.9

(based on Congressional Quarterly's list), and 3) the same overturning cases we use in this book.

Regarding the reverse cases, Brenner discovered that in 14 of the 18 datasets the strategic voting scores ranged from 81.7 to 75.7 percent. The overturning cases score was 78.7 percent. In salient cases the score was higher (83.2 percent) and in three other datasets it was lower (69.8 percent, 73.3 percent, and 74.9 percent). Thus, there is no evidence that justices in the overturning cases on the Warren Court vote more strategically than in other cases.

Brenner also investigated the affirm cases. Here, he found that the overturning cases score of 79.3 percent for the prediction strategy was the highest score for the prediction strategy of any of the 18 datasets. But we do not wish to emphasize this finding because of the mixed results we obtained for the other three Courts.

THE ORIGINAL VOTE ON THE MERITS

Not only is it useful to focus on a justice's cert vote, it is also worthwhile to compare his vote at the original vote on the merits with his vote at the final vote. Brenner[13] compared these two votes for the Vinson Court and discovered that no fluidity occurred in 86 percent of the pairs. In other words, the justices voted the same way at both votes. Strong fluidity (a shift from reverse to affirm or the converse) did result in 10 percent of the pairs of votes, and weak fluidity (a switch from nonparticipation at the original vote to affirm or reverse at the final

---

[13] Harold J. Spaeth and Saul Brenner, eds., *Studies in U.S. Supreme Court Behavior* (New York: Garland, 1990), p. 55.

Table 5.4. *Overall view of stability and fluidity: individual voting*

Court	Vinson		Warren		Burger		Rehnquist		Overall	
No fluidity	46	(88%)	333	(88%)	274	(87%)	127	(91%)	780	(88%)
Strong fluidity	5	(10%)	40	(11%)	29	(9%)	11	(8%)	85	(10%)
MIN - MAJ	(2)		(12)		(15)		(5)		(34)	
MAJ - MIN	(3)		(17)		(5)		(2)		(27)	
Shifting when the Court is shifting	(0)		(8)		(8)		(4)		(20)	
Tied at original vote	(0)		(3)		(1)		(0)		(4)	
Weak fluidity	1	(2%)	4	(1%)	12	(4%)	2	(1%)	19	(1%)
Total number of pairs	52		377		315		140		884	

vote) in 3 percent of the pairs. Brenner's[14] comparable numbers for the 1956–1967 terms of the Warren Court are 87 percent, 10 percent, and 3 percent.

It is uncertain whether the voting in the overturning cases will be more or less fluid than in cases in general, for we do not know the consequences of the salience of the overturning cases. Dorff and Brenner[15] discovered that substantially more majority-minority voting occurs in nonsalient cases than in salient ones. The salience of a case might cause a justice to vote more carefully at the original vote on the merits. But the salience of the case might also motivate a justice to shift his vote if he had failed to vote "correctly" (i.e., in accord with his views) at the original vote.

Regarding *individual* votes, we discovered that 88 percent of the votes on the Warren Court displayed no fluidity, strong fluidity appeared in 11 percent of the votes, and weak fluidity in 1 percent. Comparable numbers for the Burger Court are 87 percent, 9 percent, and 4 percent, and for the Rehnquist Court 91 percent, 8 percent, and 2 percent. The combined scores are 88 percent, 10 percent, and 2 percent, results quite similar to Brenner's. (See Table 5.4.)

Concerning *Court* votes, we discovered that the Warren Court voted the same way at both the original and final vote in 89 percent of the cases, shifted from reverse to affirm or affirm to reverse in 7 percent of the cases, and voted to reverse or affirm after a tie vote at the original vote in 4 percent of the cases. (See Table 5.5.) The comparable data for the Burger Court are 87 percent, 5 percent, and 8 percent, and for the Rehnquist Court 94 percent, 6 percent, and 0 percent. Overall we obtained scores of 88 percent, 10 percent, and 2 percent.

14   Saul Brenner, "Fluidity on the Supreme Court, 1956–1967," 26 *American Journal of Political Science* 388 (1982).
15   Robert H. Dorff and Saul Brenner, "Conformity Voting on the United States Supreme Court," 54 *Journal of Politics* 762 (1992), at 771–772.

Table 5.5. *Overall view of stability and fluidity: Court voting*

Court	Vinson		Warren		Burger		Rehnquist		Overall	
Stable voting	6	(100%)	40	(89%)	33	(87%)	16	(94%)	95	(89%)
Reverse-reverse	(5)		(36)		(25)		(10)		(76)	
Affirm-affirm	(1)		(4)		(8)		(6)		(19)	
Shifting voting	0	(0%)	3	(7%)	2	(5%)	1	(6%)	6	(6%)
Reverse-affirm	–		(1)		(0)		(0)		(1)	
Affirm-reverse	–		(2)		(2)		(1)		(5)	
Tie vote at orig-inal vote	0	(0%)	2	(4%)	3	(8%)	0	(0%)	5	(5%)
Tie-reverse	–		(2)		(3)		–		(5)	
Tie-affirm	–		(0)		(0)		–		(0)	
Total number of cases	6		45		38		17		106	

We also wanted to present data on the stability rates of the individual justices who participated in at least 20 decisions in one of our four Courts.[16] Only in the Warren and Burger Courts did a justice meet this threshold. In computing these scores we included only stable and strong fluidity pairs of votes.[17]

On the Warren Court we discovered that the five liberal justices (Brennan, Fortas, Black, Douglas, and Warren) had stability rates ranging from .98 to .93, while the four moderate or conservative justices (Stewart, White, Harlan, and Clark) ranged from .92 to .74 (see Table 5.6).

On the Burger Court, however, we found a different pattern. The two liberal justices (Brennan and Marshall) ranked first and eighth among nine justices and garnered very different scores of .97 and .83, as Table 5.7 shows.

Now that we have presented data regarding the amount of voting fluidity, we turn to the question: Under what conditions does strong fluidity occur? Here again we have sufficient data only for the Warren and Burger Courts. On the Warren Court strong fluidity most commonly occurred either when a non-liberal justice (i.e., a conservative or a moderate) voted for the winning liberal outcome at the original vote and then shifted to the losing conservative position at the final vote (13 votes) or when the non-liberal justice voted for the losing conservative

[16] No rule or convention determines how many participations are sufficient to indicate a pattern in which we can have confidence. We believe, however, that if we use a number substantially less than 20, it is likely that the idiosyncratic nature of particular cases will bias the results. The number 20 is arbitrary of course. We could have as easily used 19 or 21.

[17] This statistic omits those pairs of votes in which a justice did not not participate at conference but voted at the final vote. This situation, however, combines two very different events – nonparticipation of justices who were present at the conference and nonparticipation of absent justices. We could not separate these two kinds of nonparticipations because the docket books often do not distinguish betweeen them.

Table 5.6. *Stability rates for individual justices on the Warren Court*
(justices who participated in at least 20 decisions)

Justice	Stable Pairs	Total Pairs*	Stability Rate
1. Brennan**	40	41	.98
2. Fortas**	22	23	.96
3. Black**	42	44	.95
4. Douglas**	41	44	.93
5. Warren**	41	44	.93
6. Stewart	35	38	.92
7. White	30	34	.88
8. Harlan	35	44	.80
9. Clark	23	31	.74

* Includes stable pairs and strong fluidity pairs.
** Liberal justices.

Table 5.7. *Stability rates for individual justices on the Burger Court*
(justices who participated in at least 20 decisions)

Justice	Stable Pairs	Total Pairs*	Stability Rate
1. Brennan**	35	36	.97
2. Burger	30	31	.97
3. Rehnquist	26	28	.93
4. Stevens	21	23	.91
5. Powell	27	30	.90
6. White	33	37	.89
7. Blackmun	32	36	.89
8. Marshall**	30	36	.83
9. Stewart	18	23	.78

*Includes stable pairs and strong fluidity pairs.
**Liberal justices.

outcome at the original vote and for the winning liberal outcome at the final vote (9 votes). The various patterns are presented in Table 5.8.

It comes as no surprise, of course, that the non-liberal Warren Court justices did most of the shifting. This result was already suggested by Table 5.6. What is unexpected, however, is the numerical superiority of majority-minority votes (17) over minority-majority ones (12). This pattern differs substantially from that found by Brenner and Dorff.[18] They discovered that in the 1948 and 1952 terms of the Vinson Court minority-majority votes occurred 8.9 and 4.8 times more frequently than majority-minority votes. Why the Warren Court produced an opposite pattern is unclear. Perhaps the non-liberal justices had poorly developed ideologies and, therefore, it took them longer to vote "correctly."

On the Burger Court minority-majority voting predominated, as Table 5.9 shows. More specifically, the most numerous pattern is of non-liberal justices

[18]   Saul Brenner and Robert H. Dorff, "The Attitudinal Model and Fluidity Voting on the United States Supreme Court: A Theoretical Perspective," 4 *Journal of Theoretical Politics* 195 (1992), at 198.

Table 5.8. *Patterns of strong fluidity on the Warren Court*

Non-shifting cases

Justice	Original vote	Final vote	Original vote	Final vote	N	Outcome of case
1. LIB	LIB	CONS	MIN	MAJ	0	CONS
2. LIB	LIB	CONS	MAJ	MIN	2	LIB
3. LIB	CONS	LIB	MIN	MAJ	3	LIB
4. LIB	CONS	LIB	MAJ	MIN	2	CONS
5. NON-LIB	LIB	CONS	MIN	MAJ	0	CONS
6. NON-LIB	LIB	CONS	MAJ	MIN	13	LIB
7. NON-LIB	CONS	LIB	MIN	MAJ	9	LIB
8. NON-LIB	CONS	LIB	MAJ	MIN	0	CONS

Shifting cases

1. LIB	CONS	LIB	MAJ	MAJ	5	LIB
2. NON-LIB	CONS	LIB	MAJ	MAJ	3	LIB

Tied cases

1. NON-LIB	CONS	LIB	TIED	MAJ	3	LIB

LIB = Black, Brennan, Douglas, Fortas, Goldberg, Marshall, Warren
NON-LIB = Burton, Clark, Frankfurter, Harlan, Jackson, Minton, Reed, Stewart, White, Whittaker

Table 5.9. *Patterns of strong fluidity on the Burger Court*

Non-fluidity cases

Justice	Original vote	Final vote	Original vote	Final vote	N	Outcome of case
1. LIB	LIB	CONS	MIN	MAJ	3	CONS
2. LIB	LIB	CONS	MAJ	MIN	0	LIB
3. LIB	CONS	LIB	MIN	MAJ	1	LIB
4. LIB	CONS	LIB	MAJ	MIN	3	CONS
5. NON-LIB	LIB	CONS	MIN	MAJ	1	CONS
6. NON-LIB	LIB	CONS	MAJ	MIN	0	LIB
7. NON-LIB	CONS	LIB	MIN	MAJ	10	LIB
8. NON-LIB	CONS	LIB	MAJ	MIN	2	CONS

Shifting Cases

1. LIB	CONS	LIB	MIN	MIN	1	CONS
2. NON-LIB	LIB	CONS	MAJ	MAJ	7	CONS

Tied Cases

1. NON-LIB	CONS	LIB	TIED	MAJ	1	LIB

LIB = Brennan, Douglas, and Marshall
NON-LIB = Black, Blackmun, Burger, Harlan, O'Connor, Powell, Rehnquist, Stevens, Stewart, White

voting for the minority conservative position at the original vote and with the majority liberal outcome at the final vote (10 votes). Overall, 15 minority-majority votes were cast, as compared with 5 minority-majority votes, a reversal of the Warren Court pattern.

CONCLUSION

The major findings of this chapter are the following:

1) We found that the justices voted to grant certiorari at an overall rate of .71 in the cases formally altering precedent, a rate similar to the cert grant rate for cases in general.
2) We discovered that when the Court reversed, the justices voted strategically; i.e., in support of the error-correcting and the prediction strategies from 70.1 percent of the time in the Burger Court to 89.1 percent in the Rehnquist Court.
3) No fluidity occurred in 88 percent of the votes, strong fluidity in 10 percent, and weak fluidity in 2 percent.
4) In 89 percent of the cases the Court voted the same way at both votes, in 6 percent they shifted from affirm to reverse or the converse, and in 5 percent they originally cast a tie vote and then voted to affirm or reverse.
5) On the Warren Court the conservative and moderate justices were more likely to switch from affirm to reverse or the converse than were the liberals.
6) The Warren Court justices cast more majority-minority votes than minority-majority votes, but the opposite pattern prevailed on the Burger Court.

In short, we have presented a brief overview of the overturning cases in conference. In the next three chapters we will focus on the final vote and attempt to offer a theoretically grounded explanation for that vote.

6

Attitudinal voting

Why do the justices on the U.S. Supreme Court vote they way they do? In an attempt to answer this question scholars have advanced two major models of decision making: the legal and the attitudinal models. In Chapter 7 we will test one element of the legal model – adherence to precedent. In this chapter we describe the attitudinal model and determine the extent to which it explains the justices' votes in the overruling cases.

The attitudinal model possesses two attractive features. First, it readily lends itself to testing. Second, the testing already conducted shows that this model can predict and explain the justices' votes.[1]

Both the legal and the attitudinal models purport to explain the justices' votes and aspire to do so simply and parsimoniously. Neither model claims to represent reality. They focus instead on a set of crucial variables that presumably explain the behavior in question. Note the tension between the goals of parsimony and explanation. Extremely complex models, though perhaps more valid and reliable, are not useful because it is axiomatic that the more variables one uses the more one can decipher. Thus, for example, one arguably can explain every judicial decision on the basis of its facts and the relevant legal provision(s) at issue. But such an idiosyncratic focus would destroy a model's utility. Better to employ a handful of variables that explain a high percentage of the behavior.

THE ATTITUDINAL MODEL

The first comprehensive attitudinal model was the work of political scientist Glendon Schubert.[2] On the basis of research done by psychologist Clyde Coombs,[3] Schubert argued that the stimuli presented by the cases and the justices' policy preferences could be ordered along ideological dimensions. To illustrate, assume two police searches of two different houses, both of which were supported by probable cause and both of which uncovered similar incrimi-

[1] Harold J. Spaeth, *Supreme Court Policy Making: Explanation and Prediction* (San Francisco: W. H. Freeman, 1979), chs. 5–6; Jeffrey A. Segal and Harold J. Spaeth, *The Supreme Court and the Attitudinal Model* (Cambridge: Cambridge University Press, 1993), ch. 6.
[2] *The Judicial Mind* (Evanston, IL: Northwestern University Press, 1965).
[3] *A Theory of Data* (New York: Wiley, 1964).

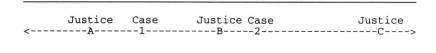

Figure 6.1. Hypothetical cases and judges in ideological space

nating evidence. A warrant was issued for the first search, but not for the second. According to Schubert, these two searches can be positioned in ideological space as illustrated by Figure 6.1. Because a warrant was obtained in the first search, this search is more protective of individual liberty than the second search. As such, it ought to be placed to the left of case 2. Depending on its facts, any case can be positioned on the line representing ideological space. The more justifiable the search, the farther to the left it will be located, and vice-versa. The justices who decide these cases can also be placed in the space. Because of their location, Justice A may be described as liberal, B as moderate, and C as conservative. According to Schubert, a justice will vote to uphold any search to the left of his point in the space and void any search to his right. A justice will be indifferent to searches located on his point. Accordingly, Justice A will vote in favor of the defendant in both cases; Justice B will uphold the search in case 1, but not that in case 2; while Justice C will find neither search objectionable.

David W. Rohde and Harold J. Spaeth advanced an alternative attitudinal model.[4] They contended that the justices' primary goals are policy ones, and that each member of the Court has preferences concerning the policy questions that the Court addresses. In deciding the cases, each justice desires that the Court's outcome approximate as closely as possible his individual policy preferences. Because they lack electoral accountability, serve for life, have no ambition for higher office, are beholden to no other governmental body, and control their own jurisdiction, the justices are able to vote in accord with their personal policy preferences in deciding cases. Central to the Rohde-Spaeth model is the construct of attitudes, which they define as a set of interrelated beliefs about at least one object and the situation in which it is encountered.[5] The attitude objects are the direct and indirect parties to the litigation; the attitude situation is the dominant legal issue in the case.

In focusing on attitudes, Rohde and Spaeth proceeded microanalytically. They placed the Court's decisions in discrete sets, based on an attitude object and situation, as specific in content as the Court's decisions permit. Thus, cases pertaining to due process qua due process, for example, can be partitioned into hearings for government employees, prisoners' rights, impartial decision makers, jurisdiction over nonresident defendants, the takings clause, and a residual notice and hearing set, along with a miscellaneous due process category. They

[4]   *Supreme Court Decision Making* (San Francisco: W. H. Freeman, 1976).
[5]   Id. at 75–76.

also assumed that sets of cases that form around similar attitude objects and situations will correlate with one another to form broader issue areas (e.g., criminal procedure, civil rights, First Amendment freedoms, judicial power, federalism) in which an interrelated set of attitudes – which they term a "value" – will explain and predict the votes of the individual justices (e.g., freedom, equality, libertarianism).

CUMULATIVE SCALING

The method most often used to operationalize the attitudinal model of judicial behavior is cumulative scaling. This technique was created during World War II by the social psychologist Louis Guttman, in association with several colleagues,[6] for the purpose of developing procedures whereby social psychological data could be ordered reliably and validly. Consider, for example, a set of three questions on a given subject to which a group of people were asked to respond either favorably or unfavorably. Further assume that 75 percent of the respondents expressed agreement with the first statement, 50 percent with the second statement, and 25 percent with the third. Cumulative scaling simply assumes that if a person endorses the most extreme statement, that person will endorse all less extreme statements (as measured by the proportion of favorable or unfavorable responses) for the statements to constitute a scale. This means that the 25 percent who supported the third statement will also favor the other two statements. Conversely, a person who opposed the statement that 75 percent supported will also oppose the statements that 50 and 25 percent supported. In other words, each respondent would reply in one of the following consistent ways: yes-yes-yes, yes-yes-no, yes-no-no, or no-no-no. Glendon Schubert first applied Guttman's technique to judicial behavior,[7] followed by S. Sidney Ulmer,[8] and Harold J. Spaeth.[9]

As applied to judicial behavior, cumulative scaling posits that if the justices' attitudes explain their votes, then once a justice begins to oppose a hypothesized attitude (e.g., a claim of double jeopardy), he should continue to do so in all cases decided by a larger negative vote than the cases in which he supported the hypothesized attitude. Thus, if a given justice voted with the majority in support of a claim of double jeopardy in all cases in which no more than two justices voted in opposition to such claims, and joined the dissenters in all double jeopardy cases decided in favor of the claimant by a vote of 6 to 3, this justice will also vote in opposition to a claim of double jeopardy in all cases in which four or

[6] Samuel A. Stouffer, Louis Guttman, Edward A. Suchman, Paul F. Lazersfeld, Shirley A. Star, and John A. Clausen, *Measurement and Prediction* (New York: Wiley, 1950).
[7] *Quantitative Analysis of Judicial Behavior* (Glencoe, IL: Free Press, 1959), ch. 5.
[8] "Supreme Court Behavior and Civil Rights," 13 *Western Political Quarterly* 288 (1960).
[9] "Warren Court Attitudes toward Business," in Glendon Schubert, ed., *Judicial Decision Making* (New York: Free Press, 1963).

Table 6.1. *Hypothetical cumulative scale*

	Justices									
Case	A	B	C	D	E	F	G	H	I	Vote
1	+	+	+	+	+	+	+	+	+	9-0
2	+	+	+	+	+	+	+	+	-	8-1
3	+	+	+	+	+	+	-	-	-	6-3
4	+	+	+	+	+	-	-	-	-	5-4
5	+	+	+	+	-	-	-	-	-	4-5
6	+	+	+	+	-	-	-	-	-	4-5
7	+	+	+	-	-	-	-	-	-	3-6
8	+	+	-	-	-	-	-	-	-	2-7
9	+	+	-	-	-	-	-	-	-	2-7
10	+	-	-	-	-	-	-	-	-	1-8
11	-	-	-	-	-	-	-	-	-	0-9

more justices oppose the claim. Table 6.1 illustrates the voting in a hypothetical cumulative scale.

Assume that the cases represent those pertaining to double jeopardy that were decided during a specific period. Case 1 unanimously upheld the claimant's allegation that he was unconstitutionally subject to double jeopardy, while case 11 indicates that the claimant lost by a vote of 9 to 0. The cases are ordered solely on the basis of the proportion of "+" votes.[10] Case 7 is less extreme than case 4 solely because fewer justices supported the claimant in 7 than in 4. Extremeness, in short, is solely a function of the number of supportive votes. Note further that each justice votes with perfect consistency in all the cases across the scale. Justice A is most liberal, voting in support of the double jeopardy claimant in the first ten cases. Conversely, Justice I is most conservative, opposing the claimant in all but case 1. Obviously, the pattern displayed in Table 6.1 did not occur by chance. When all nine justices participate in a case, 256 different voting combinations may occur.[11] Because extremeness (direction) is assigned, the number of combinations must be doubled. Thus, a 9 to 0 vote may either support or oppose the hypothesized variable that motivates the justices' behavior.

[10] Cases, of course, can also be ordered on the basis of the proportion of "−" votes. It makes no difference which way the cases are ordered so long as support or opposition to the hypothesized variable is defined consistently.

[11] The formula is $N!/R! \div (N - R)!$, where N = the number of justices, and R = number of justices voting either "+" or "−".

A cumulative scale need not display perfect voting consistency for it to be a scientifically valid scale. Guttman introduced a measure, the coefficient of reproducibility (R), to determine whether a given set of responses constitutes a scale. Because cases decided unanimously or with only a single dissent unwarrantedly inflate the coefficient, they are excluded from its calculation. The number of inconsistent votes (nonscale responses) are subtracted from the total number of participations (N) and divided by the number of participations: i.e., $R = N -$ nonscale responses / N. Although some scholars use an R of .900 as the minimum level necessary for a group of cases to consitute a scale,[12] a good argument can be made that the R ought to reach .950, and that the nonscale votes should be randomly distributed across the scale, rather than be concentrated in one or two cases or among one or two of the justices.[13] If the latter pattern prevails, the cases in question tap a variable different from the hypothesized one, or the votes of the inconsistent justice(s) tap a motivating variable different from that of the others.

Although Schubert uses as few scales as necessary,[14] we contend that each scale should be formed with a content as specific as possible.[15] Effort should be made to insure that apples are not mixed with oranges, to say nothing of combining fruit with vegetables. The focus should be on legal and semantic content which is determined as precisely as the Court's decisions permit. Gross categories should be avoided to the extent possible. For example, separate scales dealing with commercial speech, the religion clauses, and libel are preferred to a single First Amendment scale. If the cases in specific scales belong together to form a single First Amendment scale, so be it. But the deck should not be stacked in advance to favor a single broad scale.

The use of cumulative scaling to identify the attitudes that explain the justices' voting raises a serious question of their validity. Although the robustness of the constructed scales and the excellence of the attitudinal variables supports a "confident inference" that attitudes motivate behavior,[16] one cannot scientifically demonstrate that attitudes influence the votes when the attitudes are operationalized from these same votes. Circularity results. Some independent measure of attitudes is needed. In recent work, Segal and Spaeth have formulated and applied three separate and independent methods to overcome circularity, of which the most relevant for our purposes is the use of the justices' past voting to predict their votes in subsequent cases.[17]

The hypothesized variables that explain and predict the behavior of the justices

---

[12] For example, Glendon Schubert, "Judicial Attitudes and Voting Behavior: The 1961 Term of the United States Supreme Court," 28 *Law and Contemporary Problems* 100 (1963), at 120.

[13] Harold J. Spaeth and David J. Peterson, "The Analysis and Interpretation of Dimensionality: The Case of Civil Liberties Decision Making," 15 *American Journal of Political Science* 415 (1971).

[14] Op. cit. fn. 7 *supra*.   [15] Spaeth and Peterson, op. cit. fn. 13 *supra*.

[16] Joseph F. Kobylka, "Leadership on the Supreme Court of the United States: Chief Justice Burger and the Establishment Clause," 42 *Western Political Quarterly* 545 (1989), at 550.

[17] Op. cit. fn. 1 *supra*, pp. 221–226, 255–260. The other two methods are described on pp. 215–221 and 226–229.

in the cumulative scales that we have formed may be referred to as the justices' personal policy preferences. They concern such issues as civil rights and liberties, economic activity, federalism, the exercise of judicial power, and federal taxation. Because our scales are constructed as specifically in legal and semantic content as the Court's decisions permit, the justices do not, for example, display the same degree of liberalism or conservatism from one civil liberties issue to another, nor the same amount of judicial activism or restraint across issues that pertain to the exercise of judicial power.

To determine the extent to which the justices' personal policy preferences explain their votes in cases that alter precedent, we look to the presence of nonscale votes. If, for example, case 5 in Table 6.1 overruled a precedent, we would conclude that the justices' attitudes toward double jeopardy motivated their behavior because they voted in this case consistently with the other cases that formed the scale. If, on the other hand, Justice B had voted in opposition to the double jeopardy claim and Justice G had supported the claimant, we would conclude that variables that the scale does not measure motivated these two justices' votes. What these variables might be we do not know. They might pertain to the justices' attitudes toward precedent or toward a policy variable other than double jeopardy.

THE VINSON COURT

Although scholars have not attempted to scale the Vinson Court's decisions systematically, the six cases that altered precedent and the two cases in which the Vinson Court overruled itself are sufficiently few that we can supplement the few fragmentary scales that have been constructed. As a result, we are able to evaluate the justices' behavior in these few cases even though two of the cases were decided unanimously. Because of the lack of disagreement, this pair – *Oklahoma Tax Commission v. Texas Company,* 336 U.S. 342 (1949), an intergovernmental tax immunity case, and *Burstyn v. Wilson,* 343 U.S. 495 (1952), which extended the protection of the First Amendment to movies – tells us nothing about why the justices voted as they did.

The voting in a third case, *Cosmopolitan Shipping v. McAllister,* 337 U.S. 783 (1949), a Jones Act case, fits perfectly into a scale of Federal Employees' Liability Act cases constructed by Glendon Schubert.[18] The four justices who supported the injured worker – Black, Douglas, Murphy, and Rutledge – were all more economically liberal than any justice in the majority: Frankfurter, Vinson, Jackson, Burton, or Reed.

The two cases that overturned an earlier Vinson Court decision – *United States v. Rabinowitz,* 339 U.S. 56 (1950), overruling *Trupiano v. United States,* 334 U.S. 699 (1948), and *Darr v. Burford,* 339 U.S. 200 (1950), overruling *Wade v. Mayo,* 334 U.S. 672 (1948) – concern the Fourth Amendment's search and

---

[18] Op. cit. fn. 7 *supra,* p. 295.

seizure clause in a non-vehicular context and the system of comity as applied to criminal and First Amendment litigation. We have constructed a scale of the Vinson Court's decisions in both these issue areas. The 12 search and seizure cases[19] do not scale satisfactorily because of the inconsistent voting of Justice Black. He accounts for three of the six nonscale responses, with Douglas, Vinson, and Burton producing the other three. As a result, nonscale responses are not randomly distributed across the scale. Furthermore, the coefficient of reproducibility – .943 – falls below our cutoff of .950. Black, however, voted consistently in the overruling and voided cases even though he cast a dissent in both cases: in *Trupiano* – along with Vinson, Reed, and Burton – and also in *Rabinowitz*, which overruled *Trupiano*. Black explained his behavior by distinguishing the force of the judicially created exclusionary rule from the authority of the Fourth Amendment itself to bar the admissibility of illegally obtained evidence. He noted his support of the former, as evidenced by his votes in *Wolf v. Colorado*, 338 U.S. 25 (1949), but not for the latter.

In recent years, the scope of the [exclusionary] rule has been a subject of almost constant judicial controversy both in trial and appellate courts. In no other field has the law's uncertainty been more clearly manifested. To some extent that uncertainty may be unavoidable. The Trupiano Case itself added new confusions "in a field already replete with complexities." . . . But overruling that decision merely aggravates existing uncertainty.[20]

Although Black's rationale articulates a legal rather than an attitudinal policy concern, his votes in *Trupiano* and *Rabinowitz* are attitudinally consistent, even though his overall voting in search and seizure cases is not. As for Black's rationale, Jeffrey Segal has refuted the allegation – echoed by subsequent justices and commentators – that the law of the Fourth Amendment is uncertain and incoherent.[21]

The voided and overruling comity cases decided by the Vinson Court pertain to habeas corpus. Unlike search and seizure, the voting in these cases and the other few that comprise this scale is consistent.[22] We, therefore, conclude that

---

[19]   These cases listed in scale order (from most to least liberal) by case citation are *United States v. De Ri*, 332 U.S. 581; *United States v. Jeffers*, 342 U.S. 48; *District of Columbia v. Little*, 339 U.S. 1; *McDonald v. United States*, 335 U.S. 451; *United States v. Rabinowitz*, 339 U.S. 56; *Johnson v. United States*, 333 U.S. 10; *Trupiano v. United States*, 334 U.S. 699; *Harris v. United States*, 331 U.S. 145; *On Lee v. United States*, 343 U.S. 747; *Lustig v. United States*, 338 U.S. 74; *Wolf v. Colorado* and *Wolf v. Colorado*, 338 U.S. 74.

[20]   *United States v. Rabinowitz*, 339 U.S. at 67.

[21]   "Predicting Supreme Court Cases Probabilistically: The Search and Seizure Cases, 1962–1981," 78 *American Political Science Review* 891 (1984).

[22]   In scale order these cases, from most to least liberal by case citation, are *Darr v. Burford*, 339 U.S. 200; *Brown v. Allen, Speller v. Allen*, and *Daniels v. Allen*, 344 U.S. 443; *Wade v. Mayo*, 344 U.S. 672; *Albertson v. Millard*, 345 U.S. 242; and three conservatively decided solo dissent cases in which Douglas continued to cast a liberal vote: *Aircraft & Diesel Equipment v. Hirsch*, 331 U.S. 752; *Sweeney v. Woodall*, 344 U.S. 86; and *Stefanelli v. Minard*, 342 U.S. 117.

the attitudinal model explains the justices' behavior toward abstention in habeas corpus litigation.

The remaining Vinson Court decision that altered precedent is the Internal Revenue Code case *Commissioner v. Church's Estate,* 335 U.S. 632 (1949). Our efforts to scale this and the other internal revenue cases failed. The most plausible policy basis for these decisions, government versus taxpayer, failed miserably. Accordingly, we assume that the justices' votes in this issue area might be motivated by legal variables.

Our analysis of the overruling decisions of the Vinson Court, along with the two cases of its own that it overturned, presents no clear picture of why the justices' behaved as they did. Attitudinal variables seem to explain their votes in the workers' compensation case and in the two state habeas corpus cases. Attitudinal variables appear absent from the federal tax case, while the record in the two search and seizure cases seems mixed.

THE WARREN COURT

In considering attitudinal voting in the overruling decisions of the Warren Court, we divide these cases into three sets: the decisions that formally altered pre-Warren Court precedents; the cases that altered Warren Court precedents; and the votes in the altered precedents themselves. We divide the cases this way because of the possibility that attitudinal variables may be more or less evident depending not only on who is doing the overruling, but also on who is being overruled. Accordingly, we inspect the 30 Warren Court cases that overruled predecessor Courts, the 13 in which the Warren Court overruled itself, and the 15 of its decisions that these 13 overrulings voided, to ascertain the presence of nonscale votes. We shift our focus slightly here in comparison with the Vinson Court because the Warren Court – like its successors – has been successfully subject to systematic cumulative scale analysis. To determine the presence of attitudinal variables in the altering and altered decisions, we consider only these cases. If these cases fit into their respective cumulative scales so as to produce a coefficient of reproducibility (R) at or above .950, they suggest the dominance of attitudinal variables; a lesser R may suggest the presence of legal variables. In computing R, we consider only "computable" decisions – those containing at least two dissenting votes, except where a solo dissent itself spawns a nonscale response.

The 30 cases in which the Warren Court overruled pre-Warren Court decisions produce three nonscale responses, one in each of three cases. Justice Clark wrote the liberal opinion of the Court in *Mapp v. Ohio,* 367 U.S. 643 (1961), which applied the exclusionary rule to state prosecutions violative of the Fourth Amendment, thereby overruling the Vinson Court decision in *Wolf v. Colorado,* 338 U.S. 25 (1949). Justice Black cast the only dissent in *Katz v. United States,* 389 U.S. 347 (1967), another landmark Fourth Amendment case that held wiretapping to be within the Constitution's purview. Justice White was one of two dissenters (along with Harlan) in *Jones v. Alfred H. Mayer Co.*, 392 U.S. 409 (1968), which outlawed housing discrimination. The 30 cases altering pre-Warren Court precedents contain a total of 173 computable votes. With only 3 nonscale responses, the coefficient of reproducibility is an excellent .983.

The 13 decisions in which the Warren Court overruled one of its own precedents exhibit only one inconsistent vote, Warren's solo dissent in *Marchetti v. United States*, 390 U.S. 39 (1968), from a ruling that declared unconstitutional a federal occupational wagering tax statute because it ran afoul of the self-incrimination clause. If we include *Marchetti* among the computable cases, reproducibility reaches .989.

The 15 decisions in which the Warren Court overruled itself contain two nonscale votes. Whittaker was among the dissenters (with Warren, Black, and Douglas) in *Perez v. Brownell*, 356 U.S. 44 (1958), which upheld congressional authority to denaturalize citizens who voted in foreign elections. Warren voted with a minimum winning coalition – over the dissents of Frankfurter, Black, Douglas, and Brennan – to uphold the admissibility of a co-defendant's confession in *Delli Paoli v. United States*, 352 U.S. 232 (1957). With 128 computable votes cast in these overruled cases, reproducibility reaches .984.

THE BURGER COURT

Attitudinal voting is less pronounced in the 22 cases in which the Burger Court overruled decisions antedating the Warren Court. In only eight of these cases did as many as two justices dissent, and these eight cases produce four nonscale responses. R, accordingly, falls below our cutoff to .944. On the other hand, none of the cases containing inconsistent votes concerns a particularly salient issue area. Stewart's pro-state dissent and Powell's anti-state concurrence in *Machinists v. Wisconsin Employment Relations Board*, 427 U.S. 132 (1976), do not conform to their behavior in other cases involving the preemption of state court jurisdiction. Burger inconsistently associated himself with Rehnquist in a national supremacy case in which the Court declared a state law prohibiting the out-of-state shipment of minnows to violate the interstate commerce clause: *Hughes v. Oklahoma*, 441 U.S. 322 (1979). And the consistently liberal Marshall joined a dissent of Rehnquist objecting on full faith and credit grounds to the District of Columbia awarding supplemental workers' compensation to an employee who had earlier been awarded such benefits by Virginia: *Thomas v. Washington Gas Light Co.*, 448 U.S. 261 (1980). Not only were the justices unable to agree on an opinion of the Court, but Marshall and Rehnquist joined three special concurrers to hold that a Vinson Court precedent was overruled, which precedent differed from the one specified by the four justices in the plurality.[23]

---

[23] Marshall joined a Rehnquist dissent in only one case other than *Thomas: Burbank v. Lockheed Air Terminal, Inc.*, 411 U.S. 624 (1973), a decision preempting state regulation of aircraft

The 16 Burger Court decisions that overturned Warren Court precedents display acceptable attitudinal voting. The altering decisions show an $R = .951$, while the 19 overturned Warren Court decisions manifest an $R = .957$. As for the former, White's dissent in *Boys Markets v. Retail Clerks,* 398 U.S. 235 (1970), is incompatible with his voting in labor arbitration cases generally. Blackmun inconsistently dissented in *Perez v. Campbell,* 402 U.S. 637 (1971), a minimum winning supremacy clause case which held that an Arizona statute conflicted with the federal Bankruptcy Act. The plaintiff and his wife sought relief from a monetary judgment resulting from an automobile accident because of their discharge in bankruptcy. Powell uncharacteristically voted with the liberal majority in the civil rights liability case of *Monell v. Department of Social Services,* 436 U.S. 658 (1978), which held local governments subject to liability under the Civil Rights Act of 1871. Finally, White and Stevens voted inconsistently – both in dissent – in the convoluted state business regulation case of *Brown-Forman Distillers Corp. v. New York State Liquor Authority,* 476 U.S. 573 (1986). The majority ruled that a state law dictating the minimum prices that liquor producers could charge wholesalers in other states facially violated the interstate commerce clause and was not saved by the Twenty-First Amendment. Not until 1989, in *Healy v. The Beer Institute, Inc.,* 491 U.S. 324, did the Court rule that *Brown-Forman* had overruled a precedent. And when it did so, it held that the precedent that *Brown-Forman* had voided was one that it said "we need not consider the continuing validity of . . ."[24]

The foregoing set of Burger Court decisions formally altered 19 Warren Court precedents which exhibit four nonscale votes. White dissented in *Memoirs v. Massachusetts,* 383 U.S. 413 (1966), the famous obscenity case that the presently definitive *Miller v. California,* 413 U.S. 15, overturned seven years later. Douglas dissented from the pro-employee decision in *Maryland v. Wirtz,* 392 U.S. 183 (1968), the Fair Labor Standards Act case that *National League of Cities v. Usery,* 426 U.S. 833 (1976), voided.[25] In his dissent, Douglas uncharacteristically alleged "a serious invasion of state sovereignty protected by the Tenth Amendment."[26] The staunchly conservative Justice Harlan, speaking for the majority, had no difficulty sustaining the Act's application on the basis of the

---

noise. Marshall never joined even one of Rehnquist's concurrences. Conversely, Rehnquist joined twice as many of Marshall's dissents: *Guam v. Olson,* 431 U.S. 195 (1977); *Ray v. Atlantic Richfield Co.,* 435 U.S. 151 (1978); *Federal Deposit Insurance Corp. v. Philadelphia Gear Corp.,* 476 U.S. 426 (1986); and *Japan Whaling Assn. v. American Cetacean Society,* 478 U.S. 221 (1986). Rehnquist also never joined one of Marshall's concurrences. He did, however, join one of Marshall's jurisdictional dissents: *American Export Lines, Inc. v. Alvez,* 446 U.S. 274 (1980). It seems most unlikely that legal factors could account for such pronounced differences.

[24] 476 U.S. at 584, note 6. The putatively voided decision was *Joseph E. Seagram & Sons v. Hostetter,* 384 U.S. 35 (1966).

[25] *Usery,* of course, was itself overturned by the Burger Court's subsequent decision in *Garcia v. San Antonio Metropolitan Transit Authority,* 469 U.S. 528 (1985). The outcome of both cases turned on Blackmun's vote.

[26] 392 U.S. at 201.

commerce clause. Black voted inconsistently when he dissented with Frankfurter and Harlan in *Morey v. Doud,* 354 U.S. 457 (1957). The majority ruled that an Illinois statute regulating all currency exchanges except for money orders sold or issued by the American Express Company violated the equal protection clause. Lastly, Harlan's liberal concurrence in *Aguilar v. Texas,* 378 U.S. 108 (1964), does not comport with his voting in other search and seizure cases decided during the early 1960s.

We complete our assessment of the Burger Court by appraising the eight cases in which it overruled nine of its own precedents. Surprisingly perhaps, the consistency of the justices' voting is markedly higher here than it is in the other sets of Burger Court decisions. Only one nonscale vote manifested itself in the overruling decisions, that of White in *United States v. Ross,* 456 U.S. 798 (1982), and one in the voided cases, that of Stevens in *Robbins v. California,* 453 U.S. 420 (1981). The respective R's $= .981$ and $.972$, comfortably above the minimum level of scale acceptablity. Interestingly, not only did *Ross* overrule *Robbins,* the latter was, as we noted earlier, the most short lived of all the altered precedents – 11 months.[27]

One might expect nonattitudinal variables to intrude when a collegial body voids its own previous decisions, especially when, as here, the membership of the group is largely unchanged. But at least six of the justices who overruled the precedent participated in its creation, and in five of the nine overrulings eight of the justices who created the precedent also took part in its destruction.

THE REHNQUIST COURT

Of the six Rehnquist Court overrulings of decisions antedating the Warren Court, in only one did more than a single justice dissent, *American Trucking Assns. v. Scheiner,* 483 U.S. 266 (1987). It contained no nonscale votes.

The eight Rehnquist Court decisions that overruled a similar number of Warren Court precedents also show the dominance of attitudinal variables. Kennedy cast the only nonscale vote and wrote the opinion of the Court in the overruling decision, *Rodriguez de Quijas v. Shearson/American Express, Inc.,* 490 U.S. 477 (1989), a predispute agreement to arbitrate claims under the Securities Act of 1933. Douglas cast the only nonscale vote in the overruled case, an anti-employee dissent in *Parden v. Terminal Railway,* 377 U.S. 184 (1964), which concerned Alabama's waiver of sovereign immunity in a federal court suit under the Federal Employers' Liability Act. The R's $= .986$ and $.984.$

The Rehnquist Court rendered five decisions overruling Burger Court precedents. We exclude from this number *Griffith v. Kentucky,* 479 U.S. 314 (1987), which voided a Warren Court as well as a Burger Court precedent, because we

---

[27] The cases concerned the applicability of the Fourth Amendment to vehicular searches and seizures.

counted it with the Warren Court overrulings.[28] None of the overruled decisions exhibit a nonscale vote, while only Stevens cast one in the altering cases: his dissent in *Thornburgh v. Abbott,* 104 L Ed 2d 459 (1989). He authored an opinion, which Brennan and Marshall joined, holding that prison regulations censoring incoming mail inadequately protected First Amendment freedoms. The R for this group of cases is .978.

No nonscale responses appear in the highly salient Rehnquist Court death penalty case, *Payne v. Tennessee,* 115 L Ed 2d 720 (1991), that overruled two of its own precedents: *Booth v. Maryland,* 482 U.S. 496 (1987), and *South Carolina v. Gathers,* 490 U.S. 805 (1989). Like *Payne,* the overruled pair produce no attitudinally inconsistent votes.

CONCLUSION

Tables 6.2 and 6.3 summarize the justices' voting in the cases that alter precedent in the three Courts for which refined cumulative scales have been constructed. Precisely 1000 computable votes were cast, of which 976 were attitudinally consistent. Of the 24 inconsistent votes, 75 percent were cast as dissents, with each Court displaying more of them than majority votes as Table 6.2 shows. Table 6.3 shows that 17 of the 24 inconsistent votes cast by members of these three Courts occurred in overruling rather than in overruled decisions (70.1 percent). This is an unexceptional finding, however. The Warren, Burger, and Rehnquist Courts altered 109 precedents, 60 of which were decisions they themselves created. The resulting proportion, 64.5 percent, approximates the proportion of inconsistencies that are located in the overruling cases.[29] Absent a similarity between these proportions, the predominance of dissenting nonscale votes might suggest that the legal model is at least somewhat operative here; i.e., that the value of adhering to precedent outweighed attitudinal consistency in the minds of those justices casting inconsistent dissenting votes in overruling cases. Of the 17 overruling votes displayed in Table 6.3, 12 were dissents objecting to the overruling of the precedents in question (70.6 percent).

As for the 26 justices who served on these three Courts during the terms we considered, 14 cast at least one nonscale vote. White and Stevens lead with five and three votes. Black, Douglas, Powell and Warren each cast two, while Blackmun, Burger, Clark, Harlan, Kennedy, Marshall, Stewart, and Whittaker each cast one nonscale vote.

Our survey of attitudinal voting in the altering and altered decisions, as evidenced by construction of refined cumulative scales, indicates that the justices' personal policy preferences substantially explain their behavior. This does not necessarily mean that legal considerations pale by comparison. The legal and

---

[28] It makes no difference attitudinally whether we count *Griffith* as overruling a Warren or a Burger Court decision. No justice voted inconsistently.

[29] All six of the inconsistent majority votes shown in Table 6.2 occurred in decisions overruling precedent, as did 11 of the 18 nonscale dissenting votes.

Table 6.2. *Type of nonscale vote by Court*

	Warren	Burger	Rehnquist	Total
Majority	2	3	1	6
Dissent	4	12	2	18
Total	6	15	3	24

Table 6.3. *Nonscale votes in overruling and overruled cases by Court*

	Warren	Burger	Rehnquist	Total
Overruling	4	11	2	17
Overruled	2	4	1	7

attitudinal models of decision making do not diverge in all respects. Facts, for example, obviously influence the Court's decisions and are basic to both models. Whether legal variables also operate remains to be seen. We address this question in Chapter 7.

7

Personal and institutional stare decisis

According to the legal model, Supreme Court justices decide cases based on the facts of the case in light of the plain meaning of the relevant legal provision, the intent of the people who framed the provision, stare decisis, and the balancing of social interests.[1]

In this chapter we will test the extent to which the justices in the overruling cases voted in accord with one element of the legal model – stare decisis. Examining overruling cases to study the justices' adherence to precedent is a peculiar and a biased choice, for in these cases a majority of the participating justices voted to overrule a precedent.

Why did we select the overruling cases? We did so because we had no other choice. Ideally, we would also have analyzed cases in which the majority considered altering precedent, but did not do so. Unfortunately there is no way we can ascertain if such behavior occurred. The majority or plurality opinion writer rarely indicates that overruling a given precedent was considered but rejected. Indeed, for a controlling opinion to communicate this information would probably send an unwanted signal to lower court judges and future litigants, inviting them to pressure the Court to reconsider its decision.

Neither can we assume the majority considered altering a precedent simply because dissenting justices favor its abandonment. The majority and minority do not necessarily disagree on all the arguments. The majority, for example, might believe that its position does not depend on the precedent that the dissenters desire to overturn.

In contrast, when the Court overrules a precedent, all the participating justices usually express their views about its alteration. They do so either by writing their own opinion or by joining that of another justice. Only in these cases is the issue sufficiently dramatic to evoke a response from all the participating justices. Thus, we have taken advantage of the best, and perhaps the only, opportunity we have to test whether the justices adhere to precedent.[2]

---

[1] Jeffrey A. Segal and Harold J. Spaeth, *The Supreme Court and the Attitudinal Model* (Cambridge: Cambridge University Press, 1993), pp. 33–64.

[2] Alternatively, we might have inspected cases in which one of the litigants asked, but the Court refused, to overturn a precedent. Such a request, however, does not necessarily indicate that the

TESTING THE LEGAL MODEL

To test the legal model insofar as stare decisis is concerned, we assume that when a justice votes to overturn precedent his behavior conflicts with the legal model. We are compelled to make this assumption in order to test the legal model. We are aware that the lax version of stare decisis, presented in Chapter 1, allows some nonconformity to precedent. Nonetheless, such deviation is considered unusual, and defenders of the legal model do not present explicit guidelines about when it is appropriate to abandon stare decisis.

Testing the legal model also requires that we distinguish between "institutional" and "personal" stare decisis. The latter occurs when an individual justice either supports the Court's decision in case 1 (i.e., the overruled case) and opposes its overruling in case 2, or opposes the Court's decision in case 1 and favors its overruling in case 2. Institutional stare decisis takes place when a justice conforms to the Court's precedents. Four possible patterns, therefore, may result. These are specified in Table 7.1.

1) A justice may vote with the majority in the overruled case and dissent from the overruling. Such a justice adheres to both personal and institutional stare decisis.
2) A justice may dissent in the overruled case and vote with the majority to overrule. Such a justice conforms to personal stare decisis, while rejecting institutional stare decisis.
3) A justice may vote with the majority in both the overruling and the overruled decision. Here the justice conforms neither to personal stare decisis nor to institutional stare decisis.
4) A justice may dissent in both the overruled and overruling case. In this circumstance, the justice does not conform to personal stare decisis, but conforms to institutional stare decisis.

We normally perceive the first two patterns as consistent with the attitudinal model and the last two as inconsistent with such voting. But it is possible for the converse to be true. Thus, for example, we observed in Chapter 6 that Chief Justice Warren cast a nonscale vote in *Marchetti v. United States,* 390 U.S. 39 (1968), even though that vote was a dissent from an overruling in which he had been a member of the majority (type 1 voting). As a consequence, we will not use these data to test the attitudinal model. We will, however, employ it to test the legal model. As previously suggested, we will treat voting in conflict with institutional stare decisis as voting incompatible with this model.

Whether justices vote in conformity or in conflict with personal and institutional stare decisis can usually be determined by examining their votes alone. But, at times, what the justices say in their opinions may conflict with the thrust

Court considered it. Attorneys not uncommonly employ a scattershot approach in presenting their case to the Court: if one argument proves unpersuasive, others remain.

Table 7.1. *Behavioral options in overruled and overruling cases*

		Overruled case	Overruling case	Compatible with the legal model
Voted with	1)	majority	minority	yes
	2)	minority	majority	no
	3)	majority	majority	no
	4)	minority	minority	yes
		Overruled case	Overruling case	Compatible with personal stare decisis
Voted with	1)	majority	minority	yes
	2)	minority	majority	yes
	3)	majority	majority	no
	4)	minority	minority	no

of their votes. Thus, for example, a justice who dissents from both the overruled and the overruling decision (type 4) may disagree with the decision to overrule not because he has come to accept the overruled precedent, but because he disapproves of both. If so, this would not demonstrate an attachment to institutional stare decisis. A good case in point is the votes of Black and Douglas in *Lear, Inc. v. Atkins,* 395 U.S. 653 (1969). In their opinion, they state they "concur in the judgment and opinion of the Court" except for a section that addresses an issue separate from and independent of the overruling.[3]

For convenience and for analytical precision, we focus on the individual justices and the four Courts on which they sat. Our data set is reduced, however, because we exclude cases that overruled decisions antedating the Vinson Court. Some of the holdover justices on the Vinson and Warren Courts served on the Hughes and Stone Courts. We believe, however, that the overruled cases from the Hughes and Stone Courts are sufficiently distinctive to warrant exclusion. Where a single overruling voids more than one precedent, we do a multiple count. More specifically, if, for example, an overturning case voids three decisions, we treat this as a discrete set of three overruling and overruled votes.

THE VINSON COURT

As Appendix I indicates, the Vinson Court overruled only two of its own decisions, *Wade v. Mayo,* 334 U.S. 672 (1948), a comity case, and *Trupiano v.*

[3] 395 U.S. at 676.

United States, 334 U.S. 699 (1948), a Fourth Amendment case. Douglas participated in neither overruling; hence, the number of justices who voted in all four
cases is reduced to six. Vinson, Reed, and Burton dissented in the overruled
cases and voted with the majority in the overrulings, behavior compatible with
the attitudinal but not the legal model. Frankfurter voted the opposite in both
pairs of cases, a behavior compatible with both models. Black and Jackson voted
as Frankfurter did in one case and dissented in the other pair.[4] Their behavior
thus comports with the legal model. Black, moreover, stated that his dissent in
the overruling search and seizure case was motivated by institutional stare decisis.[5] Because neither Black nor Jackson cast a nonscale vote in any of these
four cases, their behavior seems to conform to the attitudinal model. We do point
out in Chapter 5, however, that Black's voting in the totality of the Vinson
Court's non-vehicular search and seizure cases is sufficiently inconsistent to
destroy the goodness of that cumulative scale. Hence, even though he cast no
nonscale vote in either *Trupiano* or *Rabinowitz,* one may nonetheless dispute his
attitudinal consistency in this issue area. We credit Jackson with a legally compatible vote in *Darr* even though his brief opinion finds neither the position of the
Darr majority nor that of the overruled *Wade v. Mayo* satisfactory.[6]

Of the 12 pairs of votes cast by the overlapping justices in these 2 pairs of
cases, 6 clearly fail to conform to the legal model: the votes of Vinson, Reed,
and Burton. Just as clearly, their voting harmonizes with the attitudinal model.
By contrast, the voting of Frankfurter, Black, and Jackson conforms to the legal
model. With the possible exception of Black's *Rabinowitz-Trupiano* votes, his
votes also conform to the attitudinal model.

As for voting compatible with personal stare decisis, only Black's minority-
minority voting in *Trupiano* and *Rabinowitz,* and that of Jackson in *Wade* and
Darr, deviate from it. Accordingly, 83.3 percent of the votes conform to personal
stare decisis. As we depart the Vinson Court, the scoreboard reads: attitudinal
model 11, maybe 12, of 12; the legal model 6 of 12; personal stare decisis 10
of 12.

THE WARREN COURT

The Warren Court formally altered 13 Vinson Court decisions in which four
different justices were holdovers. (See Table 7.2.) Frankfurter voted compatibly
with the legal model in the single overruling case in which he participated, *Mapp
v. Ohio,* 367 U.S. 643 (1961). He had authored the opinion of the Court in *Wolf v.
Colorado,* 338 U.S. 25 (1949), and joined Harlan's dissent in *Mapp.* On the
Warren Court, Justice Clark voted the same way as Frankfurter in two of the five

---

[4] Black voted majority-minority in the comity pair, and minority-minority in the search-and-seizure
set. Jackson reversed the sets.
[5] See the quotation from Black's *Rabinowitz* dissent in Chapter 6.
[6] *Darr v. Burford,* 339 U.S. 200 (1949), at 238.

Table 7.2. *Legally compatible voting in overruled*
and overruling cases, Warren Court justices

Altered precedent of:	Vinson Court	Warren Court	Total	
Legal model:	Pro-anti	Pro-anti	Pro-anti	% pro
Justice				
Black	3-11	1-16	4-27	12.9
Brennan		0-11	0-11	0.0
Burton		2-0	2-0	100.
Clark	2-3	11-3	13-6	68.4
Douglas	0-12	1-16	1-28	3.4
Frankfurter	1-0	0-2	1-2	33.3
Harlan		9-6	9-6	60.0
Stewart		3-3	3-3	50.0
Warren		1-16	1-16	5.9
Total	6-26	28-73	34-99	25.6
% pro	18.8	27.7	25.6	

Vinson Court overrulings in which he participated, dissenting from the alteration of decisions he had supported: *Jackson v. Denno,* 378 U.S. 368 (1964), which overruled the coerced confession case of *Stein v. New York,* 346 U.S. 156 (1953), and *Keyishian v. Board of Regents,* 383 U.S. 663 (1966), which overturned the security risk case of *Adler v. Board of Education,* 342 U.S. 485 (1952). Unlike Frankfurter, Clark voted incompatibly with the legal model in three cases: he voted with the majority in both the altering and the altered decision in *Construction & General Laborers' Union v. Curry,* 371 U.S. 542 (1962), which overturned *Montgomery Trades Council v. Ledbetter Erection Co.,* 344 U.S. 178 (1952); *Gray v. Sanders,* 372 U.S. 368 (1963), which voided *South v. Peters,* 339 U.S. 276 (1950); and *Fay v. Noia,* 372 U.S. 391 (1963), which overruled *Darr v. Burford,* 339 U.S. 200 (1950).

Egregiously unlike the behavior of Frankfurter and Clark was that of Douglas and Black. Douglas never voted compatibly with the legal model as majority-minority in any of his 12 participations, Black only once in his 14. While Clark voted majority-majority three times, Douglas and Black each did so only once. Indeed, Douglas voted minority-majority in all but two cases. He voted with the majority in *Gray* to overrule *Cook v. Fortson,* 329 U.S. 675 (1946), a summary per curiam that dismissed an appeal challenging Georgia's county unit election system. He also voted majority-majority in *Chimel v. California,* 395 U.S. 752 (1969), which held that the warrantless search of the defendant's house could not be constitutionally justified as a search incident to a lawful arrest.[7] It may superficially appear that his vote concurring in part and dissenting in part in *Lear,*

---

[7] *Chimel* voided *Harris v. United States,* 331 U.S. 145 (1947), in which Douglas voted with the majority.

Inc. v. Adkins, 395 U.S. 653 (1969), is minority-minority since he dissented in the overruled case, *Automatic Radio Mfg. Co. v. Hazeltine Research, Inc.,* 339 U.S. 827 (1950), which had held that licensee estoppel was the general rule under patent law. In joining Black's opinion, however, Douglas indicated his agreement with the judgment and opinion of the Court, disagreeing only with a remand to consider questions of state law antedating the issuance of the patent.[8]

Including *Lear,* Black voted antithetically to the legal model as minority-majority in 11 of the 14 Warren Court decisions that altered Vinson Court precedents. One of his three legally compatible votes occurred in his dissent from the decision in *Lee v. Florida,* 392 U.S. 378 (1968), refusing to overrule the holding of *Schwartz v. Texas,* 344 U.S. 199 (1952), that wiretap evidence was admissible in state courts notwithstanding contrary language in the Federal Communications Act of 1934. Black's other two legally congruent votes also pertained to the overruling of search and seizure decisions. He dissented in *Chimel,* thereby refusing to overrule either *Harris* or *United States v. Rabinowitz,* even though he had also dissented in the latter, as we discuss above.[9]

Although the votes of Douglas and Black do not conform to the legal model, they comport well with personal stare decisis: 90.3 and 89.7 percent, respectively, as Table 7.3 shows. Because they cast all but six of the relevant votes, Douglas and Black account for the fact that in overruling the Vinson Court, the Warren Court justices support personal stare decisis more than three-fourths of the time, but the legal model only a quarter of the time.

Apart from the contents of Tables 7.2 and 7.3, we may observe definite patterns in the justices' votes. Clark, for example, always voted with the majority in the overruled case. If we count their *Lear* votes as minority-majority, Douglas ended up in the majority in each of his 12 participations, Black in 11 of his 14. In 10 of these 11 overrulings, moreover, Black's majority position vindicated his dissent in the overruled case.

The Warren Court overruled 17 of its own precedents, 2 of which were voided twice: *Crooker v. California,* 357 U.S. 433 (1958), and *Cicenia v. LaGay,* 357 U.S. 504 (1958). The voiding decisions were *Escobedo v. Illinois,* 378 U.S. 478 (1964), and *Miranda v. Arizona,* 384 U.S. 436 (1966). *Escobedo* overruled them in part, while *Miranda* finished the job.[10] Because we are concerned with how holdover justices voted in the overruling as well as the overruled cases in which they participated, we double count *Crooker* and *Cicenia.* Nothing required the participating justices to vote the same in the 2 overruling cases.

Nine of the 17 Warren Court justices confronted a case that their colleagues were about to alter formally, ranging from Black, Douglas, and Warren, who participated in all 17, to Burton and Frankfurter, who voted in but a pair of these

---

[8] 395 U.S. at 676–677.

[9] In overruling *Rabinowitz,* which had overruled *Trupiano, Chimel* became an overruling of an overruling.

[10] See 378 U.S. at 492, and 384 U.S. at 479, note 48.

Table 7.3. *Voting compatible with personal stare decisis*
in overruled and overruling cases, Warren Court justices

Altered precedent of:	Vinson Court	Warren Court	Total	
Personal stare decisis:	Pro-anti	Pro-anti	Pro-anti	% pro
Justice				
Black	12-2	16-1	28-3	90.3
Brennan		7-4	7-4	63.6
Burton		2-0	2-0	100.
Clark	2-3	11-3	13-6	68.4
Douglas	10-2	16-1	26-3	89.7
Frankfurter	1-0	2-0	3-0	100.
Harlan		9-6	9-6	60.0
Stewart		3-3	3-3	50.0
Warren		15-2	15-2	88.2
Total	25-7	81-20	106-27	79.7
% pro	78.1	80.2	79.7	

cases. (See Table 7.2.) Although the justices increased the frequency with which they adhered to the legal model when overruling their own precedents, as distinct from those of the Vinson Court – 27.7 percent versus 18.8 percent (see Table 7.2) – the rise hardly evidences the operation of the legal model. As was true in the Vinson Court, the justices' behave either in harmony with or in opposition to the legal model. Only Stewart and Harlan are even-handed, at 50 percent and 60 percent, respectively. Indeed, only Burton, with his 2 votes, and Clark, with 11 of his 14, consistently vote compatibly with the legal model. The other five – Black, Brennan, Douglas, Frankfurter, and Warren – cast only 3 of their 64 votes congruously (4.7 percent), of which 2 were cast by Black and Douglas.

Black and Douglas each cast a legally supportive vote (dissent-dissent) in *Swift & Co. v. Wickham,* 382 U.S. 111 (1965). They disagreed with an aspect of the overruled case, *Kesler v. Dept. of Public Safety,* 369 U.S. 153 (1962), that they had originally supported: "I agree that this case was properly heard by a three judge District Court but dissent from the Court's holding that Utah may . . . enforce the payment of a judgment already discharged under the Federal Bankruptcy Act."[11] In their opinion in the overruling case they said: "I regret that I am unable to join in that decision. My objection is not that the Court has not given *Kesler* 'a more respectful burial' . . . but that the Court has engaged in unwarranted infanticide."[12] Justice Black also cast another vote dissenting from both an overruling and overruled decision. In his opinion, however, he made no reference whatsoever to the overruled decision, *Westinghouse Employees v. Westinghouse Corp.,* 348 U.S. 437 (1955). His dissent in the overruling case merely objected to the majority's ruling that state courts were not preempted from maintaining suits brought by individual employees for employer breach of a

[11]   369 U.S. at 182.   [12]   382 U.S. at 133 (citation omitted).

collective bargaining contract.[13] As a result, we count Black's vote as sustaining the overruling (as minority-majority) and, hence, incompatible with the legal model. After all, he dissented from the creation of *Westinghouse* and that should suffice. His other eight colleagues all agreed that the *Westinghouse* "holding is no longer authoritative as precedent."[14] Under the circumstances, Black's reiteration of his original position would have been redundant.

The remaining legally compatible vote cast by the five justices who least frequently voted compatibly with the legal model was Warren's dissent in *Marchetti v. United States,* 390 U.S. 39 (1968). Not only was Warren in the majority in the overruled case, *Lewis v. United States,* 348 U.S. 419 (1955), his *Marchetti* vote was an attitudinally nonscale response, as we explain in Chapter 6.

The patterns displayed in Table 7.2, though striking, do not tell the whole story. Except for the infrequently participating Burton, no justice voted compatibly with the legal model more than two-thirds of the time: the most consistent justice, Clark, voted with the legal model only 68.4 percent of the time. Conversely, four justices fall woefully below 25 percent: Black 12.9 percent, Warren 5.9, Douglas 3.4, and Brennan 0.0. The legal model obviously explains little of what is going on. Overall, barely a quarter of the Warren Court's votes conform to the legal model. Further analysis reveals additional patterning. Clark, for example, invariably voted with the majority in the overruled cases – a pattern that he also displayed in the overruled Vinson Court decisions. Harlan also voted with the majority in the overruled cases. When the Warren Court formally altered Vinson Court precedents, Douglas invariably found himself with the majority, while Black was similarly positioned in 11 of his 14 votes, as we note above. Furthermore, their presence in the majority vindicated their votes in the overruled decisions, nine of which were dissents. When the Warren Court altered its own precedents, Douglas and Black had always been in the minority in the overruled cases.[15] Additionally, Douglas came out on top in 16 of the 17 overrulings, Black in 15 of 17. Warren and Brennan display a similar pattern. Brennan was in the minority in 7 of the 11 overruled decisions, Warren in 13 of 16. At the overruling stage, however, Brennan was always among the majority; so also was Warren except for *Marchetti.*

Table 7.3 shows that the Warren Court justices do not vary their personal stare decisis voting between their Vinson and Warren Court overrulings: 78.1 percent versus 80.2 percent. All of the justices attain at least 50 percent. Of the four justices who overturned Vinson Court precedents, only Clark appreciably varies his proportion between it and the Warren Court. Along with Clark, Burton, Harlan, and Stewart combine personal stare decisis with a modicum of attachment to the legal model. Their pro and anti votes are identical on both tables.

---

[13]   *Smith v. Evening News Assn.,* 371 U.S. 195 (1962), at 201–205.   [14]   Id. at 199.
[15]   When the Warren Court altered Vinson Court precedents, Black had been in the overruled majority once, Douglas twice.

Antithetical behavior results from Black, Brennan, Douglas, Frankfurter, and Warren. Collectively, their pro-personal stare decisis voting of 85.2 percent (69 of 81) dwindles to a paltry 7.7 percent pro-legal model.

The patterns we have discovered thus far in this chapter neatly portray what is happening in the overruled and overruling decisions, but they do not explain why it is occurring. We surmise that the justice's ideological orientation may be the key that unlocks the explanatory door. Explanation, however, is the subject of the next chapter. We first need to determine whether the patterned behavior of the Warren Court also manifests itself on the Burger and Rehnquist Courts. They, after all, have not been decisional clones of the Warren Court.

THE BURGER COURT

Although the Burger Court formally altered eight Vinson Court decisions, in only one overruling, *Braden v. 30th Judicial Circuit,* 410 U.S. 484 (1973), did a holdover justice participate in the overturned case: Douglas in *Ahrens v. Clark,* 335 U.S. 188 (1948).[16] Surprisingly, given Douglas's behavior on the Warren Court, he silently voted with the majority to overrule a majority of which he had been part. Indeed, he had written the Court's opinion in the overruled case. Not only are his votes overall incompatible with the legal model, he had previously voted majority-majority in only 2 of 29 instances, and one of these voided a summarily dismissed appeal.[17]

The Burger Court formally altered 19 Warren Court precedents in 16 decisions. We add to this set the vote of Douglas in the overruled Vinson Court case discussed in the preceding paragraph, but not the case itself. The usable $N = 17$. Two cases partly overruled by *Burks v. United States,* 437 U.S. 1 (1978), contain no overlapping justices: *Sapir v. United States,* 348 U.S. 373 (1955), and *Yates v. United States,* 354 U.S. 298 (1957).[18] One case, *Illinois v. Gates,* 462 U.S. 213 (1983), overruled two precedents: *Aguilar v. Texas,* 378 U.S. 108 (1964), and *Spinelli v. United States,* 393 U.S. 410 (1969).

Although a much higher proportion of the Burger Court justices participated in the alteration of decisions in which they had earlier taken part than was true of the Warren Court justices (12 of 13[19] versus 9 of 17), the proportion of legally

---

[16] The other seven Vinson Court decisions that the Burger Court voided are *Joseph v. Carter & Weekes Stevedoring Co.,* 330 U.S. 422 (1947); *Industrial Commission of Wisconsin v. McCartin,* 330 U.S. 622 (1947); *United States v. Yellow Cab Co.,* 332 U.S. 218 (1947); *Goesaert v. Cleary,* 335 U.S. 464 (1948); *UAW v. Wisconsin Employment Relations Board,* 336 U.S. 245 (1949); *Kiefer-Stewart v. Joseph E. Seagram & Sons,* 340 U.S. 211 (1951); and *Spector Motor Service v. O'Connor,* 340 U.S. 602 (1951).

[17] *Cook v. Fortson,* 329 U.S. 675 (1946), overruled by *Gray v. Sanders,* 372 U.S. 368 (1963). The other instance concerned the overturning of *Harris v. United States,* 331 U.S. 145 (1947), by *Chimel v. California,* 395 U.S. 752 (1969).

[18] They were overruled to the extent that a defendant, by reason of the double jeopardy clause, does not waive his right to a judgment of acquittal by moving for a new trial.

[19] The only exception was the Court's junior justice, O'Connor.

Table 7.4. *Legally compatible voting in overruled*
and overruling cases, Burger Court justices

Altered precedent of:	Warren Court	Burger Court	Total	
Legal model:	Pro-anti	Pro-anti	Pro-anti	% pro
Justice				
Black	1-1		1-1	50.0
Blackmun		2-7	2-7	22.2
Brennan	8-8	6-3	14-11	56.0
Burger		1-8	1-8	11.1
Douglas	2-4	0-1	2-5	28.6
Harlan	1-1		1-1	50.0
Marshall	2-0	6-3	8-3	72.7
Powell		1-5	1-5	16.7
Rehnquist		1-5	1-5	16.7
Stevens		0-5	0-5	0.0
Stewart	1-11	0-4	1-15	6.3
White	2-7	3-6	5-13	27.8
Total	17-32	20-47	37-79	31.9
% pro	34.7	29.9	31.9	

congruent votes that the Burger Court justices cast in cases overruling Warren Court decisions does not vary much from the overruling votes of the Warren Court, as Table 7.4 indicates (31.9 percent versus 25.6 percent). Again like the Warren Court, the Burger Court justices exhibited no more support of the legal model in their own overruled decisions than they did in those of their predecessor (29.9 percent versus 34.7 percent). Consistent with this finding, the five justices who participated in the alterations of precedents of both Courts did not appreciably vary their voting proportions. The Burger Court additionally altered nine of its own decisions in eight overrulings.[20]

Three justices participated in overrulings on both Courts: Black, Douglas, and Brennan. All three exhibited greater attachment to the legal model in their voting on the Burger Court than they did on the Warren Court even though Black participated but twice. Indeed, Brennan raised his proportion from zero on the Warren Court to second highest on the Burger Court, 56.0 percent. The Burger Court leader in legally congruent voting was, surprisingly enough, another liberal, Justice Marshall. Least adherent to the legal model were Stevens at zero, Stewart at 6.3 percent, and Burger at 11.1 percent. Also antithetical were Powell and Rehnquist at 16.7 percent, Blackmun at 22.2 percent, and White at 27.8 percent.

Voting compatible with personal stare decisis differs not only from that of the

---

[20] An early Rehnquist Court decision, *Pope v. Illinois*, 481 U.S. 497 (1987), said that *Rose v. Clark*, 478 U.S. 570 (1986), overruled *Jackson v. Virginia*, 443 U.S. 307 (1979), and *Marks v. United States*, 430 U.S. 188 (1977).

Table 7.5. *Voting compatible with personal stare decisis*
in overruled and overruling cases, Burger Court justices

Altered precedent of:	Warren Court	Burger Court	Total	
Personal stare decisis:	Pro-anti	Pro-anti	Pro-anti	% pro
Justice				
Black	2-0		2-0	100.
Blackmun		3-6	3-6	33.3
Brennan	9-7	5-4	14-11	56.0
Burger		1-8	1-8	11.1
Douglas	4-2	1-0	5-2	71.4
Harlan	2-0		2-0	100.
Marshall	2-0	6-3	8-3	72.7
Powell		1-5	1-5	16.7
Rehnquist		2-4	2-4	33.3
Stevens		2-3	2-3	40.0
Stewart	4-8	1-3	5-11	31.3
White	5-4	4-5	9-9	50.0
Total	28-21	26-41	54-62	46.6
% pro	57.1	38.9	46.6	

Warren Court justices, but also from the Burger Court justices' legally harmonious behavior. While 79.7 percent of the votes cast by the Warren Court justices accorded with personal stare decisis, only 46.6 percent of those of the Burger Court justices so conformed. (See Table 7.5.) Moreover, the Warren Court justices did not distinguish between overrulings of their own and the predecessor Court, as Table 7.3 indicates. But on the Burger Court, the justices voted markedly more compatibly with personal stare decisis in their Warren Court overrulings (57.1 percent) than they did in their own (38.9 percent). This overall pattern, however, does not correlate with a high degree of legally congruent voting, as a comparison of Tables 7.4 and 7.5 demonstrates.

The negative association between voting in conformity with the legal model and voting compatible with personal stare decisis is not particularly manifest in the voting of the individual justices, however, as it was on the Warren Court. The justice who voted most often in accord with the legal model, Marshall, displays the same proportion of personal stare decisis, 72.7 percent. So also do Brennan (56.0 percent), Powell (16.7 percent), and Burger (11.1 percent). Apart from the infrequently participating Black and Harlan, the others, except Blackmun, raise their personal stare decisis markedly above their legal voting levels (Rehnquist, Stevens, Stewart, Douglas, and White).

The voting paradigms displayed in Table 7.1 characterize the Burger Court justices as they did those sitting on the Warren Court. The three justices who most often participated in the cases altering Warren Court precedents – Brennan, Stewart, and White – voted with the majority in the overruling decisions 16 of 16 times, 11 of 12, and 7 of 9. By contrast, the other four justices who have entries in the first columns of Tables 7.4 and 7.5 were collectively in the majority of an overruling decision with only 1 of their 11 votes.[21] As for its own alterations, a surprisingly high proportion were majority-majority: 37 of 67 (55.2 percent). By contrast, only 20 of the 48 of the Burger Court alterations of Warren Court decisions were such (41.7 percent), along with a mere 6 of the 32 cast in Warren Court alterations of Vinson Court decisions (18.8 percent), and only 18 of the 101 cast when it altered its own precedents (17.8 percent). Accompanying this predilection for majority-majority voting are three cases in which the same justice wrote the Court's opinion in both the overruled and overruling case: Rehnquist in the double jeopardy cases, *United States v. Scott,* 437 U.S. 82 (1978), overruling *United States v. Jenkins,* 420 U.S. 358 (1975); Rehnquist again in civil rights liability cases, *Daniels v. Williams,* 474 U.S. 327 (1986), overruling in part *Parratt v. Taylor,* 451 U.S. 527 (1981); and Powell in *Rose v. Clark,* 478 U.S. 570 (1986), a harmless error case, overruling *Marks v. United States,* 430 U.S. 188 (1977). In Powell's defense, however, his opinion said nothing about the voiding of *Marks.* An early Rehnquist Court decision, *Pope v. illinois,* 481 U.S. 497 (1987), made this announcement. Even so, Powell silently joined White's overruling opinion in *Pope.*

In other respects, Stevens and Stewart always voted with the overruling majority when the Burger Court altered its own precedents, while Blackmun did so in seven of his nine participations. At the other extreme, Burger and White were in the overruled majority eight of nine times. Powell and Rehnquist, compatibly with their proclivity for writing the opinion of the Court that overruled their own such opinions, were simultaneously in both the overruled and overruling majority in four of five participations. Only Brennan and Marshall distributed their voting across all four paradigms of Table 7.1. No other justice behaved similarly except for Black in his Warren Court votes in cases altering Vinson Court precedents.

THE REHNQUIST COURT

One Rehnquist Court decision overruled two Vinson Court precedents, but no personnel overlapped.[22] One of the eight Rehnquist Court alterations of Warren Court precedents also contains no overlap, *Rodriguez de Quijas v. Shearson/American Express Inc.,* 490 U.S. 477 (1989), overruling *Wilko v. Swan,* 346 U.S. 427 (1953). Only 3 of the 11 Rehnquist Court justices (through Souter) participate in any of these cases: Brennan, Marshall, and White, as Table 7.6 indicates. Marshall conformed to the legal model in his two votes, Brennan did so in two of his five, and White in only one of seven. The resulting percentage of 35.7 substantially exceeds that of the Warren Court justices (see Table 7.2), while

---

[21] Douglas's vote overruling a Vinson Court case also placed him with the majority.

[22] *American Trucking Assns. v. Scheiner,* 483 U.S. 266 (1987), overruled *Aero Mayflower Transit Co. v. Board of Railroad Comrs.,* 332 U.S. 495 (1947), and *Capitol Greyhound Lines v. Brice,* 339 U.S. 542 (1950).

Table 7.6. *Legally compatible voting in overruled
and overruling cases, Rehnquist Court justices*

Altered precedent of:	Warren Court	Burger Court	Rehnquist Court	Total
Legal model:	Pro-anti	Pro-anti	Pro-anti	% pro
Justice				
Blackmun		6-1	2-0	88.9
Brennan	2-3	3-1	1-0	60.0
Marshall	2-0	4-2	2-0	80.0
O'Connor		0-2	0-2	0.0
Rehnquist		1-5	0-2	12.5
Scalia			0-2	0.0
Stevens		4-1	2-0	85.7
White	1-6	1-7	0-2	11.8
Total	5-9	19-19	7-8	31-36
% pro	35.7	50.0	46.7	46.3

slightly surpassing that of the Burger Court justices (see Table 7.4). Conversely, all three adhere to personal stare decisis, especially Marshall and White. Collectively, they display less attachment to personal stare decisis than the Warren Court justices but more than those of the Burger Court (compare Table 7.7 with Tables 7.3 and 7.5). With but a single exception between them, Brennan and Marshall voted with the majority in the overruled cases. White voted conversely: with the majority in all but one overruling decision.

Six Rehnquist Court decisions formally altered eight Burger Court precedents, one of which had also overruled a Warren Court case: *Griffith v. Kentucky,* 479 U.S. 314 (1987). We count it here as well as there. Half of the altered decisions concern abortion: *Roe v. Wade,* 410 U.S. 113 (1973); *Colautti v. Franklin,* 439 U.S. 379 (1979); *Akron v. Akron Center for Reproductive Health,* 462 U.S. 416 (1983); and *Thornburgh v. American College of Obstetricians and Gynecologists,* 476 U.S. 747 (1986). This disproportion skews voting congruently with the legal model as well as personal stare decisis. Fully half the 38 votes cast by the seven participating justices conform to the former, as do 84.2 percent to the latter. No other Court ranks as high. Blackmun, Stevens, Marshall, and Brennan cast all but two of the legally compatible votes, while no justice fell below 75 percent in support of personal stare decisis. As expected, Blackmun, Marshall, Stevens, and Brennan were overwhelmingly in the majority in the overturned cases (19 of 22) and simultaneously with the losers in the overruling decisions (5 of 22). White, Rehnquist, and O'Connor exhibit the opposite pattern, casting 11 of 16 dissenting votes in the altered cases, and 14 of 16 majority votes to overturn.

The single instance in which the Rehnquist Court altered its own precedents,

Table 7.7. *Voting compatible with personal stare decisis*
in overruled and overruling cases, Rehnquist Court justices

Altered precedent of:	Warren Court	Burger Court	Rehnquist Court	Total
Legal model:	Pro-anti	Pro-anti	Pro-anti	% pro
Justice				
Blackmun		6-1	2-0	88.9
Brennan	3-2	3-1	1-0	70.0
Marshall	2-0	5-1	2-0	90.0
O'Connor		2-0	2-0	100
Rehnquist		5-1	2-0	87.5
Scalia			2-0	100
Stevens		5-0	2-0	100
White	5-2	6-2	1-1	70.6
Total	10-4	32-6	14-1	56-11
% pro	71.4	84.2	93.3	83.6

Payne v. Tennessee, 115 L Ed 2d 720 (1991), which voided *Booth v. Maryland,* 482 U.S. 496 (1987), and *South Carolina v. Gathers,* 490 U.S. 805 (1989), saw seven of the *Payne* justices participate in both *Booth* and *Gathers,* and one, Brennan, take part in only *Booth.* Blackmun, Brennan, Marshall, and Stevens all voted majority-minority, compatibly with the legal model and personal stare decisis; O'Connor, Rehnquist, and Scalia voted the opposite: minority-majority – incompatible with the legal model, but congruent with personal stare decisis. White voted with O'Connor et al. in *Booth,* and majority-majority in *Gathers.* Legal voting is 46.7 percent (7 of 15), while adherence to personal stare decisis soars to 93.3 percent (14 of 15).

CONCLUSION

This chapter has examined the extent to which the justices of the Vinson, Warren, Burger, and Rehnquist Courts voted compatibly with the legal model and personal stare decisis when they voted in both the overruling and overruled cases. Needless to say, we do not infer that the findings in these cases apply across the board. All four Courts manifested more support for personal stare decisis than for the legal model. The Warren and Burger Courts were least supportive of the legal model: 25.6 and 31.9 percent. The Rehnquist Court reached 46.3 percent, while the Vinson Court justices split their 12 votes equally. This record hardly betokens attachment to the legal model. Nor does the behavior of the individual justices belie our judgment. Perusal of Tables 7.2, 7.4, and 7.6 shows inconstancy on the part of the justices who sat on more than one Court (i.e., Black, Blackmun, Brennan, Douglas, Stevens, and Stewart), as well as those who did not. Others were consistently hostile to the legal model; i.e., Rehnquist and White. The situation is similar for justices who sat on overrulings from only a single Court; i.e., Burger, O'Connor, Powell, and Warren. Even an otherwise legally support-ive justice such as Clark sharply varied his support depending on which Court was being overruled, Vinson or Warren.[23] Apart from the infrequently participat-ing Burton ($N = 4$), only two justices consistently voted compatibly with the legal model, Marshall at a most respectable 76.2 percent (16 of 21 votes) and Harlan at a much more modest 58.8 percent (10 of 17).

A basically opposite pattern emerges from our examination of voting congru-ent with personal stare decisis. To the extent that personal stare decisis theoreti-cally conforms to the attitudinal model this finding comes as no surprise, given the justices' nonadherence to the legal model. But not all justices discriminate in their degree of support/nonsupport for the two behaviors. On the Warren Court, Clark, Harlan, and Stewart voted compatibly with both the legal and attitudinal models at identical frequencies: 68.4, 60.0, and 50.0 percent. So also Brennan and Marshall on the Burger Court: 56.0 and 72.7 percent; and Blackmun on the Rehnquist Court: 88.9 percent. Other Rehnquist Court justices varied their sup-port for the legal model and personal stare decisis somewhat: Brennan, Marshall, and Stevens. Conversely, others staunchly voted incompatibly with both: Black-mun, Burger, Powell, Rehnquist, Stevens, and Stewart on the Burger Court. Interestingly, no members of the Warren or Rehnquist Courts simultaneously opposed the legal model and personal stare decisis.

Associated with the foregoing behavior is a pronounced patterning of the justices' membership in the majority and minority vote coalitions of the over-ruled and overruling cases. The justices may exercise one of four options when they participate in a case that formally alters a case in which they earlier took part. As Table 7.1 reveals, they may vote 1) majority-minority, which is compati-ble with both the legal model and personal stare decisis; 2) minority-majority, which is compatible with personal stare decisis but not with the legal model; 3) majority-majority, which is compatible with neither; or 4) minority-minority, which is compatible with the legal model, but incompatible with personal stare decisis. Table 7.8 specifies the frequency of each.

Minority-majority voting (38.7 percent) predominates by 8 percent over majority-minority (30.2 percent) and by 10 percent over majority-majority (28.4 percent). Only minority-minority voting (2.7 percent) varies hugely from the other three patterns. A somewhat higher percentage of the overruling votes supported alteration, 67.1 (220 of 328), than had been cast to establish the precedent in the first place, 58.5 (192 of 328). But again, these patterns conceal more than they reveal. The Warren Court, for example, cast more minority-majority votes than the others combined, 75 out of a total of 127 (59.1 percent). Indeed, when overruling itself, the Warren Court cast more of these votes (55)

---

[23]   Frankfurter also differentiated between the Vinson and Warren Courts, although his three partici-pations are too few to repose any confidence in.

Table 7.8. *Crosstabulation of majority and minority votes in overruled and overruling cases*

		Overruled Majority	Overruled Minority	Totals
Overruling	Majority	93 (28.4%)	127 (38.7%)	220 (67.1%)
	Minority	99 (30.2%)	9 (2.7%)	108 (32.9%)
	Totals	192 (58.5%)	136 (41.5%)	328

Table 7.9. *Frequency of the justices' overruled and overruling votes, by justice*

Justice	Majority-minority	Minority-majority	Majority-majority	Minority-minority	Total
Black	4 (11.4)	27 (77.1)	1 (2.9)	3 (8.6)	35
Blackmun	10 (55.6)	1 (5.6)	7 (38.9)		18
Brennan	18 (39.1)	10 (21.7)	16 (34.8)	2 (4.3)	46
Burger	1 (11.1)		8 (88.9)		9
Burton	2 (50.0)	2 (50.0)			4
Clark	13 (68.4)		6 (31.6)		19
Douglas	2 (5.6)	29 (80.6)	4 (11.1)	1 (2.8)	36
Frankfrter	3 (60.0)	2 (40.0)			5
Harlan	10 (58.8)	1 (5.9)	6 (35.3)		17
Jackson	1 (50.0)			1 (50.0)	2
Marshall	14 (66.7)	3 (14.3)	2 (9.5)	2 (9.5)	21
O'Connor		4 (100)			4
Powell	1 (16.7)		5 (83.3)		6
Reed		2 (100)			2
Rehnquist	2 (14.3)	7 (50.0)	5 (35.7)		14
Scalia		2 (100)			2
Stevens	6 (50.0)	3 (25.0)	3 (25.0)		12
Stewart	4 (18.2)	4 (18.2)	14 (63.6)		22
Vinson		2 (100)			2
Warren	1 (5.9)	14 (82.4)	2 (11.8)		17
White	7 (20.0)	14 (40.0)	14 (40.0)		35
Totals	99	127	93	9	328

than the non-Warren Courts combined (52). Relatedly, the Burger Court cast 58 of the 93 majority-majority votes (62.4 percent), and when overruling itself, it exceeded the number of majority-majority votes cast by all the non-Burger Courts: 37 to 35. The Rehnquist Court justices voted majority-majority only 16.4 percent of the time, compared with the Burger Court's 50 percent. And while the Warren Court justices were voting minority-majority 56.4 percent of the time, the Rehnquist justices were doing so at a rate of 46.3 percent.

The prior patterns, of course, are a composite of the individual justices' voting, which is displayed in Table 7.9. Definite patterns again emerge. Well over half the minority-majority votes, for example, were cast by Douglas, Black, and Warren (70 of 127). Indeed, Black cast more than three-fourths of his votes compatibly with this pattern, Douglas and Warren more than 80 percent of theirs. We suspect that these votes occurred in liberal decisions that overruled conservative precedents. The opposite reasoning presumably applies to the minority-majority voting of such conservatives as O'Connor, Scalia, and Rehnquist: to void liberal precedents. We similarly suspect that Brennan's and Marshall's penchant for voting majority-minority is also attitudinally rooted: that these justices dissented from decisions of the Burger and Rehnquist Courts that overruled liberal precedents. Note that none of Brennan's 11 overruling votes on the liberal Warren Court were majority-minority. Like Brennan and Marshall on the Burger and Rehnquist Courts, Clark and Harlan also voted predominately majority-minority on the Warren Court. Overall, they cast 68.4 and 58.8 percent of their votes in this way. We again suspect that these votes were motivated by ideological proclivities: as conservative objections to liberal overrulings.

Not all the voting exhibited in Table 7.9 lends itself to such a ready explanation, particularly the majority-majority propensities of Stewart and Burger (63.6 and 88.9 percent). We do not, however, discount the possibility that attitudinal variables operate here also. Something must explain the distinctive paradigms that the Courts and the individual justices display. To this undertaking we now turn.

8

Ideology

Our analyses thus far have established that when the justices formally alter precedent they vote markedly more compatibly with the attitudinal model than with the legal model. But we have not determined what attitudinal variables cause them to behave this way. We suspect that it may concern the ideology of the individual justices, and by extension, that of the Court as well. If ideology explains the justices' attitudinal voting, that ideology is most likely to be the one that describes the behavior of other American political elites: liberal and conservative. Thus, we hypothesize that conservative Courts and justices will vote to overrule liberal decisions and vice-versa.

We do not expect a perfect fit, of course. Conservative and liberal Courts will occasionally overturn decisions of the same ideological stripe. And of course over time the definition of "liberal" and "conservative" will change. As a result, we expect that overrulings of nineteenth or early twentieth century decisions may pertain to issues that either do not lend themselves to today's ideological definitions or do so only tangentially. But overall we anticipate an inverse relation between a Court's ideological direction and that of the decisions it overrules. We also expect the same inverse relation for the individual justices (e.g., conservative justices vote to overrule liberal decisions, and vice-versa). We define "liberal" and "conservative" compatibly with conventional usage.[1]

THE VINSON COURT

Two of the four Vinson Court decisions that overturned pre-Vinson Court precedents were decided unanimously and are therefore of no guidance ideologically: *Oklahoma Tax Comn. v. Texas Co.*, 336 U.S. 342 (1949), an intergovernmental tax immunity case, and *Burstyn v. Wilson,* 343 U.S. 495 (1952), subjecting movies to the strictures of the First Amendment. Of the other two, an Internal

---

[1] For a complete specification, see Harold J. Spaeth, *Documentation to the United States Supreme Court Judicial Database, 1953–1991 Terms* (Ann Arbor: Interuniversity Consortium for Political and Social Research, 1993), pp. 69–71. Essentially, a liberal vote supports persons accused or convicted of crime, and favors civil liberty and civil rights claimants. In economic matters, a liberal vote is anti-business, pro-competition, pro-union, and pro-liability. In federal-state conflicts, it is pro-United States and anti-state, and in exercising judicial power it is activist.

Revenue Code case, *Commissioner v. Church's Estate,* 335 U.S. 632 (1949), is the more problematical ideologically. Efforts to cumulatively scale federal revenue cases have largely been unavailing on the basis of a pro-government (liberal)/anti-taxpayer (conservative) basis. Nonetheless, if we consider ideological direction simply on the basis of the proportion of the pro- and anti-government or taxpayer votes the Vinson Court justices cast, the votes in *Church's Estate* match up well. Four of the six who voted with the pro-government majority most often vote that way, along with Jackson, who is tied with Frankfurter for sixth place, and Douglas, who is least supportive of the government overall. Accordingly, the three dissenters – Reed, Frankfurter, and Burton – rank fifth, tied for sixth, and eighth in their support for the liberal position in federal tax cases. In the other overruling in which the Vinson Court altered a pre-Vinson Court precedent, *Cosmopolitian Shipping v. McAllister,* 337 U.S. 783 (1949), the ideological fit is perfect. The Court's five economic conservatives voted pro-business against the Court's four economic liberals in a Jones Act case denying an injured seaman compensation for his injuries. Although Jones Act cases have not been scaled as such, cases dealing with its counterpart – the Federal Employers Liability Act – have been.[2] No knowledgeable scholar disputes that Black, Douglas, Murphy, and Rutledge were economic liberals, while Frankfurter, Jackson, Vinson, Reed, and Burton were economic conservatives.

The pair of Vinson Court decisions that overruled a precedent of its own making fit without any inconsistent votes into the cumulative scale to which they belong. The overruled precedents – *Trupiano v. United States,* 334 U.S. 699 (1948), and *Wade v. Mayo,* 334 U.S. 672 (1948) were established before the deaths of liberal justices Murphy and Rutledge in 1949. In overruling *Trupiano,* Vinson, Reed, and Burton picked up the votes of Murphy's and Rutledge's conservative replacements, Clark and Minton. As further evidence of the ideological voting in *Trupiano* and its sequel, *United States v. Rabinowitz,* 339 U.S. 56 (1950), both cases fit into a cumulative scale of the Vinson Court's search and seizure cases without any inconsistent voting.[3] In this scale, the members of the *Rabinowitz* majority and the *Trupiano* minority show themselves to be markedly more conservative (anti-civil liberties) than any of the other Vinson Court justices.[4]

A similar pattern characterizes the other pair of Vinson Court alterations. Vinson, Reed, and Burton again joined with Clark and Minton in *Darr v. Burford,* 339 U.S. 200 (1950), to overrule *Wade v. Mayo,* 334 U.S. 672. Although the issue here pertained to comity rather than civil liberties, the question of

---

[2] Glendon Schubert, *Quantitative Analysis of Judicial Behavior* (Glencoe, IL: Free Press, 1959), pp. 290–297.

[3] Overall, the 12 nonunanimous non-vehicular search-and-seizure cases do not scale, however. The coefficient of reproducibility, .943, falls slightly below the .95 cutoff, due in large part to Black's three nonscale votes.

[4] It is worthy of note that in one of its final decisions, *Chimel v. California,* 395 U.S. 752 (1969), the liberal Warren Court overruled *Rabinowitz.*

abstention did arise in the context of habeas corpus petitions. In comity cases, the ideological dimension is judicial activism/restraint, with liberals voting in support of the exercise of judicial power, conservatives the opposite. Not all questions of judicial power contain the federalism component, however, as comity does. The liberal position here is pro-federal/anti-state, conservative the opposite. Accordingly, the conservative *Darr* majority voted pro-restraint and pro-state.[5] Adding to the ideological explanation is the construction of a perfect cumulative scale of the six multiple dissent Vinson Court comity cases that arose in a criminal, civil rights, or First Amendment context.[6]

Analysis of the Vinson Court cases overruled by the Warren, Burger, and Rehnquist Courts further supports our ideological explanation. All 14 Vinson Court decisions that the Warren Court overruled were conservatively decided. Interestingly, none of them were decided unanimously. Twenty-eight of the 35 dissenting votes in these cases were cast by Douglas, Black (10 each), Murphy, and Rutledge (4 each). Frankfurter cast five votes and Jackson three. Although neither Frankfurter nor Jackson was liberal, they were sufficiently moderate regarding certain issues to dissent from conservative outcomes. They did so in *Darr v. Burford,* discussed above, where they joined Black in dissent, Douglas not participating. Frankfurter joined Black and Douglas in *Stein v. New York,* 346 U.S. 156 (1953), an involuntary confession case, and in *United States v. Kahriger,* 345 U.S. 22 (1953), a self-incrimination case, and both he and Jackson dissented in the two search-and-seizure cases overruled by the Warren Court's decision in *Chimel v. California: Harris v. United States,* 331 U.S. 145 (1947), and *United States v. Rabinowitz,* also discussed above.[7]

A similar ideological pattern governs the Burger Court's alteration of Vinson Court precedents. Although the Burger Court was markedly less liberal than the Warren Court, it nonetheless voided only conservative Vinson Court decisions, except for *Wisconsin Industrial Comn. v. McCartin,* 330 U.S. 622 (1947), a unanimously decided interstate relations matter, an issue area to which ideological labels have not been applied. Two other altered Vinson Court decisions also were decided unanimously: *Bryan v. United States,* 338 U.S. 552 (1950), which concerned the Federal Rules of Criminal Procedure, and *Kiefer-Stewart Co. v.*

---

[5] *Darr* suffered the same fate as *Rabinowitz:* an overruling by the liberal Warren Court. *Fay v. Noia,* 372 U.S. 391 (1963), provided the occasion. But unlike *Rabinowitz, Darr* was ultimately resurrected when the Rehnquist Court overruled *Fay v. Noia* in *Coleman v. Thompson,* 115 L ed 2d 640 (1991).

[6] The Vinson Court also decided conservatively three comity cases with only a solo dissent; Douglas cast all of the dissents.

[7] The other Vinson Court cases that the Warren Court overturned were *Wolf v. Colorado,* 338 U.S. 25 (1949), a search-and-seizure case; *Montgomery Trades Council v. Ledbetter Erection Co.,* 344 U.S. 178 (1952), a judicial power case; *Cook v. Fortson,* 329 U.S. 675 (1946), dealing with reapportionment; *South v. Peters,* 339 U.S. 276 (1950), about standing to sue; *Adamson v. California,* 332 U.S. 46 (1947), about self-incrimination; *Adler v. Board of Education,* 342 U.S. 485 (1952), about security risks; *Schwartz v. Texas,* 344 U.S. 199 (1952), about search-and-seizure; *MacDougall v. Green,* 335 U.S. 281 (1948), about ballot access; and *Automatic Radio Mfg. Co. v. Hazeltine Research, Inc.,* 339 U.S. 827 (1950), a patent case.

Joseph E. Seagram & Sons, 340 U.S. 211 (1951), an antitrust case. Eighteen of the 22 dissenting votes in the seven conservatively decided cases were cast by Black, Rutledge (5 each), Douglas, and Murphy (4 each). Clark cast one in *Spector Motor Service v. O'Connor,* 340 U.S. 602 (1951), a state tax case, an issue on which he voted liberally.[8] The other three dissents were cast by Frankfurter, Burton, and Vinson in *Carpenters v. United States,* 330 U.S. 395 (1947). The issue here was anticompetitive activities by a labor union. In such cases ideological direction is problematic: is a liberal vote pro-union or pro-competition? It cannot be both. The *Carpenters* dissenters voted against the union. To that extent their votes comported with their general economic conservativism. A study of the justices' voting has shown that they, plus Jackson, who did not participate, were the most conservative economically of all the Vinson Court justices.[9] Unlike the Warren Court alterations of Vinson Court decisions, the Burger Court primarily overturned those involving an economic issue. Along with the unanimously decided *Bryan v. United States,* only two of the other nine concerned civil liberties: *Ahrens v. Clark,* 335 U.S. 188 (1948), a habeas corpus case, and the (in)famous sex discrimination case, *Goesaert v. Cleary,* 335 U.S. 464 (1948).[10]

The Rehnquist Court overturned only two Vinson Court precedents, both as a result of its decision in *American Trucking Assns. v. Scheiner,* 483 U.S. 266 (1987). Unlike the alterations wrought by its predecessors, this pair was liberally decided: *Aero Mayflower Transit Co. v. Board of Railroad Comrs.,* 332 U.S. 495 (1947), a unanimous decision, and *Capital Greyhound Lines v. Brice,* 339 U.S. 542 (1950). Both concerned state taxation, and the dissenters in *Brice* were the two Vinson Court justices who most frequently voted pro-business: Frankfurter and Jackson.[11]

To the extent that ideological measures apply, the voting of the Vinson Court justices in the cases altering precedent supports an ideological explanation: the justices voted the way they did because of their conservative or liberal personal policy preferences toward the dominant issue the cases contained.

THE WARREN COURT

The Warren Court's alteration of pre-Vinson Court precedents reveals the same pattern as did its Vinson Court overrulings: the voiding of conservative prece-

---

[8] Harold J. Spaeth, "Warren Court Attitudes toward Business," in Glendon Schubert, ed., *Judicial Decision Making* (New York: Free Press, 1963), p. 92.

[9] Jeffrey A. Segal, Lee Epstein, Charles M. Cameron, and Harold J. Spaeth, "Ideological Values of Justices Revisited: A Research Note," paper presented at the 1994 meeting of the Midwest Political Science Association, Chicago.

[10] The other unmentioned overrulings all concerned economic issues: *Joseph v. Carter & Weekes Stevedoring Co.,* 330 U.S. 422 (1947), a state tax case; *United States v. Yellow Cab Co.,* 332 U.S. 218 (1947), an antitrust case, and *UAW v. Wisconsin Employment Relations Board,* 336 U.S. 245 (1949), a labor-management dispute.

[11] Op. cit. fn. 8 *supra.*

dents. Because the Warren Court not uncommonly overruled more than a single precedent when it voided earlier decisions, and because a given ruling altering precedent may void those from a number of different Courts, our ideological focus contains a bit of overlap. That is, we cannot sharply distinguish the decisions of the Warren Court that overruled pre-Vinson, Vinson, and Warren Court precedents because a given case, say *Reid v. Covert*, 354 U.S. 1 (1957), overruled two of the Warren Court's own precedents as well as one antedating the Vinson Court. Similarly, *Marchetti v. United States* overturned a decision of the Vinson Court as well as one of its own. With this caveat in mind, we continue our ideological analysis by dividing the 43 overruling decisions of the Warren Court into two components: those overruling decisions antedating the Warren Court (30) and those in which the Warren Court formally altered its own precedents (13). Any decision that simultaneously overruled a pre-Warren and a Warren Court precedent is included among the latter group of 13.

Of the 30 Warren Court decisions altering pre-Warren Court decisions, 28 unequivocally produce a liberal outcome, including all 9 in which the decision was unanimous: *Brown v. Board of Education*, 347 U.S. 483 (1954), which overruled the separate but equal doctrine; *United States v. Raines*, 362 U.S. 17 (1960), a voting rights case; *Continental Ore Co. v. Union Carbide & Carbon Corp.*, 370 U.S. 690 (1962), an antitrust case; *Construction & General Laborers' Union v. Curry*, 371 U.S. 542 (1962), which concerned federal preemption of state court jurisdiction; *Gideon v. Wainwright*, 372 U.S. 335 (1962), extending the right to counsel to indigents accused of felonies; *Ferguson v. Skrupa*, 372 U.S. 726 (1962), which voided an overlooked leftover from the era of laissez faire involving state regulation of business; *Pointer v. Texas*, 380 U.S. 400 (1965), which made the Sixth Amendment's right to confront and cross-examine adverse witnesses binding on the states; *Peyton v. Rowe*, 391 U.S. 54 (1968), a habeas corpus case; and *Brandenburg v. Ohio*, 395 U.S. 444 (1969), which formulated the modern definition of the clear and present danger test.

One nonunanimous overruling produced a problematic ideological outcome because it contains two discrete issues, one of which was resolved conservatively, the other liberally: *Lear, Inc. v. Adkins*, 395 U.S. 653 (1969). The majority liberally ruled that state contract law could not require patent licensees to pay royalties while challenging the patent's validity in state courts. Such a requirement, they said, would frustrate overriding federal policies. Although the Court was unanimous on this issue of federal supremacy, Black, Douglas, and Warren disagreed with the majority's refusal to decide "the question whether the States have power to enforce contracts under which someone claiming to have a new discovery can obtain payment for disclosing it while his patent application is pending."

The national policy expressed in the patent laws, favoring free competition and narrowly limiting monopoly, cannot be frustrated by private agreements among individuals, with or without the approval of the State.[12]

[12]   395 U.S. at 676, 677.

This liberal dissent, however, applied only to the economic component of the decision, not to the specific holding of the overruled decision, *Automatic Radio Mfg. Co. v. Hazeltine Research, Inc.,* 339 U.S. 827 (1950). Douglas and Black had dissented from *Hazeltine* and their opinion, joined also by Warren, explicitly approved the overruling.[13] Consequently, we treat *Lear* as a decision that produced a unanimous liberal outcome.

The 19 nonunanimous overruling decisions that generated a liberal outcome contained 49 dissents, the single conservative decision 3. With but a single exception, *Katz v. United States,* 389 U.S. 347 (1967), at least two justices dissented. Harlan, consistently the most conservative member of the Warren Court,[14] dissented in all but two of them, *Katz* and *Chimel v. California,* 395 U.S. 752 (1969). Both concerned the Fourth Amendment. Stewart cast eight dissents, Clark seven, White six, Frankfurter five, Black four, and Whittaker two. Although Clark was moderately liberal on economic issues, he was stauchly conservative toward criminal procedure, civil liberties, and civil rights.[15] All seven of his dissents fell into the latter areas. Five pertained to criminal procedure: *Elkins v. United States,* 364 U.S. 206 (1960), a search-and-seizure case; *James v. United States,* 366 U.S. 213 (1961), which concerned the construction of a criminal statute; *Fay v. Noia,* 372 U.S. 391 (1963), a habeas corpus matter; *Malloy v. Hogan,* 378 U.S. 1 (1978), which made the self-incrimination clause of the Fifth Amendment binding on the states; and the involuntary confession case, *Jackson v. Denno,* 378 U.S. 368 (1964). One each concerned citizenship and loyalty oaths, *Schneider v. Rusk,* 377 U.S. 163 (1964), and *Keyishian v. Board of Regents,* 385 U.S. 589 (1967). Frankfurter, like Harlan and Whittaker, a strong conservative on the Warren Court, dissented in all of the nonunanimously decided cases in which he participated: *Vanderbilt v. Vanderbilt,* 354 U.S. 416 (1957), a due process case; the criminal procedure cases, *Elkins* and *James; Mapp v. Ohio,* 367 U.S. 643 (1961), which concerned the admissibility in state court of unconstitutionally secured evidence; and the reapportionment case of *Baker v. Carr,* 369 U.S. 186 (1962).[16] Harlan joined Frankfurter in all five of these decisions, as did Clark in *Elkins* and *James.* Whittaker also dissented in *Elkins* and *Mapp.*

Although Black was generally liberal on criminal procedure and First Amendment issues, he voted conservatively toward search and seizure and various civil rights issues. His four conservative dissents so illustrate: he cast the sole dissent in *Katz,* and joined with White in two other search-and-seizure cases: *Lee v. Florida,* 392 U.S. 378 (1968), and *Chimel v. California,* 395 U.S. 752 (1969).

---

[13] Id. at 676.

[14] David W. Rohde and Harold J. Spaeth, *Supreme Court Decision Making* (San Francisco: W. H. Freeman, 1976), pp. 140–145; Harold J. Spaeth, *Supreme Court Policy Making: Explanation and Prediction* (San Francisco: W. H. Freeman, 1979), pp. 132–135.

[15] Id.

[16] Frankfurter had written the prevailing opinion in the cases overruled by *Mapp* and *Baker v. Carr: Wolf v. Colorado,* 338 U.S. 25 (1948), and *Colegrove v. Green,* 328 U.S. 549 (1946).

His other dissent occurred in the case that declared poll taxes unconstitutional as a condition for voting, *Harper v. Virginia Board of Elections*, 383 U.S. 663 (1966).

White and Stewart were ideological moderates on the Warren Court.[17] Their voting in cases that overturned conservative decisions supports this finding: White dissented in 6 of the 12 cases in which he participated (50 percent), Stewart in 8 of 18 (44.4 percent). The more conservative Harlan, Frankfurter, Whittaker, and Clark, by comparison, dissented in 31 of their 40 participations (77.5 percent), while the generally liberal Black did so in 4 of his 19 (21.1 percent). White and Stewart both dissented in *Schneider v. Rusk*, the denaturalization case, and voted to uphold the loyalty oath in *Keyishian*. White also dissented in *Malloy v. Hogan* and the search-and-seizure case of *Lee v. Florida*. In all four of these decisions, at least two other justices joined him in dissent. He and Black dissented in another search-and-seizure case, *Chimel v. California*, and he and Harlan dissented in the housing discrimination case, *Jones v. Alfred H. Mayer Co.*, 392 U.S. 409 (1968).

Like White's first four dissents, Stewart's first five dissents all came in cases in which at least three justices dissented: *Fay v. Noia, Malloy v. Hogan, Jackson v. Denno, Harper v. Virginia Board of Elections*, and *Keyishian v. Board of Regents*. Clark and Harlan were generally kindred spirits. But after Clark's retirement at the end of the 1966 term, Harlan alone occupied right field, along with Black, on search-and-seizure issues. Stewart's final three conservative dissents all occurred in cases in which Harlan also dissented: *Duncan v. Louisiana*, 391 U.S. 145 (1968), which required a jury trial in state court for all criminal cases which, if tried in federal court, would require a jury; *Moore v. Ogilvie*, 394 U.S. 814 (1969), a ballot access case; and *Benton v. Maryland*, 395 U.S. 784 (1969), which incorporated the double jeopardy clause of the Fifth Amendment into the due process clause of the Fourteenth Amendment.

The sole Warren Court decision which conservatively altered a pre-Warren Court precedent was *Warden v. Hayden*, 387 U.S. 294 (1967), in which the Court's three most liberal members – Douglas, Warren, and Fortas – dissented from Brennan's opinion of the Court abolishing the Fourth Amendment rule prohibiting the seizure of "mere evidence," as distinct from the seizure of instrumentalities, fruits, or contraband.[18]

We therefore conclude from this assessment of the voting in the decisions in which the Warren Court altered pre-Warren Court precedents that the justices voted the way they did in these cases because of their ideology. When conservative and moderate justices refused to vote to overrule, they did so when the majority voided a conservative precedent. In the single instance when a conser-

[17] Rohde and Spaeth, op. cit. fn. 14 *supra;* Spaeth, op. cit. fn. 14 *supra.*
[18] Overruled was the unanimously decided case of *Gouled v. United States*, 255 U.S. 298 (1921). The liberal Justice John Clarke wrote the Court's opinion. Among those justices joining it were Oliver Wendell Holmes and Louis Brandeis.

vative majority formally altered a liberal precedent, the dissenters were the Court's three most liberal justices.

We may also note that on balance these Warren Court overrulings were among that Court's most salient, although some of them were not listed by CQ, including *Brandenburg v. Ohio,* which is mentioned below. Certainly the issues they contained were not mundane except for the single case involving preemption of state court jurisdiction, the state business regulation case, and the one pertaining to national supremacy. Fifteen of the remaining 27 concerned criminal procedure, including 6 that incorporated provisions of the Bill of Rights into the due process clause of the Fourteenth Amendment – *Gideon, Mapp, Malloy v. Hogan, Duncan v. Louisiana, Pointer v. Texas,* and *Benton v. Maryland.* Eight addressed civil rights, including *Brown v. Board of Education,* the major housing discrimination case, and two of the initial decisions leading to the one-person, one-vote standard for legislative districting and apportionment. Two concerned the First Amendment, including *Brandenburg v. Ohio;* one concerned due process, and one the Clayton Antitrust Act. If issues are ever resolved ideologically, these cases are prime candidates.

The 13 decisions in which the Warren Court formally altered its own precedents display an ideological voting pattern similar to that manifest in the Warren Court's overrulings of the decisions of earlier Courts. Eleven of the 13 decisions were decided liberally, including two that were unanimous: *Murphy v. Waterfront Commission,* 378 U.S. 52 (1964), a self-incrimination case, and *Carafas v. LaVallee,* 391 U.S. 234 (1968), a habeas corpus decision.

As before, we can discount the ideological significance of the conservatively decided cases. *Smith v. Evening News Assn.,* 371 U.S. 195 (1962), involved a question of the preemption of state court jurisdiction in the context of a labor-management dispute. The litigation was more ideologically complex than the typical labor-management preemption case because the liberal position federally (pro-U.S./anti-state) did not run in tandem with the economic dimension (pro-union). Over a solo dissent by Black, the Court ruled that the state court had jurisdiction of an employee's suit alleging violation of a collective bargaining agreement. In this regard, the decision was conservative. Black, as the Court's most liberal member on preemption – i.e., pro-federal – cast an attitudinally consistent vote as did the other justices.[19] But from the standpoint of the altered precedent – *Westinghouse Employees v. Westinghouse Corp.,* 348 U.S. 437 (1955) – *Smith* may be counted as liberal with Black rendering a conservative dissent – i.e., favoring restraint – to an overruling of a judgment that the federal courts lacked jurisdiction under the National Labor Relations Act over a suit brought by a union to enforce "uniquely personal" employee rights.[20]

---

[19] As a member of the Warren Court, Black never upheld state court jurisdiction over a labor dispute except for one unanimously decided case in which the state court had ruled in favor of the union: *Dowd Box Co. v. Courtney,* 368 U.S. 502 (1962). No other justice had as consistent an anti-state record as he.

[20] 371 U.S. at 198.

The other conservative decision was *Swift & Co. v. Wickham,* 382 U.S. 111 (1965). Douglas, Black, and Clark dissented from the dismissal of a direct appeal to the Supreme Court, and the majority's holding that appellate review rested in the court of appeals. The majority's pro-restraint posture substantially expanded the authority of single-judge district courts at the expense of three-judge courts, and concomitantly enhanced the appellate authority of the courts of appeals rather than that of the Supreme Court.

Neither *Smith* nor *Swift* can be considered a particularly important decision. Neither is listed by CQ. The bulk of the nine nonunanimous liberal overrulings, however, were important, though only two of them met CQ standards:[21] *Reid v. Covert,* 354 U.S. 1 (1957), the celebrated court martial case; *Escobedo v. Illinois,* 378 U.S. 478 (1964), and its successor, *Miranda v. Arizona,* 384 U.S. 436 (1966); *Harris v. United States,* 382 U.S. 162 (1965), involving the Federal Rules of Criminal Procedure; *Spevack v. Klein,* 385 U.S. 511 (1967), a self-incrimination case; *Afroyim v. Rusk,* 387 U.S. 253 (1967), which held Congress without power to divest a person of citizenship absent voluntary renunciation; *Camara v. Municipal Court,* 387 U.S. 523 (1967), the Fourth Amendment case barring prosecution of persons who refuse a warrantless code enforcement inspection of their residences; *Marchetti v. United States,* 390 U.S. 39 (1968), which applied the self-incrimination clause to a prosecution for evading payment of an occupational gambling tax; and *Bruton v. United States,* 391 U.S. 123 (1968), setting aside a conviction resulting from a joint trial as a violation of the confrontation clause of the Sixth Amendment.

Of the 28 dissenting votes in these nine cases, all but 1 were cast by the conservative and moderate members of the Court. The single exception was Warren's nonscale vote in *Marchetti.* In five of the nine cases – *Escobedo, Miranda, Harris, Spevack,* and *Afroyim* – the same four justices dissented: Harlan, Clark, Stewart, and White. Overall, Clark dissented in 7 of the 8 in which he participated, Burton in 1 of 1, Harlan in 7 of 11, and Stewart and White in 6 of 10. As appears true of the pre-Warren Court alterations, when the Warren Court overturned itself, ideology seems to be the explanation for the justices' voting.

THE BURGER COURT

We expected the Burger Court to maintain the ideological patterning of the Warren Court in its overruling decisions. But in contrast to the Warren Court, we expected to find a less extreme distribution between liberal and conservative overrulings. Because most decisions prior to the Warren Court were conservatively decided by modern standards, we expected the Burger Court to have formally altered an appreciable number of conservative decisions notwithstanding its own moderately conservative orientation. Because the Burger Court be-

[21] See Appendix I.

came more conservative as it aged, we expected most of the decisions that overruled its own precedents to produce conservative outcomes.

We adhered to a tripartite breakdown of the Burger Court overrulings instead of the bipartite breakdown that we used to assess those of the Warren Court: pre-Warren Court overrulings, alteration of Warren Court precedents, and the overturning of its own precedents.

A greater proportion of the pre-Warren alterations were unanimous than was the case with any other subset of the data we have considered thus far: 11 of 22. Somewhat surprisingly, perhaps, 9 of the 11 were liberally decided. But only one of them concerned civil liberties, while one was a patent case, four concerned state taxation; another dealt with state business regulation; and two dealt with liability under admiralty and maritime law. Apart from the tax cases, these were *Moragne v. States Marine Lines, Inc.*, 398 U.S. 375 (1975), holding that maritime law permits a cause of action for the wrongful death of a seaman; *Blonder-Tongue Laboratories, Inc. v. University of Illinois Foundation*, 402 U.S. 313 (1971), a patent infringement case; *Braden v. 30th Judicial Circuit*, 410 U.S. 484 (1973), authorizing the filing of habeas corpus petitions outside the district of petitioner's confinement; *North Dakota State Board of Pharmacy v. Snyder's Drug Stores*, 414 U.S. 156 (1973), involving state business regulation; *United States v. Reliable Transfer Co.*, 421 U.S. 397 (1975), which voided the admiralty rule of divided damages, a rule whose origins date back at least 850 years. The other liberally decided overrulings that unanimously produced a liberal result all pertained to the authority of the states to impose taxes affecting interstate and foreign commerce. *Michelin Tire Corp. v. Wages*, 423 U.S. 276 (1976), overthrew the original package doctrine of *Low v. Austin*, 13 Wallace 29 (1871), thereby permitting the states to levy non-discriminatory ad valorem taxes on imported goods. *Complete Auto Transit v. Brady*, 430 U.S. 274 (1977), upheld a state tax on interstate businesses operating within a state. *Washington Revenue Dept. v. Stevedoring Assn.*, 435 U.S. 734 (1978), overruled a Vinson Court decision and upheld a state tax on the interstate aspects of stevedoring. And *Limbach v. Hooven & Allison Co.*, 466 U.S. 353 (1984), held that collateral estoppel does not preclude a state's imposition of a state ad valorem personal property tax where the previous ruling has been undermined by later Supreme Court decisions.

By contrast with the issues contained in the Burger Court's liberal unanimous alterations, both of those decided conservatively concerned civil liberties, albeit neither was salient: *United States v. One Assortment of 89 Firearms*, 465 U.S. 354 (1984), held that neither the double jeopardy clause nor the doctrine of collateral estoppel precludes a subsequent in rem forfeiture proceeding following acquittal on criminal charges concerning the same firearms; and *United States v. Miller*, 471 U.S. 130 (1985), ruled that a conviction on charges narrower than – but included within – the indictment does not violate the Fifth Amendment's grand jury guarantee.

The nonunanimous half of the Burger Court's 22 pre-Warren Court overrulings were divided between 8 liberal and 3 conservative outcomes. Overall, they appear on balance to be markedly more salient than the unanimous alterations, although much less so than those of the Warren Court. Eight of the 13 justices cast at least one dissent in these cases, White and the four who served the most briefly on the Burger Court – Black, Harlan, O'Connor, and Douglas – alone excepted. Rehnquist, the most conservative member of the Burger Court, dissented in six of these eight cases, Burger in three, and Powell and Stevens in two.

One liberal overruling continued the Burger Court's focus on state taxation: *Commonwealth Edison Co. v. Montana,* 453 U.S. 609 (1981). Over the dissent of Powell, Blackmun, and Stevens, the majority ruled that Montana's 30 percent severance tax on coal, most of which was shipped to energy-poor states, did not violate the Constitution. Two of the three civil liberties overrulings attained major dimensions. In *Virginia State Board of Pharmacy v. Virginia Citizens Consumer Council,* 425 U.S. 748 (1976), a non-CQ-listed case, the Court for the first time unequivocally constitutionalized commercial speech. Rehnquist alone dissented. *Craig v. Boren,* 429 U.S. 190 (1976), formulated the intermediate level of scrutiny which courts apply to sexually discriminatory statutes and policies, thereby replacing the minimal rational basis test which had previously held sway. The other civil liberty case was *Braden v. 30th Judicial Circuit Court,* 410 U.S. 484 (1973), which allowed prisoners to bring habeas corpus petitions outside the district of their confinement. Rehnquist, along with Burger and Powell, dissented.

The other four liberal overrulings occurred in *Machinists v. Wisconsin Employment Relations Commission,* 427 U.S. 132 (1976), which preempted state court jurisdiction of a labor dispute, Rehnquist and Stewart dissenting; *Shaffer v. Heitner,* 433 U.S. 186 (1977), which sounded the death knell of federal quasi in rem jurisdiction; *Hughes v. Oklahoma,* 441 U.S. 322 (1979), a national supremacy case, which voided a state law prohibiting out-of-state shipment of in-state minnows, Rehnquist and Burger dissenting; and *Thomas v. Washington Gas Light Co.,* 448 U.S. 261 (1980), which held that the full faith and credit clause did not bar an injured worker from receiving compensation benefits from the District of Columbia after recovering them from Virginia. Rehnquist and Marshall dissented. The sole dissenter in *Shaffer v. Heitner* was Brennan and, from an ideological standpoint, his vote could as justifiably be labelled liberal as conservative. *Shaffer's* issue, state court jurisdiction of out-of-state defendants, triggers due process questions. Except for the takings clause, the liberal position under due process is anti-government/pro-litigant. Such a posture clearly comports with conventional understanding, as when litigation turns on the adequacy of a hearing, the rights afforded incarcerated persons, or the impartiality of a governmental decision maker. And though fairness underlies the ability of a state court to render judgment over a nonresident defendant, it also governs the plaintiff's ability to garner satisfaction for injuries or misdeeds suffered. Hence, one can as plausibly, if not as consistently, define the contacts needed to establish state court jurisdiction over the defendant more favorably to the plaintiff as the liberal position.[22]

From an ideological standpoint, only Marshall's vote concurring in Rehnquist's dissent in *Thomas* is surprising.[23] Accordingly, 16 of the 17 dissenting votes in the liberal alterations conform to ideological expectations. The same may be said for the seven dissents cast in the three conservatively decided alterations. Douglas dissented alone in *Andrews v. Louisville & Nashville R. Co.,* 406 U.S. 320 (1972), a case that disallowed a discharged employee to bring a breach of contract suit in state court, thereby forcing him to adhere to the procedures set forth in the Railway Labor Act. Brennan, Marshall, and Stevens dissented in *Michigan v. Long,* 463 U.S. 1032 (1983), the search-and-seizure case that fundamentally altered the relationship between state and federal courts, and in *Copperweld Corp. v. Independence Tube Corp.,* 467 U.S. 752 (1984), a Sherman Act case that held that a parent corporation and its wholly owned subsidiary were legally incapable of conspiring with each other.

The Burger Court displayed its conservative orientation in its alteration of Warren Court precedents. This pattern does not surprise us. The Warren Court was predominately liberal; if its decisions were to be overruled, they would likely be altered by conservative decisions. Ten of the 16 were such.

Of the overrulings that produced a liberal result, only one was decided unanimously: *Burks v. United States,* 437 U.S. 1 (1978), a double jeopardy case barring a second trial once a court has found the evidence insufficient to sustain the jury's verdict. Three of the five nonunanimous liberal alterations pertained to civil rights and liberties: *Taylor v. Louisiana,* 419 U.S. 522 (1975), a sex discrimination case that overruled the Warren Court's holding in *Hoyt v. Florida,* 368 U.S. 57 (1961), that women could constitutionally be exempted from jury service; *Monell v. Dept. of Social Services,* 436 U.S. 658 (1978), which revoked the immunity of local governments from suit under the Civil Rights Act of 1871; and *Batson v. Kentucky,* 476 U.S. 79 (1986), which subjected peremptory jury challenges excluding blacks to the strictures of the equal protection clause. Rehnquist dissented from all three decisions; Burger from *Monell* and *Batson.*

The other two liberal overrulings came in *Perez v. Campbell,* 402 U.S. 637 (1971), a bankruptcy matter, and *Brown-Forman Distillers Corp. v. New York State Liquor Authority,* 476 U.S. 573 (1986), denying a state the authority to dictate the minimum prices that distillers could charge wholesalers in other states. *Perez,* decided before the appointments of Rehnquist and Powell, saw Burger, Harlan, Blackmun, and Stewart dissent; while White and Stevens joined Rehnquist in *Brown-Forman.* Ten of the 12 dissents in these cases conform

---

22   To be precise, Brennan labelled his *Shaffer* opinion as "concurring in part and dissenting in part" (433 U.S. at 219). In *World-Wide Volkswagen Corp. v. Woodson,* 444 U.S. 286 (1980), at 301, however, Brennan tags his *Shaffer* opinion as a dissent.
23   Marshall's vote was also nonscale.

to ideological patterning, the nonscale votes of White and Stevens in *Brown-Forman* alone excepted.

Two conservative outcomes were unanimously decided: *New Orleans v. Dukes,* 427 U.S. 297 (1976), grandfathering some pushcart vendors while prohibiting all others, and *Trammel v. United States,* 445 U.S. 40 (1980), restricting marital testimonial privileges by vesting the decision to disclose adverse testimony exclusively in the witness spouse. The eight nonunanimous alterations of liberal Warren Court decisions comprise an important set of cases. Although *Boys Markets v. Retail Clerks,* 398 U.S. 235 (1970), was a substantively unimportant labor-management arbitration case, the uncharacteristic candor (for that time, at least) with which Justices Brennan, Black, and Stewart articulated the alleged bases for overruling the precedent at issue provided the case with more publicity than it might otherwise have gained. Brennan, who had dissented from the Warren Court's decision, wrote for the Court:

> Nor can we agree that conclusive weight should be accorded to the failure of Congress to respond to *Sinclair* [the precedent being overruled] on the theory that congressional silence should be interpreted as acceptance of the decision. . . . Therefore, in the absence of any persuasive circumstances evidencing a clear design that congressional inaction be taken as acceptance of *Sinclair,* the mere silence of Congress is not a sufficient reason for refusing to reconsider the decision.[24]

To which Black, who had authored the Court's opinion in the overturned case, responded: "Nothing at all has changed, in fact, except the membership of the Court and the personal views of one Justice."[25] That one justice was Stewart, who lamely explained: "An aphorism of Mr. Justice Frankfurter provides me refuge: 'Wisdom too often never comes, and so one ought not to reject it merely because it comes late.'"[26]

The other liberal decisions undone by the Burger Court include *Miller v. California,* 413 U.S. 15 (1973), a CQ-listed case, in which the Court redefined the law of obscenity to ease state prosecutions. In *Edelman v. Jordan,* 415 U.S. 651 (1974), also listed by CQ, another minimum winning coalition formed – as in *Miller* – and the Court ruled that the Eleventh Amendment precluded state payment of retroactive welfare benefits even though the state culpably failed to

---

[24] 398 U.S. at 241–242. It is instructive to compare the quoted langauge as a rationale for decision with that which the majority articulated in the baseball antitrust case two years later. Characterizing the baseball antitrust decisions of 1922 and 1952 as "an anomaly" and "an aberration," Justice Blackmun, in the Court's opinion, nevertheless observed that courts do not necessarily have an obligation to correct them because "there is merit in consistency even though some might claim that beneath that consistency is a layer of inconsistency." And if there is "any inconsistency or illogic in all this, it is an inconsistency and illogic of long standing that is to be remedied by the Congress and not by this Court." Why? Because "we continue to be loath, 50 years after *Federal Baseball [v. National League,* 259 U.S. 200 (1922)], and almost two decades after *Toolson [v. New York Yankees,* 346 U.S. 356 (1953)], to overturn those cases judicially when Congress, by its positive inaction [*sic!*], has allowed those decisions to stand for so long" (*Flood v. Kuhn,* 407 U.S. 258 [1972], at 282, 284, 283–284).

[25] 398 U.S. at 256.   [26] Id. at 255.

comply with federal processing regulations. *Hudgens v. National Labor Relations Board*, 424 U.S. 507 (1976), held that the First Amendment did not protect labor union picketing on the premises of a privately owned shopping center. And the CQ-listed *National League of Cities v. Usery*, 426 U.S. 833 (1976), subsequently overruled, voided the minimum wage and maximum hour provisions of the Fair Labor Standards Act insofar as they applied to state and local governmental employees. This is the only case in which a single Court overruled a precedent and then overruled the precedent it had created. This result occurred because Blackmun changed his vote.[27] *Continental T.V., Inc. v. GTE Sylvania Inc.*, 433 U.S. 36 (1977), replaced a per se antitrust rule governing the number and location of franchised retailers with a "rule of reason." The final overrulings both concerned the Fourth Amendment. *United States v. Salvucci*, 448 U.S. 83 (1980), abandoned the automatic standing rule that allowed defendants to challenge an incriminating search and replaced it with a requirement that they demonstrate an expectation of privacy in the searched premises. *Illinois v. Gates*, 462 U.S. 213 (1983), substituted the totality of the circumstances as the proper standard for determining probable cause for the issuance of a search warrant.

Of the 23 dissenting votes that accompanied these decisions, Marshall and Brennan cast 14. Marshall dissented in all seven in which he participated; Brennan in all but *Boys Markets*. Douglas dissented in two of his three participations; Stevens in two of four. Blackmun dissented in *Edelman*, the poverty law case; Stewart in *Miller;* White in *Usery* and *Boys Markets;* and Black in *Boys Markets* also. With the exception of White's nonscale *Boys Markets'* vote, the others admit of ideological explanation.

The eight decisions in which the Burger Court altered its own precedents continue the disproportionate production of conservative outcomes that also attended its overruling of Warren Court precedents. Only two of its self-alterations resulted in a liberal outcome, and one of these – the unanimously decided *Illinois v. Milwaukee*, 406 U.S. 91 (1972) – is marginally such at best. The case arose under the Supreme Court's original jurisdiction, alleging that six governmental bodies in Wisconsin were polluting Lake Michigan. In an opinion by the Court's foremost environmentalist, Justice Douglas, the justices refused to decide the issue since it did not involve a suit between states. We nonetheless count the decision as a liberal one because it is more environmentally protective than its overruled decision of the previous year, *Ohio v. Wyandotte Chemicals Corp,,* 401 U.S. 493 (1971).[28] There the Court had held, over Douglas's dissent, that the pollution of Lake Erie did not implicate important questions of federal law. In *Illinois v. Milwaukee*, however, the Court ruled that federal common law con-

---

[27]   A single membership change had also occurred – O'Connor's replacement of Stewart. Stewart had voted with the *Usery* majority; O'Connor – a strong supporter of states' rights – dissented from *Usery*'s overruling.

[28]   The Court did not identify either the overruling or the overruled decision until 1987 in *International Paper Co. v. Ouellette*, 479 U.S. 481, at 488.

trolled interstate water pollution and that the federal district courts were the appropriate forum for the resolution of such disputes.

The unequivocally liberal overruling occurred, as noted above, in the voiding of *Usery*. That minimum winning coalition was replaced by an opposite one when Blackmun changed his vote in *Garcia v. San Antonio Metropolitan Transportation Authority*, 469 U.S. 528 (1985).

Only one of the Burger Court's six conservative self-alterations was decided unanimously: *Daniels v. Williams*, 474 U.S. 327 (1986), which held that negligent acts by state officials that cause loss or injury do not "deprive" persons of liberty or property under the Fourteenth Amendment. A civil rights and liberties focus also characterizes four of the five nonunanimous alterations. *Gregg v. Georgia*, 428 U.S. 153 (1976), re-established the constitutionality of the death penalty, albeit under highly restrictive circumstances. *United States v. Scott*, 437 U.S. 82 (1978), held that the double jeopardy clause does not bar the government from retrying a person who has successsfully terminated his trial without a determination of guilt or innocence. *United States v. Ross*, 456 U.S. 798 (1982), extended the scope of warrantless searches based on probable cause to include a vehicle's compartments and containers. *Rose v. Clark*, 478 U.S. 570 (1986), applied harmless error analysis to a jury instruction that unconstitutionally shifted the burden of proof to a person convicted of murder. The non-civil liberties alteration was *Oregon v. Corvallis Sand & Gravel Co.*, 429 U.S. 363 (1977), which held that state rather than federal common law governed the ownership of navigable riverbeds.

Compatibly with ideological expectations, Brennan and Marshall cast the bulk of the dissents in these cases (10 of 15). Both did so in all five. Stevens dissented in *Scott*, Blackmun in *Rose v. Clark*. White, a national supremacist in economic matters,[29] dissented in *Corvallis* and also in *Scott* and *Ross*. Although he ranked as fourth most liberal in search and seizure on the Burger Court after Douglas's retirement – behind Marshall, Brennan, and Stevens – he was also the most attitudinally inconsistent of the justices, as his *Ross* vote indicates.[30]

Although the ideological configuration of the Burger Court's alterations is somewhat more complex than that of the Warren Court, it appears no less clear that ideology explains why the Court and the justices voted the way they did.

THE REHNQUIST COURT

Because the Rehnquist Court handed down less than half as many overruling decisions as the Warren and Burger Courts, we might have found less ideological patterning because of the relatively small N. On the other hand, the Rehnquist

---

[29] Timothy M. Hagle and Harold J. Spaeth, "Ideological Patterns in the Justices' Voting in the Burger Court's Business Cases," 55 *Journal of Politics* 492 (1993), at 500.

[30] Jeffrey A. Segal, "Supreme Court Justices as Human Decision Makers: An Individual-Level Analysis of the Search and Seizure Cases," 48 *Journal of Politics* 938 (1986), at 943.

Court did not shift its orientation from moderate to liberal as did the Warren Court, or from moderate to conservative as did the Burger Court. Hence, we expected to find that the Rehnquist Court overwhelmingly altered its predecessors' liberal decisions.

Four of the six decisions that overturned pre-Warren Court precedents were decided unanimously, three conservatively and one liberally. *Puerto Rico v. Bransted,* 483 U.S. 219 (1987), ruled that federal courts can compel governors to extradite fugitives. *Gulfstream Aerospace Corp. v. Mayacamas Corp.,* 485 U.S. 271 (1988), held that a federal district court order denying a motion to stay or dismiss because of pending state action is unappealable. *Collins v. Youngdahl,* 497 U.S. 37 (1990), ruled the ex post facto clause inapplicable to the reformation of a jury verdict because it did not criminalize innocent action, increase punishment after commission of a crime, or retroactively deprive a person of existing defense. The alteration producing a liberal effect was arguably even less salient than the conservative ones. *Exxon Corp. v. Central Gulf Lines, Inc.,* 114 L ed 2d 649 (1991), voided a mid-nineteenth century rule precluding admiralty jurisdiction from extending to claims arising from agency contracts.

One of the two nonunanimous overrulings clearly produced a liberal outcome insofar as federal-state relations are concerned: *South Carolina v. Baker,* 485 U.S. 505 (1988). Over the lone dissent of Justice O'Connor, arguably the strongest supporter of states' rights among the justices,[31] the Court ruled that the doctrine of intergovernmental tax immunity no longer precludes federal taxation of state and local municipal bonds. The other nonunanimous overruling, *American Trucking Assns. v. Scheiner,* 483 U.S. 266 (1987), voided two liberally decided Vinson Court decisions upholding state business taxes. From this perspective, *Scheiner* produced a pro-business (conservative) outcome. The dissenters – Rehnquist, Powell, O'Connor, and Scalia – viewed the decision as anti-state, however. From this perspective, the decision may be perceived as pro-federal as well as pro-competition (liberal). As such, it fits both ideologically and attitudinally.

One of the eight Warren Court decisions that the Rehnquist Court overruled concerned a state tax like the tax in the *Scheiner* case discussed immediately above: *Tyler Pipe Industries, Inc. v. Washington Dept. of Revenue,* 483 U.S. 232 (1987). In voiding a tax imposed only on in-state goods sold out of state, the majority's decision favored the taxpaying businesses, a conservative outcome. But from a competitive and federal standpoint the decision was liberal. The two dissenters – Rehnquist and Scalia – objected to the majority's use of the interstate commerce clause to void the state law. From this perspective – again like *Scheiner* – the decision fits both ideologically and attitudinally.

Six of the other seven Warren Court alterations unequivocally produced a conservative outcome. The sole liberal decision, *Griffith v. Kentucky,* 479 U.S. 314 (1987), made *Batson v. Kentucky,* which itself overruled a Warren Court

---

[31]   Op. cit. fn. 29 *supra,* pp. 501–502.

decision, retroactively applicable to cases pending on direct review or not yet final.[32] Rehnquist, O'Connor, and White dissented.

Four of the six conservative decisions concerned civil liberties. *Solorio v. United States*, 483 U.S. 435 (1987), broadened the jurisdiction of courts martial by extending it to include military personnel regardless of whether the offenses themselves were service connected. *Alabama v. Smith*, 490 U.S. 794 (1989), upheld a harsher sentence after trial following a defendant's withdrawal of his guilty plea. *Coleman v. Thompson*, 115 L ed 2d 640 (1991), virtually eliminated collateral appeals – writs of habeas corpus – to federal district courts if state prisoners have failed to adhere to state procedural rules.[33] *Keeney v. Tamayo-Reyes*, 118 L Ed 2d 318 (1992), still further restricted state prison inmates' access to the federal courts via writs of habeas corpus. On a claim that their attorney failed to develop material facts, petitioners now must show a cause for such failure and show that actual prejudice resulted.

The Rehnquist Court conservatively decided both of the Warren Court's non-civil liberties cases that it overruled by a 5-to-4 vote. *Welch v. Dept. of Highways and Public Transportation*, 483 U.S. 468 (1987), ruled that the Jones Act did not abrogate the states' Eleventh Amendment immunity from suit by an injured state employee. The other decision, *Rodriguez de Quijas v. Shearson/American Express, Inc.*, 490 U.S. 477 (1989), held that the Securities Act of 1933 permits brokers to enforce customer agreements requiring arbitration of claims.

The patterning of the dissenting votes in these six conservative decisions is highly uniform: Marshall dissented in all five in which he participated, Brennan in three of his four, and Stevens and Blackmun in five of their six. The only decision in which all four failed to dissent was *Alabama v. Smith*, to which only Marshall dissented. The only other dissents in these cases were the uncharacteristic liberal votes of O'Connor and Kennedy in *Tamayo-Reyes*.

The five decisions voiding Burger Court precedents all produced conservative outcomes. They all pertained to civil rights and liberties.[34] *Thornburgh v. Abbott*, 490 U.S. 401 (1989), held that officials could constitutionally ban publications detrimental to prison security. *Ward's Cove Packing Co. v. Atonio*, 490 U.S. 642 (1989), relieved employers of the burden of justifying racially disparate practices as business necessities under the 1964 Civil Rights Act.[35] *Webster v. Reproductive Health Services*, 492 U.S. 490 (1989), authorized government to impose additional abortion restrictions, as did *Planned Parenthood v. Casey*, 120

---

[32] *Griffith* also overruled a Burger Court decision, *Williams v. United States*, 401 U.S. 646 (1971). Consequently, we could justifiably have considered *Griffith* to be a Rehnquist Court alteration of a Burger Court precedent rather than of a Warren Court precedent.

[33] As mentioned in an earlier chapter, *Coleman* was the culminating decision in an overruling (*Fay v. Noia*, 372 U.S. 391 [1963]) of an overruling (*Darr v. Burford*, 339 U.S. 200 [1950]) of an overruling (*Wade v. Mayo*, 334 U.S. 672 ([1948]).

[34] If we include *Griffith v. Kentucky*, which also overruled a Warren Court decision, the total becomes six of six.

[35] Enactment of the Civil Rights Act of 1991 overturned the Court's decision, however.

Table 8.1. *Ideologically compatible voting
in nonunanimous decisions altering precedent*

Court	Vote			Direction	
	Compatible	Incompatible	Unclear	Liberal	Conservative
Vinson	32	2	0	1	3
Warren	279	1	0	30	2
Burger	248	5	8	16	17
Rehnquist	140	2	0	2	14
				--	--
Totals	701	10	8	49	36

L Ed 2d 674 (1992). Although the major thrust of *Planned Parenthood* was liberal, the overruled decisions were even more so. Two of the justices otherwise in the majority dissented from the overrulings. The final decision, *California v. Acevedo,* 114 L Ed 2d 619 (1991), cleaned up the fallout generated by the Burger Court's overruling in *United States v. Ross* of one of its own decisions, *Robbins v. California,* 453 U.S. 420 (1981), by ruling that the Fourth Amendment permits the warrantless search of a paper bag found in an automobile trunk if probable cause indicates it to contain contraband.

The dissenting votes in these cases were even more ideologically structured than in the other Rehnquist Court overrulings. Stevens dissented in all five; Marshall in the four in which he participated; Brennan in his three; Blackmun in three of five; and White in *Acevedo.*

Only one Rehnquist Court decision overruled precedents of its own creation: *Payne v. Tennessee,* 115 L Ed 2d 720 (1991), a death penalty case that we discussed at some length in Chapter 1. The case was decided conservatively. As in the other Rehnquist Court alterations, the dissenters were the three most liberal members following the retirement of Brennan: Marshall, Stevens, and Blackmun.

CONCLUSION

Our examination of the ideological direction of the overruling cases shows that the justices overwhelmingly overturn decisions because of their ideology. We discovered that 701 out of 719 votes (97 percent) in nonunanimous overturning decisions were compatible with the justices' ideology. (See Table 8.1.) Conservative justices, such as Rehnquist, Burger, Harlan, and Franfurter, voted against civil rights and liberties claims, voted in favor of business in economic activity cases, supported states' rights rather than federal authority, and favored judicial restraint. In contrast, liberal justices, such as Warren, Brennan, Marshall, and Douglas, voted in favor of civil rights and liberties, supported labor unions and workers over their employers, championed the application of the antitrust laws and economically competitive practices, favored national supremacy over states' rights, and supported judicial activism. Moderate justices, such as Stewart, White, Stevens, and Blackmun, voted moderately.

The Courts, of course, reflected the ideology of their members. In their non-unanimous overruling decisions, the Warren Court produced a liberal outcome in 30 of 32 cases (94 percent), while the Rehnquist Court rendered conservative decisions in 14 of 16 cases (87 percent). (See Table 8.1.) In contrast, the decisions of the Burger Court were split evenly (51 percent conservative).

In summary, the justices and the Courts vote the way they do in the overruling cases because of ideology.

9

Conclusion

Although stare decisis is a fundamental part of the legal model, up to now no one has examined it empirically in a comprehensive study. Doctrinal and philosophical studies abound, of course. But we found only four published empirical articles on this topic. Not only are some of the findings of these four studies open to question, but the authors of these studies failed to agree on their list of overruling and overruled cases. One of the four studies used the list collected by the Congressional Research Service, but this list is unreliable, mainly because its compilers failed to specify the criteria they employed to determine whether a given case ought to be placed on the list. We compiled our own list of cases covering a period of 46 terms – the Vinson, Warren, and Burger Courts, and the first 6 terms of the Rehnquist Court. We also listed the cases these overturning cases altered. For someone who has not conducted research on this topic, it might appear easy to identify the overruling and the overruled cases. This is not true. We had to formulate rules for the selection of cases and determine whether a given case conforms to the rules or not.

We first ascertained some of the characteristics of the overruling and overruled cases. We discovered that half the overruled decisions survived less than 21 years, while approximately 10 percent antedated 1900. Of the four Courts we inspected, the Warren Court overturned the most recent precedents and was most likely to overturn its own precedents. We also found that older precedents tended to be overturned by a much larger vote than newer precedents. The Warren Court generated a higher proportion of salient overrulings than the other three Courts. Almost two-thirds of the overrulings were based on constitutional grounds, a markedly higher proportion than is true of decisions that did not alter precedent. The dominant issue in the overruling cases of the Warren Court was civil liberties, a proportion again that was much higher than in the Warren Court's decisions overall. Justices Brennan, Rehnquist, and White wrote the most overruling majority opinions, while Frankfurter, Harlan, and Minton wrote the most majority opinions that were overruled.

We also discovered that in the overturning cases the justices voted to grant certiorari at an overall rate of approximately .70, a rate similar to the cert grant rate for cases in general. We also found that when the Court reversed, the justices in their certiorari voting were likely to vote strategically; i.e., in accord with the error-correcting and prediction strategies. In almost 90 percent of the votes in the overruling cases the justices voted for the same outcome at the original vote on the merits as they voted for at the final vote. When fluidity in voting occurred, the moderate and conservative justices on the Warren Court were more likely to switch than their liberal counterparts. Warren Court justices as a group were more likely to shift from support for the majority at the original vote on the merits to support for the minority at the final vote. The opposite pattern prevailed among Burger Court justices.

The most important part of our study, however, does not concern these discrete findings. Rather, it addresses the question: Why do the justices in the overturning and overturned cases vote the way they do? In an attempt to answer this question we tested the attitudinal model and one element of the legal model, i.e., adherence to stare decisis.

When we examined cumulative scales in which the content of the scales is defined as specifically as the data will allow, we discovered that attitudinal variables or, more precisely, the justices' personal policy preferences substantially explained their voting. More specifically, we found that over 97 percent of the votes in the overruling and overruled cases were attitudinally consistent.

But the scalability of the justices' voting in the overruling and the overruled cases does not disconfirm the possible relevance of the legal model in influencing the voting. As we point out, the legal and the attitudinal models do not diverge in all respects. Case facts, for example, are grist for both. In an attempt to test the element of the legal model most pertinent to our study, we investigated the extent to which the justices followed personal stare decisis as well as institutional stare decisis. The former occurs when a justice either votes with the majority in the overturned case and dissents in the overturning case or vice versa. Institutional stare decisis takes place when a justice upholds the Court's precedents. Thus, four patterns are possible. 1) A justice votes with the majority in the overruled case and opposes its overruling (majority-minority voting). This behavior conforms to both personal and institutional stare decisis. 2) A justice dissents in the overruled case and votes with the majority to overrule (minority-majority). This behavior accords with personal stare decisis but not with institutional stare decisis. 3) A justice votes with the majority in both the overruled and overruling cases (majority-majority). This behavior conforms to neither type of stare decisis. 4) A justice dissents in both the overruled and overruling cases (minority-minority). This behavior is contrary to personal stare decisis while conforming to institutional stare decisis.

We cannot test the attitudinal model by focusing on these four behaviors because none of these patterns necessarily conflicts with it. But because the second and third patterns deviate from the legal model, we can determine the extent to which individual justices fail to conform to it. Our analyses show that the justices were more likely to support personal stare decisis than the institutional variety. The justices on the Warren and Burger Courts displayed less support for the legal model (25.6 and 31.9 percent) than did the justices on the Rehnquist and Vinson Courts (46.3 and 50 percent). Apart from the infrequently participating Burton, only two justices consistently voted compatibly with the legal model: Marshall, at a high 76.2 percent, and Harlan, at a more modest 58.8 percent. Clark, who was generally supportive of the legal model, manifested such behavior in only two of five Vinson Court overrulings. Other justices either vacillated in their degree of support for the legal model from one Court to another (Black, Blackmun, Brennan, Douglas, Stevens, and Stewart) or were consistently hostile (Burger, O'Connor, Powell, Rehnquist, Warren, and White).

Of the four voting patterns identified above, minority-majority voting predominates (38.7 percent), followed by majority-minority voting (30.2 percent), and majority-majority (28.4 percent). Minority-minority voting occupies a distant fourth place (2.7 percent). Overall, then, two-thirds of the votes fail to conform to the legal model (i.e., 38.7 and 28.4). Further analysis shows that the justices on the Warren Court cast more minority-majority votes than the justices on the three other Courts combined: 75 of 127, 70 of which were cast by Douglas, Black, and Warren. We suspected that these votes were cast in cases that overturned conservative decisions, and that the minority-majority voting of more recently serving justices such as O'Connor, Rehnquist, and Scalia occurred in cases that voided liberal precedents. We also suspected that the majority-minority voting of Justices Brennan and Marshall took place because they objected to the Burger and Rehnquist Court penchant for overruling liberal decisions.

If what we have guessed is true, then the individual justices' ideologies – and by extension those of the Courts as well – ought to explain why they voted as they did. If ideology – an attitudinal variable – is extant, it is most likely to be that which guides American political elites generally: liberalism and conservatism. Accordingly, liberal Courts should overrule conservative precedents, and conservative Courts those that are liberal. This hypothesis was supported. The Vinson, Warren, Burger, and Rehnquist Courts overwhelmingly overturned precedents because of the ideology – the personal policy preferences – of their members. Conservative justices, such as the majority of those who sat on the Rehnquist Court, formally altered liberal precedents. In contrast, the liberal overrulings of the later Warren Court voided conservative precedents. Moderate justices – such as Blackmun, Stevens, and White – fell on both sides of the divide, manifesting less consistent support for either liberal or conservative outcomes than justices such as Brennan, Douglas, Marshall, and Warren, on the liberal side, or Burger, Frankfurter, Harlan, and Rehnquist, on the conservative side. In short, our overall findings support the attitudinal model over the legal model.

But this book does not offer the final word regarding whether the legal model influences the justices' votes. We have examined only one element of the legal model – stare decisis. And we have primarily focused only on cases that altered precedent.

Additional quantitative research is needed. We suggest three projects. First, researchers might examine the published fact-pattern studies or generate studies of new issue areas to ascertain the extent to which the key variables that explain the votes are based on the four elements of the legal model: precedent, the plain meaning of the relevant legal provision in the case, intent, and balancing. Second, investigators might inspect the briefs filed by counsel to determine whether the legal arguments advanced influence the justices' votes. A researcher might, for example, examine the same case in different courts to learn whether different legal arguments lead to different results. Here, of course, the ideology of the judges must be controlled. Finally, in Chapter 1 we mentioned Supreme Court decisions that have so influenced our understanding of the Constitution or have so changed American society that the likelihood of their being overturned approximates zero. If we wish to understand Supreme Court decision making, we ought to investigate not only the issues that the Court decides, but also those that the Court is unlikely to resolve. There are a host of questions relating to this subject that social scientists might explore.

Some of the research suggested above will prove to be exceedingly difficult and may not be worth the effort. But if we want to know whether legal variables influence the justices' votes, we have no choice but to conduct this or similar research. Perhaps it is time to stop asserting that legal variables are obviously important in the Court's decision making. Perhaps it is time to start testing whether these variables are, in fact, important.

Appendix I

Overruling and overruled decisions of the
Vinson, Warren, Burger, and Rehnquist Courts

Overruling cases	Legal provision	Issue	Overruled cases
VINSON COURT			
1948			
Comr v. Estate of Church, 335 U.S. 632 (1949)	Internal Revenue Code	Federal tax	*May v. Heiner,* 281 U.S. 238 (1930)
Oklahoma Tax Comn. v. Texas Co., 336 U.S. 342 (1949)	—	National supremacy	*Choctaw, Oklahoma & Gulf R. Co. v. Harrison,* 235 U.S. 292 (1914)
			Indian Oil Co. v. Oklahoma, 240 U.S. 522 (1916)
			Howard v. Gipsy Oil Co., 247 U.S. 503 (1918)
			Large Oil Co. v. Howard, 248 U.S. 549 (1919)
			Oklahoma v. Barnsdall Refineries, 296 U.S. 521 (1936)
Cosmopolitan Shipping Co. v. McAllister, 337 U.S. 783 (1949)	Jones Act	Governmental liability	*Hust v. Moore-McCormack Lines,* 328 U.S. 707 (1946)
1949			
United States v. Rabinowitz, 339 U.S. 56 (1950)	4th Amendment	Search and seizure	*Trupiano v. United States,* 334 U.S. 699 (1948)
Darr v. Burford, 339 U.S. 200 (1950)	Habeas corpus	Comity	*Wade v. Mayo,* 334 U.S. 672 (1948)
1951			
Burstyn v. Wilson, 343 U.S. 495 (1952)	1st Amendment	1st Amendment	*Mutual Film Corp. v. Ohio Industrial Comn.,* 236 U.S. 230 (1915)

Warren Court case	Subject	Category	Related cases
1953			
*Brown v. Board of Education, 347 U.S. 483 (1954)	Equal protection clause	School desegregation	*Plessy v. Ferguson, 163 U.S. 537 (1896); Cumming v. County Board of Education, 175 U.S. 528 (1899); Gong Lum v. Rice, 275 U.S. 78 (1927)
1956			
Reid v. Covert, 354 U.S. 1 (1957)	Code of military justice	Military	In re Ross, 140 U.S. 453 (1891); Kinsella v. Krueger, 351 U.S. 470 (1956); Reid v. Covert, 351 U.S. 487 (1956)
Vanderbilt v. Vanderbilt, 354 U.S. 416 (1957)	Full faith and credit	Due process-jurisdiction	Thompson v. Thompson, 226 U.S. 551 (1913)
1959			
United States v. Raines, 362 U.S. 17 (1960)	Title 28/15th Amendment/civil rights act	Voting	*United States v. Reese, 92 U.S. 214 (1876)
*Elkins v. United States, 364 U.S. 206 (1960)	4th Amendment	Search and seizure	*Weeks v. United States, 232 U.S. 383 (1914); Center v. United States, 267 U.S. 575 (1925); Byars v. United States, 273 U.S. 28 (1925); Feldman v. United States, 322 U.S. 487 (1944)
1960			
James v. United States, 366 U.S. 213 (1961)	Internal Revenue Code	Criminal law	Commissioner v. Wilcox, 327 U.S. 404 (1946)
*Mapp v. Ohio, 367 U.S. 643 (1961)	4th Amendment	Search and seizure	*Wolf v. Colorado, 338 U.S. 25 (1949)
1961			
*Baker v. Carr, 369 U.S. 186 (1962)	Case or controversy requirement	Reapportionment-ment/standing to sue	*Colegrove v. Green, 328 U.S. 549 (1946)
Continental Ore v. Union Carbide & Carbon Corp., 370 U.S. 690 (1962)	Clayton Act	Antitrust	American Banana Co. v. United Fruit Co., 213 U.S. 347 (1909)
1962			
Smith v. Evening News Assn., 371 U.S. 195 (1962)	National Labor Relations Act	Preemption of state court jurisdiction	Westinghouse Employees v. Westinghouse Corp., 348 U.S. 437 (1955)
Construction & General Laborers' Union v. Curry, 371 U.S. 542 (1962)	National Labor Relations Act/Title 28	Preemption of state court jurisdiction/Supreme Court jurisdiction	Montgomery Trades Council v. Ledbetter Erection Co., 344 U.S. 178 (1952)

Appendix I (*cont.*)

Overruling cases	Legal provision	Issue	Overruled cases
Gideon v. Wainwright, 372 U.S. 335 (1962)	Right to counsel	Right to counsel	*Betts v. Brady*, 316 U.S. 455 (1942)
Gray v. Sanders, 372 U.S. 368 (1963)	Equal protection/Title 28/case or case controversy requirement	Reapportionment/ mootness/district court jurisdiction/standing to sue	Cook v. Fortson, 329 U.S. 675 (1946) South v. Peters, 339 U.S. 276 (1950)
Fay v. Noia, 372 U.S. 391 (1963)	Habeas corpus	Habeas corpus/involuntary confession	Darr v. Burford, 339 U.S. 200 (1950)
Ferguson v. Skrupa, 372 U.S. 726 (1963)	Due process clause/equal protection	State business regulation	Adams v. Tanner, 244 U.S. 590 (1917)
1963			
Schneider v. Rusk, 377 U.S. 163 (1964)	Immigration Act/due process	Denaturalization	Mackenzie v. Hare, 239 U.S. 299 (1915)
Malloy v. Hogan, 378 U.S. 1 (1964)	Self-incrimination	Self-incrimination	*Twining v. New Jersey*, 211 U.S. 78 (1908) Adamson v. California, 332 U.S. 46 (1947)
Murphy v. Waterfront Comm, 378 U.S. 52 (1964)	Equal protection	Self-incrimination/immunity from prosecution	Jack v. Kansas, 199 U.S. 372 (1905) United States v. Murdock, 284 U.S. 141 (1931) Feldman v. United States, 322 U.S. 487 (1944) Knapp v. Schweitzer, 357 U.S. 371 (1958) Mills v. Louisiana, 360 U.S. 230 (1959)
Jackson v. Denno, 378 U.S. 368 (1964)	Due process clause	Involuntary confession	Stein v. New York, 346 U.S. 156 (1953)
Escobedo v. Illinois, 378 U.S. 478 (1964)	Right to counsel	Right to counsel	Crooker v. California, 357 U.S. 433 (1958) Cicenia v. Lagay, 357 U.S. 504 (1958)
1964			
Pointer v. Texas, 380 U.S. 400 (1965)	Confrontation and cross-examination	Confrontation	West v. Louisiana, 194 U.S. 258 (1904)
1965			
Swift & Co. v. Wickham, 382 U.S. 111 (1965)	Title 28	Supreme Court jurisdiction	Kesler v. Dept of Public Safety, 369 U.S. 153 (1962)
Harris v. United States, 382 U.S. 162 (1965)	Rules of Criminal Procedure	Contempt/Rules of Criminal Procedure	Brown v. United States, 359 U.S. 41 (1959)

Case	Subject	Subject	Case
*Harper v. Virginia Bd of Elections, 383 U.S. 663 (1966)	Equal protection	Voting	*Breedlove v. Suttles, 302 U.S. 277 (1937)
*Miranda v. Arizona, 384 U.S. 436 (1966)	Self-incrimination	Miranda warnings	Crooker v. California, 357 U.S. 433 (1958) Cicenia v. Lagay, 357 U.S. 504 (1958)
1966			
Spevack v. Klein, 385 U.S. 511 (1967)	Self-incrimination	Self-incrimination/attorney licensing	Cohen v. Hurley, 366 U.S. 117 (1961)
*Keyishian v. Bd of Regents, 385 U.S. 589 (1967)	1st Amendment	Loyalty oath/mootness	Adler v. Board of Education, 342 U.S. 485 (1952)
Afroyim v. Rusk, 387 U.S. 253 (1967)	Citizenship clause/Immigration Act	Denaturalization	Perez v. Brownell, 356 U.S. 44 (1958)
*Warden v. Hayden, 387 U.S. 294 (1967)	4th Amendment	Search and seizure	Gouled v. United States, 255 U.S. 298 (1921)
Camara v. Municipal Court, 387 U.S. 523 (1967)	4th Amendment	Search and seizure	Frank v. Maryland, 359 U.S. 360 (1959)
1967			
*Katz v. United States, 389 U.S. 347 (1967)	4th Amendment	Search and seizure	*Olmstead v. United States, 277 U.S. 438 (1928)
Marchetti v. United States, 390 U.S. 39 (1968)	Internal Revenue Code/self-incrimination	Self-incrimination	United States v. Kahriger, 345 U.S. 22 (1953) Lewis v. United States, 348 U.S. 419 (1955)
Peyton v. Rowe, 391 U.S. 54 (1968)	Habeas corpus	Habeas corpus	McNally v. Hill, 293 U.S. 131 (1934)
Bruton v. United States, 391 U.S. 123 (1968)	Confrontation and cross-examination	Confrontation	Delli Paoli v. United States, 352 U.S. 232 (1957)
*Duncan v. Louisiana, 391 U.S. 145 (1968)	Jury trial	Right to jury trial	*Maxwell v. Dow, 176 U.S. 581 (1900)
Carafas v. LaVallee, 391 U.S. 234 (1968)	Habeas corpus	Habeas corpus/mootness	Parker v. Ellis, 362 U.S. 574 (1960)
Lee v. Florida, 392 U.S. 378 (1968)	Federal Communications Act	Search and seizure	Schwartz v. Texas, 344 U.S. 199 (1952)
*Jones v. Alfred H. Mayer Co., 392 U.S. 409 (1968)	13th Amendment	Desegregation	Hodges v. United States, 203 U.S. 1 (1906)
1968			
Moore v. Ogilvie, 394 U.S. 814 (1969)	Equal protection	Ballot access/mootness	MacDougall v. Green, 335 U.S. 281 (1948)
Brandenburg v. Ohio, 395 U.S. 444 (1969)	1st Amendment	1st Amendment	*Whitney v. California, 274 U.S. 357 (1927)
Lear, Inc. v. Adkins, 395 U.S. 653 (1969)	Collateral estoppel	Patents/national supremacy	Automatic Radio Mfg Co. v. Hazeline Research, 339 U.S. 827 (1950)
*Chimel v. California, 395 U.S. 752 (1969)	4th Amendment	Search and seizure	Harris v. United States, 331 U.S. 145 (1947) *United States v. Rabinowitz, 339 U.S. 56 (1950)
*Benton v. Maryland, 395 U.S. 784 (1969)	Double jeopardy	Double jeopardy/standing to sue	*Palko v. Connecticut, 302 U.S. 319 (1937)

Appendix I (*cont.*)

Overruling cases	Legal provision	Issue	Overruled cases
BURGER COURT			
1969			
Boys Markets v. Retail Clerks, 398 U.S. 235 (1970)	Norris-La Guardia Act	Arbitration/labor-management dispute	*Sinclair Refining Co. v. Atkinson*, 370 U.S. 195 (1962)
Moragne v. States Marine Lines, 398 U.S. 375 (1970)	—	Election of remedies	*The Harrisburg v. Rickards*, 119 U.S. 199 (1886)
1970			
Blonder-Tongue Laboratories v. University of Illinois Foundation, 402 U.S. 313 (1971)	Collateral estoppel	Patents	*Triplett v. Lowell*, 297 U.S. 638 (1936)
Perez v. Campbell, 402 U.S. 637 (1971)	Bankruptcy Code	Bankruptcy/national supremacy	*Kesler v. Dept. of Public Safety*, 369 U.S. 153 (1962)
			Reitz v. Mealey, 314 U.S. 33 (1941)
1971			
Illinois v. Milwaukee, 406 U.S. 91 (1972)	Title 28	Environment protection	*Ohio v. Wyandotte Chemicals Corp.*, 401 U.S. 493 (1971)
Andrews v. L & N R. Co., 406 U.S. 320 (1972)	Railway Labor Act	Election of remedies	*Moore v. Illinois Central R. Co.*, 312 U.S. 630 (1941)
1972			
Lehnhausen v. Lake Shore Auto Parts, 410 U.S. 356 (1973)	Equal protection	State tax	*Quaker City Cab Co. v. Pennsylvania*, 277 U.S. 389 (1928)
Braden v. Circuit Court, 410 U.S. 484 (1973)	Habeas corpus	Habeas corpus	*Ahrens v. Clark*, 335 U.S. 188 (1948)
Miller v. California, 413 U.S. 15 (1973)	1st Amendment	State obscenity	*A Book Named "John Cleland's Memoirs of a Woman of Pleasure" v. Massachusetts*, 383 U.S. 412 (1966)
1973			
North Dakota Pharmacy Board v. Snyder's Drug Stores, 414 U.S. 156 (1973)	Due process clause/Title 28	State business regulation	*Liggett Co. v. Baldridge*, 278 U.S. 105 (1929)
Edelman v. Jordan, 415 U.S. 651 (1974)	11th Amendment	Poverty law	*Shapiro v. Thompson*, 394 U.S. 618 (1969)

Case			Overruled case
1974			
*Taylor v. Louisiana, 419 U.S. 522 (1975)	Jury trial/case or controversy	Sex discrimination	*Hoyt v. Florida, 368 U.S. 57 (1961)
United States v. Reliable Transfer Co., 421 U.S. 397 (1975)	Tort Claims Act	Government liability	The Schooner Catherine v. Dickinson, 17 Howard 170 (1854)
1975			
*Michelin Tire v. Wages, 423 U.S. 276 (1976)	Export-import clause	State tax	*Low v. Austin, 13 Wallace 29 (1871)
Hudgens v. NLRB, 424 U.S. 507 (1976)	1st Amendment/National Labor Relations Act	1st Amendment	Amalgamated Food Employees Union v. Logan Valley Plaza, 391 U.S. 308 (1968)
Virginia State Board of Pharmacy v. Virginia Citizens Consumer Council, 425 U.S. 748 (1976)	1st Amendment	Commercial speech	Valentine v. Chrestensen, 316 U.S. 52 (1942)
*National League of Cities v. Usery, 426 U.S. 833 (1976)	Interstate commerce/Fair Labor Standards	Fair Labor Standards Act	Maryland v. Wirtz, 392 U.S. 183 (1968)
Machinists v. Wisconsin Employment Relations Comm., 427 U.S. 132 (1976)	National Labor Relations Act	Preemption state court jurisdiction	UAW v. Wisconsin Employment Relations Board, 336 U.S. 245 (1949)
New Orleans v. Dukes, 427 U.S. 297 (1976)	Equal protection/Title 28	State business regulation	Morey v. Doud, 354 U.S. 457 (1957)
*Gregg v. Georgia, 428 U.S. 153 (1976)	8th Amendment	Death penalty	McGautha v. California, 402 U.S. 183 (1971)
1976			
*Craig v. Boren, 429 U.S. 190 (1976)	Equal protection/case or controversy requirement/21st Amendment	Sex discrimination/mootness/standing to sue	Goesaert v. Cleary, 335 U.S. 464 (1948)
Oregon ex rel. State Land Board v. Corvallis Sand & Gravel Co., 429 U.S. 363 (1977)	—	Federalism	Bonelli Cattle Co. vs Arizona, 414 U.S. 313 (1973)
*Complete Auto Transit, Inc. v. Brady, 430 U.S. 274 (1977)	Interstate commerce	State tax	Spector Motor Service v. O'Connor, 340 U.S. 602 (1951)
Continental T.V., Inc. v. GTE Sylvania Inc., 433 U.S. 36 (1977)	Sherman Act	Antitrust	United States v. Arnold, Schwinn & Co., 388 U.S. 365 (1967)
Shaffer v. Heitner, 433 U.S. 186 (1977)	Due process clause	Due process-jurisdiction	Pennoyer v. Neff, 95 U.S. 714 (1878) Harris v. Balk, 198 U.S. 215 (1905)

Appendix I (*cont.*)

Overruling cases	Legal provision	Issue	Overruled cases
1977			
Washington Revenue Dept. v. Stevedoring Assn., 435 U.S. 734 (1978)	Interstate commerce/export-import clause	State tax	*Puget Sound Stevedoring Co. v. State Tax Comn.*, 302 (1978) U.S. 90 (1937) *Joseph v. Carter & Weekes Stevedoring Co.*, 330 U.S. 422 (1947)
Monell v. Dept. of Social Services, 436 U.S. 658 (1978)	Civil rights act	Civil rights liability	*Monroe v. Pape*, 365 U.S. 167 (1961)
Burks v. United States, 437 U.S. 1 (1978)	Double jeopardy	Double jeopardy	*Bryan v. United States*, 338 U.S. 552 (1950) *Sapir v. United States*, 348 U.S. 373 (1955) *Yates v. United States*, 354 U.S. 298 (1957) *Forman v. United States*, 361 U.S. 416 (1960)
United States v. Scott, 437 U.S. 82 (1978)	Double jeopardy	Double jeopardy	*United States v. Jenkins*, 420 U.S. 358 (1975)
1978			
Hughes v. Oklahoma, 441 U.S. 322 (1979)	Interstate commerce	National supremacy	*Geer v. Connecticut*, 161 U.S. 519 (1896)
1979			
Trammel v. United States, 445 U.S. 40 (1980)	—	Federal Rules of Civil Procedure	*Hawkins v. United States*, 358 U.S. 74 (1958)
United States v. Salvucci, 448 U.S. 83 (1980)	4th Amendment/exclusionary rule	Search and seizure	*Jones v. United States*, 362 U.S. 257 (1960)
Thomas v. Washington Gas Light Co., 448 U.S. 261 (1980)	Full faith & credit	Election of remedies	*Industrial Comn. of Wisconsin v. McCartin*, 330 U.S. 622 (1947)
1980			
Commonwealth Edison Co. v. Montana, 453 U.S. 609 (1981)	Interstate commerce/supremacy clause	State tax	*Heisler v. Thomas Colliery Co.*, 260 U.S. 245 (1922)
1981			
United States v. Ross, 456 U.S. 798 (1982)	4th Amendment	Vehicle search and seizure	*Robbins v. California*, 453 U.S. 420 (1981)

	4th Amendment	Search and seizure	Aguilar v. Texas, 378 U.S. 108 (1964) Spinelli v. United States, 393 U.S. 410 (1969) Number indeterminable
1982 Illinois v. Gates, 462 U.S. 213 (1983)			
Michigan v. Long, 463 U.S. 1032 (1983)	4th Amendment/—	Vehicle search and seizure/Supreme Court jurisdiction	
1983 United States v. One Assortment of 89 Firearms, 465 U.S. 354 (1984)	Double jeopardy/collateral estoppel/firearms statute	Double jeopardy	Coffey v. United States, 116 U.S. 436 (1886)
Limbach v. Hooven & Allison Co., 466 U.S. 353 (1984)	Export-import clause/collateral estoppel	State tax	Hooven & Allison Co. v. Evatt, 324 U.S. 652 (1945)
Copperweld Corp. v. Independence Tube, 467 U.S. 752 (1984)	Sherman Act	Antitrust	United States v. Yellow Cab Co., 332 U.S. 218 (1947) Kiefer-Stewart Co. v. Joseph E. Seagram & Sons, 340 U.S. 211 (1951)
1984 *Garcia v. San Antonio Metropolitan Transit Authority, 469 U.S. 528 (1985)	Fair Labor Standards Act/interstate commerce	Fair Labor Standards Act/national supremacy	*National League of Cities v. Usery, 426 U.S. 833 (1976)
United States v. Miller, 471 U.S. 130 (1985)	Grand jury	Criminal procedure	Ex parte Bain, 121 U.S. 1 (1887)
1985 Daniels v. Williams, 474 U.S. 327 (1986)	Due process clause	Civil rights liability	Parratt v. Taylor, 451 U.S. 527 (1981)
*Batson v. Kentucky, 476 U.S. 79 (1986)	Equal protection	Desegregation	Swain v. Alabama, 380 U.S. 202 (1965)
Brown-Forman Distillers Corp. v. New York State Liquor Authority, 476 U.S. 573 (1986)	Interstate commerce/21st Amendment	State business regulation	Joseph E. Seagram & Sons v. Hostetter, 384 U.S. 35 (1966)
Rose v. Clark, 478 U.S. 570 (1986)	Harmless error rule	Extra-legal jury influences	Bollenbach v. United States, 326 U.S. 607 (1946) Carpenters v. United States, 330 U.S. 395 (1947) Marks v. United States, 430 U.S. 188 (1977) Jackson v. Virginia, 443 U.S. 307 (1979)

Appendix I (*cont.*)

Overruling cases	Legal provision	Issue	Overruled cases
REHNQUIST COURT			
1986			
Griffith v. Kentucky, 479 U.S. 314 (1987)	Retroactivity	Retroactivity of new constitutional rights	Desist v. United States, 394 U.S. 244 (1969); Williams v. United States, 401 U.S. 646 (1971)
Puerto Rico v. Branstad, 483 U.S. 219 (1987)	Extradition clause/extradition act	Subconstitutional fair procedure	*Kentucky v. Dennison, 24 How. 66 (1861)
Tyler Pipe Industries, Inc. v. Dept. of Revenue, 483 U.S. 232 (1987)	Interstate commerce	State tax	General Motors Corp. v. Washington, 377 U.S. 436 (1964)
American Trucking Assns., Inc. v. Scheiner, 483 U.S. 266 (1987)	Interstate commerce	State tax	Aero Mayflower Transit Co. v. Georgia PSC, 295 U.S. 285 (1935); Aero Mayflower Transit Co. v. Bd of RR Comrs, 332 U.S. 495 (1947); Capitol Greyhound Lines v. Brice, 339 U.S. 542 (1950)
Solorio v. United States, 483 U.S. 435 (1987)	Governance of the armed forces	Military	O'Callahan v. Parker, 395 U.S. 258 (1969)
Welch v. Texas Highway Dept, 483 U.S. 468 (1987)	11th Amendment	Governmental liability	Parden v. Terminal Railway of Alabama, 377 U.S. 184 (1964)
1987			
Gulfstream Aerospace Corp. v. Mayacamas Corp., 485 U.S. 271 (1988)	Title 28	Judicial administration	Enelow v. New York Life Insurance Co., 293 U.S. 379 (1935); Ettelson v. Metropolitan Life Ins. Co., 317 U.S. 188 (1942)
*South Carolina v. Baker, 485 U.S. 505 (1988)	Internal Revenue Code/10th Amendment	National supremacy	*Pollock v. Farmers' Loan & Trust Co., 157 U.S. 429 (1895)

Year / Case	Provision at issue	Subject	Precedent overruled
1988			
Thornburgh v. Abbott, 490 U.S. 401 (1989)	1st Amendment	1st Amendment	Procunier v. Martinez, 416 U.S. 396 (1974)
Rodriguez de Quijas v. Shearson/American Express, Inc., 490 U.S. 477 (1989)	Securities Act	Securities regulation	Wilko v. Swan, 346 U.S. 427 (1953)
Ward's Cove Packing Co., Inc. v. Atonio, 490 U.S. 642 (1989)	Civil rights act	Employment discrimination	*Griggs v. Duke Power Co., 401 U.S. 424 (1971)
Alabama v. Smith, 490 U.S. 794 (1989)	Double jeopardy	Double jeopardy	Simpson v. Rice, 395 U.S. 711 (1969)
*Webster v. Reproductive Health Services, 492 U.S. 490 (1989)	Due process clause	Abortion	*Roe v. Wade, 410 U.S. 113 (1973)
			Colautti v. Franklin, 439 U.S. 379 (1979)
1989			
Collins v. Youngblood, 497 U.S. 37 (1990)	Ex post facto clause	Criminal procedure	Kring v. Missouri, 107 U.S. 221 (1883)
			Thompson v. Utah, 170 U.S. 343 (1898)
1990			
California v. Acevedo, 114 L Ed 2d 619 (1991)	4th Amendment	Vehicle search and seizure	Arkansas v. Sanders, 442 U.S. 753 (1979)
Exxon Corp. v. Central Gulf Lines, Inc., 114 L Ed 2d 649 (1991)	Title 28	Judicial administration	Minturn v. Maynard, 17 How. 477 (1855)
**Coleman v. Thompson, 115 L Ed 2d 640 (1991)	—	Habeas corpus	*Fay v. Noia, 372 U.S. 391 (1963)
**Payne v. Tennessee, 115 L Ed 2d 720 (1991)	8th Amendment	Death penalty	Booth v. Maryland, 482 U.S. 496 (1987)
			South Carolina v. Gathers, 490 U.S. 805 (1989)
1991			
Keeney v. Tamayo-Reyes, 118 L Ed 2d 318 (1992)	—	Habeas corpus	Townsend v. Sain, 372 U.S. 293 (1963)
**Planned Parenthood v. Casey, 120 L Ed 2d 674 (1992)	Due process clause	Abortion	*Akron v. Akron Center for Reproductive Health, Inc., 462 U.S. 416 (1983)
			*Thornburgh v. American College of Obstetricians and Gynecologists, 476 U.S. 747 (1986)

Note: A dash indicates no statutory or constitutional provision at issue.

*A salient case according to the Congressional Quarterly's *Guide to the United States Supreme Court.*

**A salient case according to *Congressional Quarterly Weekly Report.*

Appendix II

Cases overruled by the Vinson, Warren, Burger, and Rehnquist Courts

THE VINSON COURT

The Vinson Court was by far the least active in altering precedents. During its life span of seven terms, it formally altered precedent on only six occasions,[1] the first of which did not occur until its third term. But in this term, 1948, it handed down three of its overrulings: *Commissioner v. Estate of Church,* 335 U.S. 632 (1949), an internal revenue tax case, overruled *May v. Heiner,* 281 U.S. 238 (1930), which had itself overruled a number of earlier decisions. *Oklahoma Tax Commission v. Texas Co.,* 336 U.S. 342 (1949), is the first in a lengthy string of state tax cases we consider. This one, based on intergovernmental tax immunity, upheld the state's taxes against lessees of mineral rights on allotted and restricted Indian lands. Overruled was a set of five decisions, dating from 1914 to 1936.[2] *Cosmopolitan Shipping Co. v. McAllister,* 337 U.S. 783 (1949), concerned the Jones Act liability of a wartime general agent appointed by the United States for injuries suffered by a seaman. The Court denied liabilty and overruled *Hust v. Moore-McCormack Lines,* 328 U.S. 707 (1946).

The next term, 1949, produced two overruling decisions, both of which were of considerable importance: *United States v. Rabinowitz,* 339 U.S. 56 (1950), a CQ-listed case, and *Darr v. Burford,* 339 U.S. 200 (1950). *Rabinowitz* initiates our ongoing concern with the Fourth Amendment. Armed with an arrest warrant, officers searched the desk, safe, and file cabinets of an office open to the public. The Vinson Court majority held the seized evidence admissible as a search incident to a lawful arrest, overruling *Trupiano v. United States,* 334 U.S. 699 (1948), a precedent of its own making. "The relevant test," said the majority, "is not whether it is reasonable to procure a search warrant," as *Trupiano* had held, "but whether the search was reasonable."[3] *Darr* constitutes the first of our habeas

---

[1] Actually seven, but as we point out in note 12, we do not count *Rutkin v. United States,* 343 U.S. 130 (1952), as a Vinson Court overruling because its language is much more equivocal than that of the Warren Court decision, *James v. United States,* 366 U.S. 213 (1961).

[2] *Choctaw, Oklahoma & Gulf R. Co. v. Harrison,* 235 U.S. 292 (1914); *Indian Oil Co. v. Oklahoma,* 240 U.S. 522 (1916); *Howard v. Gipsy Oil Co.,* 247 U.S. 503 (1918); *Large Oil Co. v. Howard,* 248 U.S. 549 (1919); and *Oklahoma v. Barnsdall Refineries,* 296 U.S. 521 (1936).

[3] 339 U.S. at 66.

corpus cases. The same five-member majority as in *Rabinowitz* ruled that a state court prisoner must exhaust his direct appeals before petitioning for a writ of habeas corpus except in special circumstances as to which the prisoner bears the burden of proof. The decision overruled the inconsistent aspects of *Wade v. Mayo,* 334 U.S. 672 (1948), which was also one of the Vinson Court's own precedents. The short life of *Trupiano* and *Wade* – less than two years – appears to have been due to the deaths of Justices Murphy and Rutledge and their replacement by Justices Clark and Minton.

The final Vinson Court overruling was *Burstyn v. Wilson,* 343 U.S. 495 (1952). The First Amendment, the Court stated, applies to motion pictures, thereby preventing a New York censor from banning a film because he deemed it "sacrilegious." *Mutual Film Corp. v. Ohio Industrial Comn.,* 236 U.S. 230 (1915), was overruled.

THE WARREN COURT

The first decision of the Warren Court to overrule a precedent, the landmark case of *Brown v. Board of Education,* 347 U.S. 483 (1954), belies our statements about the clarity of the language the Court uses when it alters precedent. While it is indisputable that *Brown* impacted previous case law, the Chief Justice's unanimous opinion fails to use an operative word for an alteration of precedent. Nonetheless, *Brown's* holding "that in the field of public education the doctrine of 'separate but equal' has no place"[4] necessarily forces us to conclude that at least the two public education cases upholding separation that the opinion mentions – *Cumming v. County Board of Education,* 175 U.S. 528 (1899), and *Gong Lum v. Rice,* 275 U.S. 78 (1927) – are no longer good law . Although it may be arguable, we also view *Brown* as appreciably narrowing the scope of the salient case of *Plessy v. Ferguson,* 163 U.S. 537 (1896), even if it did not completely void it.[5] As we note, the Court unequivocally ruled that the *Plessy* separate but equal doctrine has no place in public education.

Like *Brown, Reid v. Covert,* 354 U.S. 1 (1957), also involved multiple overrulings: *In re Ross,* 140 U.S. 453 (1891), which the plurality solipsistically stated "should be left as a relic from a different era,"[6] and two companion cases from the preceding term that reached an opposite result in the court martial of civilian dependents for capital offenses overseas: *Kinsella v. Krueger,* 351 U.S. 470, and *Reid v. Covert,* 351 U.S. 487 (1956). Only one of the overruled precedents with which we are concerned had a shorter life than these two – one day less than a

---

[4]   347 U.S. at 495.

[5]   Apparently *Gayle v. Browder,* 352 U.S. 903 (1956), a summary per curiam decision, fully overruled *Plessy.* It did so, however, on the authority of *Brown* and two other summary per curiam decisions.

[6]   354 U.S. at 12.

year.[7] Two weeks after the preceding overruling, the Court ruled that a 1913 decision that alimony rights did not survive an ex parte divorce "can no longer be considered controlling."[8]

During its first six terms (1953–1958) the Warren Court displayed markedly less activism than either the Vinson Court or its own subsequent history exhibited: a grand total of three overruling decisions, two of which occurred in a single term, 1956. But beginning with the 1959 term, the Warren Court got into an overruling gear that characterized not only it, but the Burger and Rehnquist Courts as well.

The first overruling of the 1960s, appropriately enough, occurred in a civil rights case, *United States v. Raines*, 362 U.S. 17 (1960). In nebulously worded language, the Court voided the CQ-listed case of *United States v. Reese*, 92 U.S. 214 (1876): "To the extent *Reese* did depend on an approach inconsistent with what we think the better one and the one established by the weightiest of the subsequent cases, we cannot follow it here."[9] Following on the heels of *Raines* was the salient case of *Elkins v. United States*, 364 U.S. 206 (1960), which overruled the several precedents that had established the silver platter doctrine admitting into federal court evidence seized by state officials in violation of the Fourth Amendment.[10]

The final overrulings before the onset of the Warren Court's liberal heyday in the 1961 term[11] were the last decisions in which Justices Frankfurter and Whittaker both participated: *James v. United States*, 366 U.S. 213 (1961), and the landmark case of *Mapp v. Ohio*, 367 U.S. 643 (1961). Both overruled a Vinson Court precedent: *James*, a decision narrowly defining the taxability of embezzled money, and *Mapp*, the admissibility in state criminal trials of illegally seized evidence.[12]

---

[7]   The precedent with the shortest lifespan, 11 months, was created and overruled by the Burger Court: *Robbins v. California*, 453 U.S. 420 (1981), overruled by *United States v. Ross*, 456 U.S. 798 (1982).

[8]   *Vanderbilt v. Vanderbilt*, 354 U.S. 416 (1957), at 419. The overruled decision was *Thompson v. Thompson*, 226 U.S. 551 (1913).

[9]   362 U.S. at 24. One might fairly argue that on its face this langauge smacks of a distinguished rather than an overruled precedent. In the context of the full opinion, however, *Reese's* niggardly construction of the penal provisions of federal civil rights legislation appears completely interred.

[10] A companion case to Elkins, *Rios v. United States*, 364 U.S. 253, may also be read to have overruled the silver platter doctrine. References in *Rios* to *Elkins*, however, indicate that the former overruled nothing not already voided by the latter.
      Partially overruled were *Weeks v. United States*, 232 U.S. 383 (1914); *Byars v. United States*, 273 U.S. 28 (1925); and *Feldman v. United States*, 322 U.S. 487 (1944); along with *Center v. United States*, 267 U.S. 575 (1925).

[11] Jeffery A. Segal and Harold J. Spaeth, "Decisional Trends on the Warren and Burger Courts," 73 *Judicature* 103 (1989), at 104.

[12] As observed in note 1, we would have considered another Vinson Court decision, *Rutkin v. United States*, 343 U.S. 130 (1952), to have overruled *Commissioner v. Wilcox*, 327 U.S. 404 (1946), given language in that case limiting *Wilcox* "to its facts" (327 U.S. at 138). But *James* uses the undebatable word "overruled" with reference to *Wilcox* (366 U.S. at 222). Hence our choice of *James* as the overruling decision.
      Mapp, of course, overruled *Wolf v. Colorado*, 338 U.S. 25 (1949).

Although Justice Brennan's majority opinion in the major case of *Baker v. Carr,* 369 U.S. 186 (1962), adroitly avoids declaring the salient case of *Colegrove v. Green,* 328 U.S. 549 (1946), a dead letter, Frankfurter's dissent does so.[13] Also overruling a precedent in the 1961 term was *Continental Ore Co. v. Union Carbide & Carbon Corp.,* 370 U.S. 690 (1962), discussed previously as an example of a subsequent decision asserting that an earlier one had overruled a precedent, even though nothing in the earlier decision so stipulates.[14]

Beginning with the 1962 term, the justices overruled precedents in 34 decisions in the seven remaining terms of the Warren Court, reaching their peak in the 1967 term with 8 separate overrulings. Six overruling decisions were handed down during the 1962 term. *Smith v. Evening News Assn,,* 371 U.S. 195 (1962), involving the preemption of state court jurisdiction under the National Labor Relations Act, is the second Warren Court decision to overrule one of its own precedents:[15] *Westinghouse Employees v. Westinghouse Corp.,* 348 U.S. 437 (1955). Three of the next four all overruled one or more Vinson Court decisions. *Construction & General Laborers' Union v. Curry,* 371 U.S. 542 (1962), which, like *Evening News,* is also a preemption case, overruled *Montgomery Trades Council v. Ledbetter Erection Co.,* 344 U.S. 178 (1952). *Gideon v. Wainwright,* 372 U.S. 335 (1963), the landmark right-to-counsel case, overruled the CQ-listed case of *Betts v. Brady,* 316 U.S. 455 (1942). *Gray v. Sanders,* 372 U.S. 368 (1963), was also a major decision involving one-person, one-vote. As was true of *Baker v. Carr,* the other overruling reapportionment decision, the majority opinion in *Gray* again overruled precedents sub silentio – *Cook v. Fortson,* 329 U.S. 675 (1946), and *South v. Peters,* 339 U.S. 276 (1950). Justice Harlan, in dissent, makes the fact of their overruling overt, however (372 U.S. at 383). The highly controversial and salient habeas corpus case, *Fay v. Noia,* 372 U.S. 391 (1963, altered *Darr v. Burford,* 339 U.S. 200 (1950). Some 28 years later, the Rehnquist Court, in *Coleman v. Thompson,* 115 L Ed 2d 640 (1991), accorded *Fay* the same treatment *Fay* had accorded the Vinson Court precedent.[16] The final 1962 term decision, *Ferguson v. Skrupa,* 372 U.S. 726 (1963), relegated to history's dustbin one of the last tottering remnants of laissez-faire economics: *Adams v. Tanner,* 244 U.S. 590 (1917).

The Court behaved in a slightly less activist manner in the 1963 term, formally altering precedents in five decisions. *Schneider v. Rusk,* 377 U.S. 163 (1964), was mentioned above as an overruling documented by the dissent. *Malloy v. Hogan,* 378 U.S. 1 (1964), a landmark decision, made the self-incrimination clause of the Fifth Amendment binding on the states, in the process overruling the salient *Twining v. New Jersey,* 211 U.S. 78 (1908), and *Adamson v. Califor-*

---

[13]   369 U.S. at 277.

[14]   The language ascribing overruling status to *Continental Ore* appears in *Kirkpatrick & Co. v. Environmental Techtonics Corp.,* 493 U.S. 400 (1990). The overruled decision was *American Banana Co. v. United Fruit Co.,* 213 U.S. 347 (1909). The actual language in *Continental Ore,* 370 U.S. at 704–705, smacks of distinguishing a precedent, rather than overruling it.

[15]   The first was *Reid v. Covert,* 354 U.S. 1 (1957).

[16]   Note that *Gideon, Gray,* and *Fay* were decided the same day, March 18, 1963.

nia, 332 U.S. 46 (1947). *Murphy v. Waterfront Commission,* 378 U.S. 52, another major decision and also a self-incrimination case, overruled, inter alia, a pair of Warren Court decisions: *Knapp v. Schweitzer,* 357 U.S. 371 (1958), and *Mills v. Louisiana,* 360 U.S. 230 (1959).[17] *Jackson v. Denno,* 378 U.S. 368 (1964), involving a coerced confession, overruled a Vinson Court case, *Stein v. New York,* 346 U.S. 156 (1953). *Escobedo v. Illinois,* 378 U.S. 478 (1964), another landmark decision, this one involving the assistance of counsel, over-ruled a pair of 1958 Warren Court decisions: *Crooker v. California,,* 357 U.S. 433, and *Cicenia v. Lagay,* 357 U.S. 504.

Only a single overruling occurred during the 1964 term, *Pointer v. Texas,* 380 U.S. 400 (1965), but it was another salient incorporation case, one requiring the states to grant an accused person the right to confront and cross-examine hostile witnesses. It overruled *West v. Louisiana,* 194 U.S. 258 (1904).

The first of the four altering decisions of the 1965 term, *Swift & Co. v. Wickham,* 382 U.S. 111 (1965), departed from the landmark civil liberties deci-sions that best characterize most of the Warren Court overrulings. The overruled case, however, was another Warren Court ruling: *Kesler v. Department of Public Safety,* 369 U.S. 153 (1962).[18] The issue concerned the circumstances requiring a three-judge district court. The next case was *Harris v. United States,* 382 U.S. 162 (1965), which also overruled a Warren Court decision, *Brown v. United States,* 359 U.S. 41 (1959). It concerned the extent to which a federal judge may impose summary punishment for criminal contempt under Rule 42(a) of the Federal Rules of Criminal Procedure. The importance of the two remaining 1965 term decisions is beyond cavil: *Harper v. Virginia Board of Elections,* 383 U.S. 663 (1966), and *Miranda v. Arizona,* 384 U.S. 436 (1966). In *Harper,* a CQ-listed case, the justices used the equal protection clause of the Fourteenth Amendment to extend the provisions of the Twenty-Fourth Amendment, enacted only two years earlier, to ban poll taxes across the board, not only in federal elections.[19] As for the landmark case of *Miranda,* its use as an overruling decision is somewhat debatable, inasmuch as the overruled cases are the same two that *Escobedo* altered: *Crooker v. California,* 357 U.S. 433 (1958), and *Cicenia v. Lagay,* 357 U.S. 504 (1958). But the operative language in *Escobedo* only states that "to the extent that *Cicenia* or *Crooker* may be inconsistent with the principles announced today, they are not to be regarded as controlling."[20] And inasmuch as the scope of *Miranda* is much broader than that of *Escobedo,* one may assume that *Crooker* and *Cicenia* may have retained a spark of life. The

---

[17]   The other cases that Murphy overruled are *Jack v. Kansas,* 199 U.S. 372 (1905); *United States v. Murdock,* 284 U.S. 141 (1931); and the remainder of *Feldman v. United States,* 322 U.S. 487 (1944).

[18]   *Kesler* is a multiply counted overruling. Only a portion of it was overruled here. A Burger Court decision, *Perez v. Campbell,* 402 U.S. 637 (1971), overruled a wholly different aspect.

[19]   The decision overruled *Breedlove v. Suttles,* 302 U.S. 277 (1937), insofar as it upheld the poll tax as "a prerequisite of voting" (383 U.S. at 669).

[20]   378 U.S. at 492.

operative language of *Miranda,* however, erases any doubt: "In accordance with our holdings today . . . *Crooker* . . . and *Cicenia* . . . are not to be followed."[21]

In the 1966 term the Court rendered five overruling decisions. *Spevack v. Klein,* 385 U.S. 511 (1967), another self-incrimination case, held that individuals may not suffer loss of their entitlements for invoking the provision's protection; specifically, the disbarment of an attorney. In the process, *Spevack* overruled another Warren Court decision, *Cohen v. Hurley,* 366 U.S. 117 (1961). *Keyishian v. Board of Regents,* 385 U.S. 589 (1967), a major decision, is, surprisingly enough, given the activism of the Warren Court, one of only two overruling decisions that is based on the First Amendment.[22] Faculty and nonfaculty employees of the State University of New York were terminated for their refusal to take a prescribed loyalty oath. Although the language concerning the continued vitality of the putatively overruled case, *Adler v. Board of Education,* 342 U.S. 485 (1952), is nebulous to say the least, Clark in dissent again rather persuasively establishes the demise of *Adler.*[23] *Afroyim v. Rusk,* 387 U.S. 253 (1967), like *Schneider,* which we previously considered, is a denaturalization proceeding. Here the revocation of citizenship occurred because of voting in a foreign nation's election in violation of the Nationality Act of 1940, rather than the Immigration and Naturalization Act of 1952, which was at issue in *Schneider.* Also unlike *Schneider,* the *Afroyim* majority, rather than the dissent, clearly announced the overruling – of *Perez v. Brownell,* 356 U.S. 44 (1958), still another Warren Court decision. The other two overrulings in the 1966 term pertain to the Fourth Amendment: *Warden v. Hayden,* 387 U.S. 294 (1967), and *Camara v. Municipal Court,* 387 U.S. 523 (1967). *Hayden* is the only overruling Warren Court civil liberties decision to produce a conservative result, holding that the Constitution does not prohibit the seizure of items that have only evidential value, and in the process nullifying *Gouled v. United States,* 255 U.S. 298 (1921). *Camara* barred the prosecution of a person who refused to permit a warrantless code-enforcement search of his home, thereby overruling still another Warren Court precedent, *Frank v. Maryland,* 359 U.S. 360 (1959).

[21]   384 U.S. at 479, n. 48.

[22]   The other is *Brandenburg v. Ohio,* 395 U.S. 444 (1969). Both also declared the pertinent state law unconstitutional, thereby forming part of a relatively small subset of overruling cases that simultaneously void legislation and formally alter precedent.

[23]   The majority begins rather clearly: "[T]o the extent that *Adler* sustained the provision of the Feinberg Law constituting membership in an organization advocating forceful overthrow of government a [*sic*] ground for disqualification, pertinent constitutional doctrines have since rejected the premises upon which that conclusion rested" (385 U.S. at 595). But then there immediately follows the sentence: "*Adler* therefore is not dispositive of the constitutional issues we must decide in this case." Not dispositive because no longer good law, or not dispositive because inapposite? The following arguably tips the balance toward overruling: "Here again constitutional doctrine has developed since *Adler.* Mere knowing membership without a specific intent to further the unlawful aims of an organization is not a constitutionally adequate basis for exclusion from such positions as those held by the appellants" (Id. at 606). The helpful portion of Clark's dissent appears at 623–625.

As previously mentioned, the Warren Court was most activist in its 1967 term, rendering eight overruling decisions. The retirement of Justice Clark and his replacement by Justice Marshall at the beginning of this term ushered in the high tide of modern liberalism which lasted until the beginning of the Burger Court two years later. All eight overrulings produced a liberal outcome.

Katz v. United States, 389 U.S. 347 (1967), a CQ-listed case, marks the onset of the refocused Fourth Amendment, one that "protects people, not places."[24] *Marchetti v. United States,* 390 U.S. 39 (1968), further extended the scope of the self-incrimination clause by overruling a decision of the Vinson Court, *United States v. Kahriger,* 345 U.S. 22 (1953), along with the early Warren Court decision *Lewis v. United States,* 348 U.S. 419 (1955). *Peyton v. Rowe,* 391 U.S. 54 (1968), broadened the protection afforded by the federal habeas corpus statute; while *Bruton v. United States,* 391 U.S. 123 (1968), extended the protection provided by the Confrontation Clause. *Duncan v. Louisiana,* 391 U.S. 145 (1968), a major decision, incorporated the Sixth Amendment's right to a jury trial into the due process clause of the Fourteenth Amendment, thereby binding the states. *Carafas v. LaVallee,* 391 U.S. 234 (1968), concerned the federal habeas corpus statute, as did *Peyton.* It severely restricted the circumstances under which mootness resulted by authorizing the issuance of the writ even though petitioners had served their sentences and had been released from custody.[25] The two remaining 1967 term decisions are *Lee v. Florida,* 392 U.S. 378 (1968), a wiretapping case, which ruled inadmissible in state courts evidence procured in violation of the Federal Communications Act, and the major decision of *Jones v. Alfred H. Mayer Co.,* 392 U.S. 409 (1968). *Jones* ruled that the Civil Rights Act of 1866 prohibited all discrimination against blacks in the sale or rental of housing, notwithstanding the recent enactment of fair housing provisions in the Civil Rights Act of 1968. The restriction in scope to state action, the majority held, does not apply to legislation impacting the Thirteenth, as distinct from the Fourteenth, Amendment.

The Warren Court's final term produced five overruling decisions. *Moore v. Ogilvie,* 394 U.S. 814 (1969), extended the one-person, one-vote principle of *Baker v. Carr* and its progeny to ballot access provisions, by obviating a requirement that nominating petitions for statewide office meet a geographical distribution unrelated to population equality. *Brandenburg v. Ohio,* 395 U.S. 444 (1969), produced the modern definition of clear and present danger and with it the overruling of *Whitney v. California,* 274 U.S. 357 (1927). *Lear, Inc. v. Adkins,* 395 U.S. 653 (1969), a non-civil liberties case, lessened the protection the patent laws afforded inventors in litigation against their licensees. The CQ-listed *Chimel v. California,* 395 U.S. 752 (1969), another Fourth Amendment case, ruled that the warrantless search of an arrested person's house cannot be justified as incident to that arrest. Two notable Vinson Court decisions were

---

[24]   389 U.S. at 351.

[25]   Note that *Peyton, Bruton, Duncan,* and *Carafas* were decided the same day, May 20, 1968.

thereby overruled: *Harris v. United States*, 331 U.S. 145 (1947), and the salient case of *United States v. Rabinowitz*, 339 U.S. 56 (1950). *Rabinowitz* also has the distinction of being one of a handful of our overruled overrulings.[26] The final overruling decision of the Warren Court, the major decision of *Benton v. Maryland*, 395 U.S. 784 (1969), characteristically incorporated still another provision of the Bill of Rights into the due process clause of the Fourteenth Amendment: the double jeopardy clause of the Fifth Amendment, thereby overruling the much-debated and salient case of *Palko v. Connecticut*, 302 U.S. 319 (1937).

THE BURGER COURT

Notwithstanding its well-grounded reputation as a conservative Court and Nixon's selection of misnomered strict constructionists as replacements for Warren, Fortas, Black, and Harlan, the Burger Court proved to be as activist as its predecessor in handing down overruling decisions: 46 in a span of 17 years, as compared to Warren's 43 in 16 years. On the other hand, the Burger Court had fewer salient overrulings than the Warren Court: 20 versus 11. The Burger Court also distributed its overrulings more evenly than its predecessor did: at least one every term, to a maximum of seven in the 1975 term, and five in 1976.

During its first six terms, 1969–1974, the Burger Court handed down a constant two overrulings per term except for the 1972 term, when it rendered 3 overruling decisions. Only three of these 13 decisions have achieved landmark status: *Miller v. California*, 413 U.S. 15 (1973), which redefined obscenity; *Edelman v. Jordan*, 415 U.S. 651 (1974), a poverty law case; and *Taylor v. Louisiana*, 419 U.S. 522 (1975), a sex discrimination case.

The initial Burger Court alteration, *Boys Markets v. Retail Clerks Union*, 398 U.S. 235 (1970,) overturned a Warren Court decision, *Sinclair Refining Co. v. Atkinson*, 370 U.S. 195 (1962), signifying that the new Court would not be its predecessor's clone. Although the issue was hardly front-page news – the arbitration of labor-management disputes – the legalistic posturing the justices employed to justify their tergiversation did nothing to enhance the Burger Court's attachment to precedent. In 1962, the Warren Court had held that federal courts have no power to halt strikes over grievances that a collective bargaining agreement requires to be arbitrated. Brennan, a dissenter in *Boys Markets,* spoke for the Burger Court majority: "At the outset, we are met with respondent's contention that *Sinclair* ought not to be disturbed because the decision turned on a question of statutory construction which Congress can alter at any time. Since Congress has not modified our conclusions in *Sinclair,* even though it has been urged to do so, respondent argues that principles of *stare decisis* should govern the present case" (398 U.S. at 240, footnote omitted). Brennan then proceeded to pay lip service to precedent – "We fully recognize that important policy consider-

---

[26] It overruled *Trupiano v. United States*, 334 U.S. 699 (1948), a precedent of two years vintage.

ations militate in favor of continuity and predictability in the law" (id.) – followed by an abrupt change of tune:

> It is precisely because *Sinclair* stands as a significant departure from our otherwise consistent emphasis upon the congressional policy to promote the peaceful settlement of labor disputes through arbitration and our efforts to accommodate and harmonize this policy with those underlying the anti-injunction provisions of the Norris-LaGuardia Act that we believe *Sinclair* should be reconsidered. (Id. at 241, footnotes omitted)

Brennan thereupon asserted, albeit gratuitously, that the ubiquitous "subsequent developments" had sapped *Sinclair's* vitality. The clinching argument reads as follows:

> Nor can we agree that conclusive weight should be accorded to the failure of Congress to respond to *Sinclair* on the theory that congressional silence should be interpreted as acceptance of the decision. . . . Therefore, in the absence of any persuasive circumstances evidencing a clear design that congressional inaction be taken as acceptance of *Sinclair,* the mere silence of Congress is not a sufficient reason for refusing to reconsider the decision. (Id. at 241–242)

Ironically, the Court used the same argument – congressional silence and inaction – two years later to *uphold* a precedent: the exemption of professional baseball, alone among professional sports, from the operation of the antitrust laws.[27] In his *Boys Market* dissent, Justice Black rhetorically queried what had changed since *Sinclair.* "Nothing at all has changed, in fact, except the membership of the Court and the personal views of one Justice" (id. at 256). Clark and Warren had retired. Marshall, Clark's successor, did not participate and the three *Sinclair* dissenters – Douglas, Harlan, and Brennan – picked up the vote of Burger. The switcher, Stewart, rationalized his change of position by simply taking "refuge" in an "aphorism" of former Justice Frankfurter: "Wisdom too often never comes, and so one ought not to reject it merely because it comes late" (id. at 255).

The other 1969 term overruling, *Moragne v. States Marine Lines, Inc.,* 398 U.S. 375 (1970), was even less salient than *Boys Markets.* A unanimous Court ruled that a nineteenth century decision[28] that had held that maritime law afforded no cause of action for wrongful death was no longer good law.

In the 1970 term, the Court – again unanimously – ruled that a patentee whose patent is held invalid in a suit against an alleged infringer may not relitigate the issue in another suit against a different alleged infringer.[29] And in a 5-to-4 decision, the justices ruled that the supremacy clause voids state financial responsibility laws to the extent that they suspend bankrupt drivers' li-

---

[27] *Flood v. Kuhn,* 407 U.S. 258 (1972). To be precise, the majority, speaking through Justice Blackmun, justified the "anomaly" and "aberration" (Id. at 282) of baseball's exclusion from the antitrust laws by Congress's "positive inaction" (Id. at 283), which, obviously, is to be distinguished from plain unvarnished "inaction."

[28] *The Harrisburg v. Rickards,* 119 U.S. 199 (1886).

[29] *Blonder-Tongue Laboratories, Inc. v. University of Illinois Foundation,* 402 U.S. 313 (1971), overruling *Triplett v. Lowell,* 297 U.S. 638 (1936).

censes because motorists erase traffic accident judgments by declaring bankruptcy.[30]

The case overruled by the first of the two overrulings of the 1971 term had the second shortest life span of any of our overruled decisions: 13 months. No one knew this at the time the overruling decision was handed down, *Illinois v. Milwaukee,* 406 U.S. 91 (1972), because nothing in the opinion stated that the precedent in question, *Ohio v. Wyandotte Chemicals Corp.,* 401 U.S. 493 (1973), had been overruled. Not until 1987 did the Court so declare in *International Paper Co. v. Ouellette,* 479 U.S. 481. *Illinois v. Milwaukee* held that the Supreme Court has original, but not exclusive, jurisdiction in controversies involving political subdivisions of states. The other alteration, *Andrews v. Louisville & Nashville R. Co.,* 406 U.S. 320 (1972), overruled a 1941 decision[31] that permitted a breach of an employment contract to be tried in state court without prior resort to the remedies provided by the Railway Labor Act for the adjustment and arbitration of grievances.

The first of the three overrulings of the 1972 term, *Lehnhausen v. Lake Shore Auto Parts,* 410 U.S. 356 (1973), overturned another remnant of laissez-faire economics, *Quaker City Cab Co. v. Pennsylvania,* 277 U.S. 389 (1928), by upholding against an equal protection challenge a state constitutional amendment prohibiting the taxation of individuals' personal property, but not that of other legal entities. *Braden v. 30th Judicial Circuit Court,* 410 U.S. 484 (1973), another habeas corpus case, overruled a Vinson Court decision that required such petitions to be brought only in the district of the prisoner's confinement. The earliest of the Burger Court's landmark decisions was *Miller v. California,* 413 U.S. 15 (1973), which, in the process of redefining obscenity, overruled the Fanny Hill case and its holding that the contemporary community standards that material had to meet to be obscene comprised a single national gauge.[32]

Still another legacy of laissez-faire came tumbling down in the first of the pair of 1973 term decisions: *North Dakota State Board of Pharmacy v. Snyder's Drug Stores,* 414 U.S. 156 (1973). The Court reiterated what it had said so often since the "switch in time that saved nine":[33] that the Court will not substitute its own judgment for what a state believes is reasonably necessary to protect the interests of the public (in this case, a statute that precluded anyone not a registered pharmacist or a corporation in which registered pharmacists owned the majority

---

[30] *Perez v. Campbell,* 402 U.S. 637 (1971), overruling the remainder of *Kesler v. Dept. of Public safety,* 369 U.S. 153 (1962), and *Reitz v. Mealey,* 314 U.S. 33 (1941). The Warren Court, in *Swift Co. v. Wickham,* 382 U.S. 111 (1965), had initially overruled a portion of Kesler, a case which it had decided three years earlier.

[31] *Moore v. Illinois Central R. Co.,* 312 U.S. 630.

[32] *A Book Named "John Cleland's Memoirs of a Woman of Pleasure" v. Massachusetts,* 383 U.S. 412 (1966).

[33] We are referring to the Court's 1937 switch in favor of Roosevelt's New Deal legislation which presumably precluded Roosevelt from increasing the number of justices on the Court.

of the stock from acquiring a permit to operate a pharmacy).[34] The other 1973 term decision, *Edelman v. Jordan*, 415 U.S. 651 (1974), was a poverty law case that overruled *Shapiro v. Thompson*, 394 U.S. 618 (1969), a case decided in the final two months of the Warren Court.[35] The CQ lists both *Edelman* and *Shapiro* as salient. The majority held that the Eleventh Amendment barred the retroactive payment of benefits to recipients of Aid to the Aged, Blind, and Disabled.

The two overrulings of the 1974 term were *Taylor v. Louisiana*, 419 U.S. 522 (1975), involving sex discrimination, and *United States v. Reliable Transfer Co.*, 421 U.S. 397 (1975), an admiralty case. *Taylor* overruled the Warren Court's sole encounter with sex discrimination, *Hoyt v. Florida*, 368 U.S. 57 (1961), by declaring unconstitutional provisions that excluded women from jury service unless they previously submitted a written declaration of their desire to be considered. *Reliable Transfer* voided the oldest of our precedents, the rule of equally apportioned damages. Although the overruled case, *The Schooner Catherine v. Dickinson*, 17 Howard 170, dates only from 1854, the rule itself traces to the Laws of Oleron, which were promulgated by Eleanor of Guienne, who governed a French duchy south of Brittany in the middle of the twelfth century.[36]

The 1975 term breaks the Burger Court pattern of a pair of non-landmark overrulings per term. The Court handed down seven altering decisions in this term. The CQ lists *Michelin Tire Corp. v. Wages*, 423 U.S. 276 (1976), which overruled the salient nineteenth century precedent, *Low v. Austin*, 13 Wallace 29 (1871), which held that the import-export clause prohibited the assessment of a nondiscriminatory ad valorem tax on imports before they became mixed with the mass of property in the state, thereby losing their character as imports. In *Hudgens v. National Labor Relations Board*, 424 U.S. 507 (1976), the Court ruled that the National Labor Relations Act, rather than the First Amendment, governs employee picketing in a shopping center, thereby overruling *Amalgamated Food Employees Union v. Logan Valley Plaza*, 391 U.S. 308 (1968), which had taken a more expansive view of the Constitution. *Virginia State Board of Pharmacy v. Virginia Citizens Consumer Council*, 425 U.S. 748 (1976), belied the conservative orientation of the Burger Court by extending the protection of the First Amendment to commercial speech. Only Rehnquist dissented. The major case of *National League of Cities v. Usery*, 426 U.S. 833 (1976), limited the scope of the putatively boundless commerce clause by voiding amendments to the Fair Labor Standards Act that extended minimum wage and maximum hour provisions to state and local governmental employees. *National League of Cities* marked the first time the Court had voided a major piece of federal economic legislation since the New Deal. The ruling overturned a decision of the later Warren Court, *Maryland v. Wirtz*, 392 U.S. 183 (1968). *National League of*

---

[34]   The overruled decision was *Liggett Co. v. Baldridge*, 278 U.S. 105 (1929).

[35]   *Edelman* also overruled two Burger Court memorandum decisions, but, as previously explained, we exclude from our list of overruled precedents cases that were not orally argued.

[36]   Harold J. Spaeth, *Supreme Court Policy Making* (San Francisco: W. H. Freeman, 1979), p. 61.

Cities itself had a short life span, however. In 1985, Justice Blackmun switched his vote and resurrected *Maryland v. Wirtz*. But while alive, it clearly was a landmark.

In another labor case, the justices overruled a Vinson Court decision by holding that federal law preempts state efforts to sanction union members who refuse to work overtime as part of a bargaining strategy.[37] In *New Orleans v. Dukes*, 427 U.S. 297 (1976), the Court unanimously held that a grandfather clause exempting pushcart vendors did not deny equal protection to a newcomer. The decision overturned an early Warren Court holding, *Morey v. Doud*, 354 U.S. 457 (1957). The most momentous landmark decision of the 1975 term was the death penalty case, *Gregg v. Georgia*, 428 U.S. 153 (1976), in which an extremely divided Burger Court resuscitated the death penalty, thereby overruling a second of its own decisions, *McGautha v. California*, 402 U.S. 183 (1971).[38]

The Court rendered five altering decisions in the 1976 term. The salient case of *Craig v. Boren*, 429 U.S. 190 (1976), formulated a new, intermediate level of scrutiny applicable to classifications based on sex. In its opinion, the Court "disapproved" the Vinson Court decision of *Goesaert v. Cleary*, 335 U.S. 464 (1948).[39] In *Oregon ex rel. State Land Board v. Corvallis Sand and Gravel Co.*, 429 U.S. 363 (1977), the Court strengthened states' rights by ruling that state law rather than federal common law governs title to riverbeds within a state's boundaries. In the process, the Burger Court overruled the third of its own precedents, *Bonelli Cattle Co. v. Arizona*, 414 U.S. 313 (1973). The three justices who changed their *Bonelli* position – Burger, Blackmun, and Powell – used stare decisis itself to justify their voting with the majority: "Since one system of resolution of property disputes has been adhered to from 1845 until 1973, and the other only for the past three years, a return to the former would more closely conform to the expectations of property owners than would adherence to the latter" (429 U.S. at 382).

Also supporting states' rights was the CQ-listed case of *Complete Auto Transit, Inc. v. Brady*, 430 U.S. 274 (1977), which upheld a state tax on the privilege of doing interstate business in the state against a commerce clause challenge. *Complete Auto Transit* voided another Vinson Court case, *Spector Motor Service v. O'Connor*, 340 U.S. 602 (1951). *Continental T.V., Inc. v. GTE Sylvania Inc.*, 433 U.S. 36 (1977), continued the economic focus of the overruling decisions of the 1976 term. Here the Court overruled *United States v. Arnold, Schwinn & Co.*, 388 U.S. 365 (1967), a Warren Court decision which had held that franchise agreements between manufacturers and retailers constituted a per se violation of the Sherman Act if they barred retailers from selling in locations other than those

---

[37] *Machinists v. Wisconsin Employment Relations Commission*, 427 U.S. 132 (1976), overruling *UAW v. Wisonsin Employment Relations Board*, 336 U.S. 245 (1949).

[38] The first overruling occurred in *Illinois v. Milwaukee*, 406 U.S. 91 (1972).

[39] 429 U.S. at 210, note 23.

specified in the agreements. Instead, said the Burger Court, a rule-of-reason standard should govern. The term's final overruling, *Shaffer v. Heitner,* 433 U.S. 186 (1977), though it received virtually no mention in the mass media, revolutionized the field of civil procedure by subjecting all proceedings against out-of-state respondents to the minimum contacts test, which determines whether the parties to a lawsuit have sufficient contact with the forum state to allow the court, compatibly with due process, to resolve the dispute.[40]

In the first of its 1977 term alterations the Burger Court extended the scope of the overruling decision of the preceding year, *Complete Auto Transit,* by authorizing states to directly tax the privilege of conducting interstate business when such tax levies only on the value of in-state services, the tax is properly apportioned, and multiple burdens on interstate commerce do not occur: *Washington Revenue Dept. v. Stevedoring Assn.,* 435 U.S. 734 (1978).[41] The Court paid a second visit to civil rights in the salient case of *Monell v. Dept. of Social Services,* 436 U.S. 658 (1978), again with a liberal result, as was the case in *Craig v. Boren.* With only Rehnquist and Burger dissenting, the Court held that the Civil Rights Act of 1871 did not wholly inoculate local governments from suit for deprivation of federally protected rights, privileges, or immunities. *Monell* overruled a conservative decision of the liberal Warren Court: *Monroe v. Pape,* 365 U.S. 167 (1961).

The final two overruling decisions of the 1977 term were the first Burger Court alterations to address the constitutionally protected rights of persons accused of crime. Both concerned double jeopardy. One was decided in a liberal direction, the other conservatively. *Burks v. United States,* 437 U.S. 1 (1978), held that a second trial is precluded once an appellate court has found the evidence insufficient to sustain a verdict of guilty. *United States v. Scott,* 437 U.S. 82 (1978), permitted governmental appeals from defendants' successful motions to terminate their trials if no determination of guilt or innocence had occurred.[42]

---

[40] The focus of *Shaffer* was quasi in rem jurisdiction, where plaintiffs attach or otherwise seize property to force debtors or other injuring parties into court. Here a stockholder sued a corporation's nonresident officers and directors in Delaware, the state of incorporation. None of the activities complained of occurred therein, nor did any defendant have other contacts with the state. The plaintiff gained jurisdiction under a statute that provided that the stock of any Delaware corporation could be attached because it was irrebuttably presumed to be located there. The Court's decision overruled the classic nineteenth century case of *Pennoyer v. Neff,* 95 U.S. 714 (1878), and the somewhat lesser classic, *Harris v. Balk,* 198 U.S. 215 (1905). For further discussion, see Harold J. Spaeth, "Jurisdiction," in Robert J. Janosik, ed., *Encyclopedia of the American Judicial System* (New York: Scribners, 1987), II, 836–841.

[41] Overruled were *Puget Sound Stevedoring Co. v. State Tax Comn.,* 302 U.S. 90 (1937), and *Joseph v. Carter & Weekes Stevedoring Co.,* 330 U.S. 422 (1947).

[42] Burks partially overruled four precedents, one from the Vinson Court and three from the Warren Court: *Bryan v. United States,* 338 U.S. 552 (1950); *Sapir v. United States,* 348 U.S. 373 (1955); *Yates v. United States,* 354 U.S. 298 (1957); and *Forman v. United States,* 361 U.S. 416 (1960). Scott overruled *United States v. Jenkins,* 420 U.S. 358 (1975), a case decided three terms earlier.

Beginning with the 1978 term, the overruling activity of the Burger Court returned to the level that characterized its first six terms (1969–1974), an average of two per term. During the final eight (1978–1985), the justices wrote 17 overrulings. By contrast, the middle three (1975–1977) produced 16.

The sole alteration of the 1978 term involved another commerce clause challenge to a state statute. Unlike the others that the Burger Court decided, this one voided the state law: *Hughes v. Oklahoma,* 441 U.S. 322 (1979). A nineteenth century legal fiction of state ownership of wild animals that had immunized them from federal regulation under the interstate commerce clause was ended, and with it *Geer v. Connecticut,* 161 U.S. 519 (1896).

The first of the three 1979 term overrulings narrowed the evidentiary scope of the marital privilege originally established by the common law. *Trammel v. United States,* 445 U.S. 40 (1980), modified the rule of *Hawkins v. United States,* 358 U.S. 74 (1958), by giving only the witness-spouse the option to testify adversely, not the other partner. *United States v. Salvucci,* 448 U.S. 83 (1980), narrowed the scope of the Fourth Amendment's exclusionary rule by denying automatic standing to defendants charged with crimes of possession to challenge the constitutionality of the search. Overruling a Warren Court decision, *Jones v. United States,* 362 U.S. 257 (1960), the majority held that defendants must show a reasonable expectation of privacy to mount such a challenge.

In *Thomas v. Washington Gas Light Co.,* 448 U.S. 261 (1980), a fractured Court held that the full faith and credit clause did not bar multistate workers from collecting workers' compensation from a state other than the original grantor, thereby overruling *Industrial Comn. of Wisconsin v. McCartin,* 330 U.S. 622 (1947). The justices were confronted with two inconsistent precedents. Although seven of them voted to reverse the decision of the circuit court of appeals, they could not agree which of the two inconsistent precedents to overrule, *McCartin* or *Magnolia Petroleum Co. v. Hunt,* 320 U.S. 430 (1943). The plurality, in an opinion by Stevens, which Brennan, Stewart, and Blackmun joined, said that "*Magnolia Petroleum Co. v. Hunt* should be overruled" (448 U.S. at 286). Justice White, specially concurring with Burger and Powell, "would not overrule either *Magnolia* or *McCartin*" (448 U.S. at 289). The dissenters, Rehnquist and Marshall, in an opinion by the former, "believe that *Magnolia* was correctly decided" and that "*McCartin* is analytically indefensible" (448 U.S. 290). A majority, therefore, would not overrule *Magnolia. McCartin* becomes the overruling decision because the two dissenters would overrule it, and because the four-member plurality said that *McCartin* "represents an unwarranted delegation to the States of this Court's responsibility for the final arbitration of full faith and credit questions" (448 U.S. at 271).

The only precedent formally altered during the 1980 term occurred as a result of the decision in *Commonwealth Edison Co. v. Montana,* 453 U.S. 609 (1981). The case concerned still another interstate commerce challenge to a state tax. Citing *Complete Auto Transit,* discussed above, as authority, the majority upheld a severance on each ton of coal mined in the state, and "disapproved . . . [a]ny contrary statements" (453 U.S. at 617) in a 1922 decision, *Heisler v. Thomas Colliery Co.*, 260 U.S. 245.[43]

The sole alteration of the 1981 term, *United States v. Ross*, 456 U.S. 798 (1982), pertained to the automobile exception to the Fourth Amendment's warrant requirement. The Court ruled that the police may conduct a warrantless search of a legitimately stopped automobile as thoroughly as a magistrate could authorize by warrant when there is probable cause to believe the automobile contains contraband. In so doing the majority voided the most short-lived of our precedents, the 11-month-old *Robbins v. California*, 453 U.S. 420 (1981). *Robbins* had required a warrant to search plastic-wrapped marijuana found in the trunk of a car.

The first of the pair of 1982 term overrulings again related to the Fourth Amendment. And instead of its own precedent, the Burger majority overruled two cases from the later Warren Court: *Aguilar v. Texas*, 378 U.S. 108 (1964), and *Spinelli v. United States*, 393 U.S. 410 (1969). The overruling decision, *Illinois v. Gates*, 462 U.S. 213 (1983), held that an approach based on the totality of the circumstances suffices to determine probable cause, rather than the more rigorous two-pronged test of *Aguilar* and *Spinelli*.

Although the other 1982 term overruling, *Michigan v. Long*, 463 U.S. 1032 (1983), also pertained to the Fourth Amendment in the form of an otherwise run-of-the-mill vehicular search-and-seizure in which the Court upheld the protective search of those portions of a car in which a weapon could be placed or hidden, its precedent-shattering quality concerned the reviewability of state court decisions. Prior to *Long*, the Court had consistently adhered to a self-imposed policy that it would not review state court decisions that rested on an adequate and independent state ground, even though they contained federal questions and, moreover, even though those questions were wrongly decided. But in *Long*, the Court created an opposite presumption:

[W]hen . . . a state court decision fairly appears to rest primarily on federal law, or to be interwoven with the federal law, and when the adequacy and independence of any possible state law ground is not clear from the face of the opinion, we will accept . . . that the state court decided the case the way it did because it believed that federal law required it to do so. (463 U.S. at 1040–1041)

As a result of this language, the ostensibly restraintist Burger Court rendered as activist a decision as any in the Court's entire history, and in the process overruled an indeterminable number of its own precedents.[44]

---

43 The plaintiff also unsuccessfully challenged the tax as contravening the supremacy clause. This part of the holding involved no alteration of precedents, however.

44 The majority opinion provides a very partial list at 463 U.S. 1038–1039. Justice Stevens, in dissent (463 U.S. at 1067, note 1), noted that a sampling of the overruled cases–some two dozen–could be found in his dissenting opinion in *South Dakota v. Neville*, 459 U.S. 553 (1983), at 566. The Court's subsequent use of *Long* suggests that the overruling occurred because of the majority's desire to review–and thereby overturn–state court decisions *upholding* the contentions of persons accused or convicted of crime. See Jeffrey A. Segal and Harold J.

The Court rendered three overrulings in the 1983 term. A unanimous Court ruled in *United States v. One Assortment of 89 Firearms*, 465 U.S. 354 (1984), that federal law did not preclude an in rem firearm forfeiture proceeding against a gun owner who had been acquitted of criminal charges involving those same firearms. The justices were also unanimous in *Limbach v. Hooven & Allison Co.*, 466 U.S. 353 (1984), which further limited the scope of the original package doctrine by extending the reach of *Michelin Tire*, discussed above. A minimum winning coalition in *Copperweld Corp. v. Independence Tube Corp.*, 467 U.S. 752 (1984), ruled that the restraints of trade addressed by the Sherman Act must involve separate entities, not a parent corporation and its wholly owned subsidiary.[45]

In the 1984 term, Blackmun rescinded the pro-states' rights position he had taken in *National League of Cities*, explored above, and again cast the deciding vote on the matter of the scope of the Fair Labor Standards Act (FLSA) under the interstate commerce clause in the CQ-listed case of *Garcia v. San Antonio Metropolitan Transit Authority*, 469 U.S. 528 (1985). As the author of the majority opinion, Blackmun performed reasonably well in rationalizing his voting switch. He observed that *National League of Cities* had held that the commerce clause did not empower Congress to enforce the FLSA "in areas of traditional governmental functions" and concluded that

> Our examination of this "function" standard . . . over the last eight years now persuades us that the attempt to draw the boundaries of state regulatory immunity in terms of "traditional governmental function" is not only unworkable but is also inconsistent with established principles of federalism and, indeed, with those very federalism principles on which *National League of Cities* purported to rest. (469 U.S. at 530, 531)

Ironically, the other members of the erstwhile *National League of Cities* majority – Burger, Rehnquist, Powell, and O'Connor – faced a Hobson's choice. In adhering to *National League of Cities* and the deference it accorded states' rights, they were forced in their dissenting opinions to actively declare the relevant portions of the FLSA unconstitutional.

The other overruling of the 1984 term addressed a matter of criminal procedure: whether an accused person's conviction violates the grand jury guarantee of the Fifth Amendment when he is convicted of charges narrower than those contained in the indictment. In *United States v. Miller*, 471 U.S. 130 (1985), the Court unanimously said no, thereby overruling *Ex parte Bain*, 121 U.S. 1 (1887).

The Burger Court rendered four overruling decisions in its final term. The most trivial was *Daniels v. Williams*, 474 U.S. 327 (1986), which held that the

Spaeth, *The Supreme Court and the Attitudinal Model* (Cambridge: Cambridge University Press, 1993), pp. 26–28.

[45] *89 Firearms* overruled *Coffey v. United States*, 116 U.S. 436 (1886); *Limbach* overruled *Hooven & Allison Co. v. Evatt*, 324 U.S. 652 (1945); and *Copperweld* overruled two Vinson Court decisions: *United States v. Yellow Cab Co.*, 332 U.S. 218 (1947), and *Kiefer-Stewart Co. v. Joseph E. Seagram & Sons*, 340 U.S. 211 (1951).

due process clause is not implicated by a prison official's negligence in causing an inmate to slip and fall. The justices thereby voided unanimously one of their five-year-old precedents, *Parratt v. Taylor,* 451 U.S. 527 (1981). At the other extreme is the major case of *Batson v. Kentucky,* 476 U.S. 79 (1986), which held that the use of peremptory challenges to exclude from the jury races different from that of the accused violates the equal protection clause. The decision overturned a conservative ruling of the liberal Warren Court: *Swain v. Alabama,* 380 U.S. 202 (1965).

In *Brown-Forman Distillers Corp. v. New York State Liquor Authority,* 476 U.S. 573 (1986), the Court struck down a New York law that unconstitutionally interfered with interstate commerce by regulating out-of-state transactions; specifically, dictating the minimum prices that distillers selling in New York could charge customers in other states. Although the opinion intimated that its decision might ultimately lead it to void a Warren Court precedent, *Joseph E. Seagram & Sons v. Hostetter,* 384 U.S. 35 (1966), the overruling did not formally occur until the Rehnquist Court so decreed in *Healy v. The Beer Institute, Inc.,* 105 L Ed 2d 275 (1989). According to our decision rules, specified above, we count *Brown-Forman* rather than *Healy* as the overruling vehicle. The final Burger Court alteration is also an ascribed one. A footnote in a Rehnquist Court decision, *Pope v. Illinois,* 481 U.S. 497 (1987), identifed *Rose v. Clark,* 478 U.S. 570 (1986), as overruling an unspecified number of decisions (481 U.S. at 504). In his dissent in Pope (481 U.S. at 510), Justice Stevens named the overturned decisions: two from the Vinson Court, *Bollenbach v. United States,* 326 U.S. 607 (1946), and *Carpenters v. United States,* 330 U.S. 395 (1947); and two from the Warren Court, *Marks v. United States,* 430 U.S. 188 (1977), and *Jackson v. Virginia,* 443 U.S. 307 (1979). The issue in Rose was the applicability of harmless error analysis to murder convictions in which the jury was unconstitutionally instructed. The majority ruled that such instructions did not always warrant a new trial.

THE REHNQUIST COURT

The 20 overruling decisions that the Rehnquist Court handed down during its first six terms (1986–1991) show it to be a bit more activist than its immediate predecessors. (See Table 3.1.) With regard to the distribution of its overrulings, the Rehnquist Court hesitated not a whit: 6 of the 20 overrulings occurred during its first term, with an additional 5 coming in 1988.

Griffith v. Kentucky, 479 U.S. 314 (1987), the Rehnquist Court's initial overruling, applied the rule of *Batson,* discussed above, retroactively to cases pending on direct review or not yet final. Although the majority opinion does not say so, Justice Powell's concurrence points out that Griffith overruled two early Burger Court decisions, *Desist v. United States,* 394 U.S. 244 (1969), and

Williams v. United States, 401 U.S. 646 (1971).[46] The other five alterations of the Rehnquist Court's first term were handed down within 48 hours of one another. *Puerto Rico v. Branstead,* 483 U.S. 219 (1987), reached back 125 years to overrule *Kentucky v. Dennison,* 24 How. 66 (1861), which held that federal courts have no power to require the governor of a state to comply with the Constitution's extradition clause ordering fugitives from justice to be delivered up. The next pair, *Tyler Pipe Industries, Inc. v. Dept. of Revenue,* 483 U.S. 232 (1987), and *American Trucking Assns., Inc. v. Scheiner,* 483 U.S. 266 (1987), voided state taxes as violative of the commerce clause. In *Tyler,* a business and occupation tax on the privilege of conducting business within the State of Washington exempted local manufacturers selling intrastate. Overruled was the Warren Court decision, *General Motors Corp. v. Washington,* 377 U.S. 436 (1964). In *Scheiner,* taxes on out-of-state trucks operating in Pennsylvania were offset for local operators. Overruled, according to the dissent, were three decisions: *Aero Mayflower Transit Co. v. Georgia Public Service Comn.,* 295 U.S. 285 (1935); *Aero Mayflower Transit Co. v. Board of Railroad Comrs.,* 332 U.S. 495 (1947); and *Capitol Greyhound Lines v. Brice,* 339 U.S. 542 (1950).

In the two remaining 1986 term overrulings, *Solorio v. United States,* 483 U.S. 435 (1987), broadened the scope of constitutionally authorized courts martial to cover all military personnel and not only those whose offenses were service connected, thereby overruling a decision rendered at the end of the Warren Court, *O'Callahan v. Parker,* 395 U.S. 258 (1969); while *Welch v. Texas Dept. of Highways and Public Transportation,* 483 U.S. 468 (1987), held that the Eleventh Amendment precludes injured seamen from suing a state in federal court because Congress has not said they may do so "in unmistakable statutory language" (483 U.S. at 475), thereby overruling still another Warren Court precedent, *Parden v. Terminal Railway of Alabama,* 377 U.S. 184 (1964).

The first of the two 1987 term alterations, *Gulfstream Aerospace Corp. v. Mayacamas Corp.,* 485 U.S. 271 (1988), concerned the appealability of a district court order denying a dismissal or stay when a similar suit was pending in state court. In denying such appeals, the justices unanimously overruled *Enelow v. New York Life Insurance Co.,* 293 U.S. 379 (1935), and *Ettelson v. Metropolitan Life Insurance Co.,* 317 U.S. 188 (1942). The other 1987 term decision, the CQ-listed case of *South Carolina v. Baker,* 485 U.S. 505 (1988), ruled that a provision of the Tax Equity and Fiscal Responsibility Act of 1982, which subjects state and local bonds to federal income tax, violates neither the Tenth Amendment nor the doctrine of intergovernmental tax immunity. Citing the Burger Court's *Garcia* decision, discussed above, the majority overruled a major

---

[46] In *Harper v. Virginia Dept. of Taxation,* 125 L Ed 2d 74, at 85, the Court states that *Griffith* also overruled the Warren Court decision *Linkletter v. Walker,* 381 U.S. 618 (1965). Nowhere does *Griffith* so state. A reading of 479 U.S. at 320–322 arguably allows one so to infer, however. We chose not to construe *Griffith* that far.

precedent dating from 1895, *Pollock v. Farmers' Loan & Trust Co.*, 157 U.S. 429.

In its second most active term, 1988, the Rehnquist Court produced five overruling decisions. *Thornburgh v. Abbott*, 490 U.S. 401 (1989), held that federal regulations rejecting incoming publications detrimental to prison security did not run afoul of the First Amendment. The decision partially overruled a Burger Court case, *Procunier v. Martinez*, 416 U.S. 396 (1974). *Rodriguez de Quijas v. Shearson/American Express, Inc.*, 490 U.S. 477 (1989), overturned a decision from the first term of the Warren Court, *Wilko v. Swan*, 346 U.S. 427 (1953), that had held unenforceable predispute agreements to arbitrate claims under the Securities Act of 1933.

The next 1988 overruling was the short-lived salient decision *Ward's Cove Packing Co., Inc. v. Atonio*, 490 U.S. 642 (1989), which coyly voided the equally salient case of *Griggs v. Duke Power Co.*, 401 U.S. 424 (1971). *Ward's Cove* was short lived because Congress expressly overturned it in the Civil Rights Act of 1991. The Burger Court had unanimously required employers to show that a policy that differentially impacted racial and ethnic minorities was "demonstrably a reasonable measure of job performance."[47] In *Ward's Cove*, however, the majority of five had required employees to prove the lack of a business necessity for the employer's policy.[48]

Alabama v. Smith, 490 U.S. 794 (1989), the penultimate overruling of the 1988 term, held that the double jeopardy clause of the Fifth Amendment does not prevent a longer sentence upon conviction at trial than a withdrawn guilty plea had called for. The decision overruled *Simpson v. Rice*, 395 U.S. 711 (1969), another end-of-the-Warren-Court decision. The 1988 term's final overruling was, of course, the landmark case of *Webster v. Reproductive Health Services*, 492 U.S. 490 (1989), which formally altered *Roe v. Wade*, 410 U.S. 113 (1973), along with one of the Burger Court's later abortion decisions: *Colautti v. Franklin*, 439 U.S. 379 (1979).

The sole overruling of the 1989 term, *Collins v. Youngblood*, 497 U.S. 37 (1990), overturned two nineteenth century decisions based on the ex post facto clause of Article I, section 10: *Kring v. Missouri*, 107 U.S. 221 (1883), and *Thompson v. Utah*, 170 U.S. 343 (1898). The majority held that a Texas law that allowed reformation of a jury verdict imposing unauthorized punishment did not violate the clause. Although the decision was unanimous, three

---

[47]   401 U.S. at 436.

[48]   "We acknowledge that some of our earlier decisions can be read as suggesting otherwise. . . . But to the extent that those cases speak of an employer's 'burden of proof' with respect to a legitimate business justification defense . . . they should have been understood to mean an employer's production–but not persuasion–burden" (104 L Ed 2d at 753). This is as close as the majority comes to indicating an overruling of *Griggs*. We deem it a formal alteration of precedent. In our judgment, a restatement by a successor Court of a reasonably clear holding of a predecessor is, as far as the alteration of precedent is concerned, a distinction without a difference.

justices believed that "that conclusion is entirely consistent with our precedents."[49]

The first of the four 1990 term overrulings again pertained to the Fourth Amendment, and again to the automobile exception thereto: *California v. Acevedo*, 114 L Ed 2d 619 (1991). The majority said that the probable cause based warrantless search of a paper bag containing marijuana in the trunk of car was permissible. The Burger Court decision *Arkansas v. Sanders*, 442 U.S. 753 (1979), was thereby voided. In *Exxon Corp. v. Central Gulf Lines, Inc.*, 114 L Ed 2d 649 (1991), the justices unanimously overturned the second-oldest precedent which we encounter, and like the oldest,[50] it also concerned admiralty law: *Minturn v. Maynard*, 17 How. 477 (1855). The issue was whether admiralty jurisdiction extends to claims arising from agency contracts. The Rehnquist Court said it does. The third overruling decision, the salient case of *Coleman v. Thompson*, 115 L Ed 2d 640 (1991), held that almost any failure by a state prison inmate to comply with state judicial procedures will bar access to the federal courts via a habeas corpus petition.[51] Like the Burger Court's decision in *National League of Cities*, discussed above, *Coleman* overruled a CQ-listed precedent, *Fay v. Noia* – established by the Warren Court – that had itself voided a Vinson Court ruling.

By far the most emotion engendering of the term's overrulings was its final one: the landmark case of *Payne v. Tennessee*, 115 L Ed 2d 720 (1991). In ruling that a capital sentencing jury could constitutionally consider victim impact evidence, the Rehnquist Court overruled two of its own precedents: *Booth v. Maryland*, 482 U.S. 496 (1987), and *South Carolina v. Gathers*, 490 U.S. 805 (1989).[52]

The first of the two 1991 term overrulings again concerned habeas corpus petitioners. In *Keeney v. Tamayo-Reyes*, 118 L Ed 2d 318 (1992), the majority overruled a Warren Court precedent, *Townsend v. Sain*, 372 U.S. 293 (1963), and held that habeas challenges to state court convictions must either show cause for the material defect in the state court proceedings and actual prejudice resulting therefrom, or show that a fundamental miscarriage of justice would result from the failure of the federal court to grant petitioner a hearing. The other overruling occurred in the major decision of *Planned Parenthood v. Casey*, 120 L Ed 2d 674

---

[49] 111 L Ed 2d at 45.

[50] *The Schooner Catherine v. Dickinson*, 17 How. 170 (1854). See the discussion of the Burger Court decision in *Reliable Transfer*, above.

[51] One may question the compatibility of *Coleman* with the ruling of *Michigan v. Long*, discussed above. In *Long*, the Court permitted access in cases of intermixed federal-state law unless the state court makes it unmistakably clear that its decision adequately rests on state law. In *Coleman*, access is denied for an inadvertent failure to comply with state procedural rules. Petitioners may gain access only if they demonstrate cause for their failure to comply with the state rule and if actual prejudice resulted from the alleged violation of federal rights. Arguably, the difference results because *Long* authorizes appeal of state court decisions decided in a liberal direction, while *Coleman* precludes appeal of conservatively decided state court decisions.

[52] See our discussion of *Payne* in Chapter 1.

(1992), wherein a majority, over the dissents of Blackmun and Stevens, expressly overruled a portion of two salient Burger Court abortion decisions: *Akron v. Akron Center for Reproductive Health, Inc.*, 462 U.S. 416 (1983), and *Thornburgh v. American College of Obstetricians and Gynecologists*, 476 U.S. 747 (1986). "To the extent Akron . . . and Thornburgh find a constitutional violation when the government requires, as it does here, the giving of truthful, non-misleading information about the nature of the procedure, the attendant health risks and those of childbirth, and the 'probable gestational age' of the fetus, those cases go too far, are inconsistent with Roe's acknowledgement of an important interest in potential life, and are overruled."[53]

---

[53]   120 L Ed 2d at 718.

Subject/name index

Case index